P9-ELW-887

Grandmother's Favorite Crochet™

Edited by Laura Scott

HOUSE of WHITE BIRCHES
PUBLISHERS SINCE 1947

Editor: Laura Scott

Editorial Assistant: Marla Freeman

Pattern Editors: Agnes Russell, Colleen McCague

Copy Editor: Cathy Reef

Photography: Nora Elsesser, Tammy Christian, Scott Campbell, Tammy Payne

Photography Assistants: Linda Quinlan, Teri Staub

Production Manager: Vicki Macy

Cover Design/Book Design/Production: Dan Kraner

Creative Coordinator: Shaun Venish

Production Coordinator: Sandra Beres

Production Assistants: Cheryl Lynch, Darren Powell

Publishers: Carl H. Muselman, Arthur K. Muselman

Chief Executive Officer: John Robinson

Marketing Director: Scott Moss

Editorial Director: Vivian Rothe

Production Director: Scott Smith

Printed in the United States of America
First Printing: 1996
Library of Congress Number: 96-77022
ISBN: 1-882138-24-4

Every effort has been made to ensure the accuracy and completeness of the instructions in this book. However, we cannot be responsible for human error or for the results when using materials other than those specified in the instructions, or for variations in individual work.

Special thanks to Roger and Naomi Muselman and Schug House Inn, Berne, Ind., Limberlost State Historical Site, Geneva, Ind., and Main Street Bed & Breakfast, Fort Recovery, Ohio, for the photo locations.

Cover project: Snowflakes Tablecloth, page 78

A Warm Welcome

Take a stroll down memory lane and bring to mind your favorite sights, smells and sounds of your grandmother's home. Are your thoughts filled with family dinners, with your aunts, uncles, cousins, Grandma and Grandpa gathered around the large dining room table? Do you remember how Grandma seemed to have an endless supply of lacy tablecloths and linen napkins adorned with delicate edgings to celebrate the occasion?

Perhaps your fondest memory is of cuddling up by the fire in one of Grandma's warm and cozy afghans with a cup of hot apple cider while Grandma read aloud. Then, being tucked into bed at night—that big, tall bed with the pretty crocheted bedspread.

Whatever your memories, hopefully they fill you with a sense of warmth, security and love. To me, Grandmother is an endless source of commitment to family. She is the rock in any crisis, the keeper of secrets whispered by young, excited grandchildren, and the maker of beautiful crocheted pieces. Always within arm's reach, Grandmother's crochet is also a treasured family tradition. After all, was not her crochet always present during thick and thin? Were her fingers not rhythmically working round upon round while attentively listening to her family share their day? And is it not her crocheted pieces for which we yearn upon her passing? Delicate doilies, exquisite tablecloths, bedspreads, cozy afghans, sweet layettes and more are all tangible pieces of her love.

In this volume, you'll find a new collection of crocheted patterns which reflect the same kinds of patterns that accompanied your grandmother throughout her life. My wish is that these pieces not only bring you joy and fulfillment, but that they will also become the same bond between you and your grandchildren that you and your grandmother share.

Laura Scott

Editor,
Grandmother's Favorite Crochet

Contents

Bedroom Comforts

Afghan Treasury

Dining Elegance

Nursery Delights

Christmas Traditions

Doily Accents

Afghan Treasury

Beautiful crocheted afghans have provided comfort and warmth to spouses, children and grandchildren in good times as well as bad. An added comfort is always to be relished when the recipient of a warm afghan realizes the love and care put into the making of this handmade treasure.

Try your hand at Tunisian crochet in this charming Victorian Hearts afghan (far left). Bands of three cream stripes stand out beautifully against a vivid raspberry background on our Raspberry Cream afghan and pillow ensemble (left). Both afghans will complement a variety of decors, from antique to contemporary. Instructions on pages 14–17.

Framed with a colorful plaid border and latticework edging, a cheerful bouquet of summer pansies is the beautiful focal point of this lovely Pansy Bouquet afghan (far right). White on White (right), with its raised floral pattern, has an elegant embossed look that suits any decor. Instructions on pages 18–21.

Crochet this romantic Heartstrings afghan (right) for your dearest! Perfectly shaped heart motifs are attached to the center of 12 chains, giving this already pretty and lacy afghan an added airy touch. A simple shell pattern for the body and border of the afghan makes it a pattern even beginning crocheters can successfully complete and enjoy. Instructions begin on page 18.

A stunning collection of bobbles, puff stitches and special treble crochet stitches comes together to create this masterpiece Climbing Roses afghan (left). An intricate pattern resembles a stony garden wall rich with character and aged with time. Pretty apricot-colored roses climb up the afghan, giving an overall cottage garden effect. Experienced crocheters will enjoy the challenge and sense of fulfillment at completing this marvelous afghan. *Instructions begin on page 23.*

Brushed yarn gives both of these afghans extra body and softness. Butterflies in Flight (upper left) captures the delicacy of these fluttering and ever-evasive creatures of flight. Snowflake Ripple (left) is worked in an attractive front post and back post double crochet ripple pattern and finished off with generous tassels. *Instructions on pages 21–23.*

If you like to take projects on the go, you'll take extra pleasure in this delightful Dainty Rosebuds afghan (right). Pretty rosebuds worked on a solid white background give this afghan a pure look perfect for a little girl's bedroom. Instructions begin on page 25.

The design in this lovely Openwork Afghan (below) has just the right amount of airiness to yield a lacy appearance while solid enough to comfortably snuggle up in. Work it in a solid color as pictured to coordinate with a favorite armchair, or in the favorite color of a loved one to give as a special gift. Instructions begin on page 24.

Raspberry Cream

Shown on page 6

Experience Level: Beginner

Size

Afghan: 42" x 58"

Pillow: 14" square

Materials

- Caron® Simply Soft® knitting worsted weight yarn: 23 oz raspberry and 11 oz cream for afghan; 4 oz cream and 3 oz raspberry for pillow
- Size G/6 crochet hook or size needed to obtain gauge
- 14" square pillow form

Gauge: 8 sc and 7 rows = 2"

To save time, take time to check gauge.

Pattern Notes: When changing colors, work off last 2 lps of first color with new color, cutting first color, leaving a 3" length of yarn.

To make a neater edge, work ends in and crochet over them as you go.

Afghan

Row 1: With cream, ch 202, sc in 2nd ch from hook, [ch 3, sk 3 chs, sc in next ch] rep across, ch 1, turn.

Row 2: Sc in first sc, [ch 3, sc in next sc] rep across.

Rows 3 & 5: Rep Row 2 with raspberry.

Rows 4, 6 & 7: Rep Row 2 with cream.

Rows 8–14: Rep Row 2 with raspberry.

[Rep Rows 1–14 in color sequence] 14 times, [rep Rows 1–7] once.

Trim all ends. Fringe if desired.

Pillow

Row 1: With raspberry, ch 66, sc in 2nd ch from hook, [ch 3, sk 3 chs, sc in next ch] rep across, ch 1, turn.

Row 2: Sc in first sc, [ch 3, sc in next sc] rep across.

Rows 3 & 5: Rep Row 2 with cream.

Rows 4, 6 & 7: Rep Row 2 with raspberry.

Rows 8–14: Rep Row 2 with cream.

[Rep Rows 1–14 in color sequence] 7 times, rep Row 2 once with raspberry. Piece should measure 28".

Finishing

Fold in half with RS tog; sew 2 side seams.

Turn RS out; insert pillow form. Sew or crochet rem side closed.

Add tassels if desired.

—Designed by Loa Ann Thaxton

Victorian Hearts

Shown on page 6

Experience Level: Intermediate

Size

42" x 68" without fringe

42" x 84" with fringe

Materials

- Cascade® 220 100 percent wool yarn (100 grams/3.5 oz per skein): 14 skeins natural #8010
- Size J (14") afghan hook
- Size J/10 crochet hook or size needed to obtain gauge

Gauge: 15 sts and 12 rows = 4" in basic afghan st

To save time, take time to check gauge.

Pattern Notes: Although gauge is not essential in an afghan, you should try to match this gauge as closely as possible. If you are getting more sts to the inch, you are working tightly and should change to a larger hook. If you are getting fewer sts to the inch, you are working loosely and should change to a smaller hook.

All panel finishing, edgings and joinings are worked with size J/10 crochet hook.

Pattern Stitch

Basic afghan st (bas): Ch required number of sts. Keeping all lps on hook, sk first vertical bar, *insert hook under next vertical bar from right to left and pull up a lp; rep from * across.

To complete this and all other rows, yo, pull yarn through the first lp on hook, *yo, pull through 2 lps on hook, rep from * across. One lp will rem on the hook at the end of the row. This lp will become the first lp of the next row.

3-dc bobble st (3dcb): Yo, draw up a lp under next bar in 2nd row below working row, yo and draw through 2 lps on hook, *yo, draw up a lp under same bar, yo and draw through 2 lps on hook, rep from * once more (4 lps on hook), yo and draw through 3 lps.

Basic afghan sts following a 3dcb are worked under the next bars in the working row.

3-hdc puff st (3hdcp): Yo, draw up a lp under next bar in 2nd row below working row, *yo, draw up a lp under same bar, rep from * once (7 lps on hook), yo and draw through 6 lps.

Note: *Basic afghan sts following a 3hdcp are worked under the next bars in the working row.*

Left Side Panel

Row 1: With afghan hook, ch 39, work even following basic afghan st instructions.

Row 2: Work even in bas.

Row 3: Draw up a lp under next bar (2 lps on hook), 3dcb, return to working row, draw up a lp under each of next 33 bars, 3dcb, return to working row, draw up a lp under each of rem 2 bars (39 lps on hook; 2 3dcb), complete row.

Row 4: Work even in basic afghan st.

Row 5: Draw up a lp under next bar (2 lps on hook), 3dcb, return to working row, draw up a lp under each of next 19 bars, 3dcb, return to working row, draw up a lp under each of next 13 bars, 3dcb, return to working row, draw up a lp under each of rem 2 bars (39 lps on hook; 3 3dcb), complete row.

Row 6: Draw up a lp under each of next 11 bars (12 lps on hook), 3hdcp, return to working row, draw up a lp under each of next 7 bars, 3dcb, return to working row, draw up a lp under each of next 3 bars, 3dcb, return to working row, draw up a lp under each of rem 14 bars (39 lps on hook; 2 3dcb and 1 3hdcp), complete row.

Rows 7–35: Working from Chart A (page 16), beg with Row 7 and work through Row 35.

Rows 36–171: Rep Rows 2–35 of Chart A 4 times. (10 double hearts and 171 rows)

Finishing

Drop lp and pick up with other hook. Sc around entire piece, working 2 sc in each corner. Be sure to have 173 sc along long side edges.

Weave in all ends.

Center Panel

Row 1: With afghan hook, ch 33, work even in basic afghan st.

Row 2: Work even in bas.

Row 3: Draw up a lp under next bar (2 lps on hook), 3dcb, return to working row, draw up a lp under each of next 27 bars, 3dcb, return to working row, draw up a lp under each of rem 2 bars (33 lps on hook; 2 3dcb), complete row.

Row 4: Work even in basic afghan st.

Row 5: Draw up a lp under next bar (2 lps on hook), 3dcb, return to working row, draw up a lp under each of next 13 bars, 3dcb, return to working row, draw up a lp under each of next 13 bars, 3dcb, return to working row, draw up a lp under each of rem 2 bars (33 lps on hook; 3 3dcb), complete row.

Rows 6–35: Working from Chart B (page 17), beg with Row 6 and work through Row 35.

Rows 36–171: Rep Rows 2–35 of Chart B 4 times. (10 hearts and 171 rows)

Finishing

Drop lp and pick up with other hook. Sc around entire piece, working 2 sc in each corner. Be sure to have 173 sc along long side edges.

Weave in all ends.

Right Side Panel

Row 1: With afghan hook, ch 39, work even in bas.

Row 2: Work even in bas.

Row 3: Draw up a lp under next bar (2 lps on hook), 3dcb, return to working row, draw up a lp under each of next 33 bars, 3dcb, return to working row, draw up a lp under each of rem 2 bars (39 lps on hook; 2 3dcb), complete row.

Row 4: Work even in bas.

Row 5: Draw up a lp under next bar (2 lps on hook), 3dcb, return to working row, draw up a lp under each of next 13 bars, 3dcb, return to working row, draw up a lp under each of next 19 bars, 3dcb, return to working row, draw up a lp under each of rem 2 bars (39 lps on hook; 3 3dcb), complete row.

Row 6: Draw up a lp under each of next 13 bars (14 lps on hook), 3dcb, return to working row, draw up a lp under each of next 3 bars, 3dcb, return to working row, draw up a lp under each of next 7 bars, 3hdcp, return to working row, draw up a lp under each of rem 12 bars (39 lps on hook; 2 3dcb and 1 3hdcp), complete row.

Rows 7–35: Working from Chart C (page 17), beg with Row 7 and work through Row 35.

Rows 36–171: Rep Rows 2–35 of Chart C 4 times. (10 double hearts and 171 rows)

Finishing

Drop lp and pick up with other hook. Sc around entire piece, working 2 sc in each corner. Be sure to have 173 sc along long side edges.

Weave in all ends.

Right Side Panel Right Edging

Row 1: With RS facing, join with a sl st in sc at lower right corner, ch 4 (counts as dc, ch 1), dc in same sc as joining (½ dc cluster made), **sk next 3 sc, dc in next sc, *ch 1, dc in same sc *, rep from * to * twice (dc cluster made), rep from ** across, ending with sk next 3 sc, dc in last sc, ch 1, dc in same sc (½ dc cluster made), fasten off. (42 dc clusters)

Weave in all ends. Set aside.

Center Panel Right Edging

Row 1: With RS facing, join with a sl st in sc at lower right corner, work as for Right Side Panel Right Edging, turn.

Rows 2 & 3: Sl st in ch-1 sp, ch 4, dc in same sp, *dc, [ch 1, dc in same sp] 3 times in 2nd ch-1 sp of next dc cluster, rep from * across, [dc, ch 1, dc] in last ½-dc cluster, turn, fasten off at end of Row 3.

Weave in all ends. Set aside.

Right Side Panel Left Edging & Joining

Rows 1 & 2: With RS facing, join with a sl st in sc at upper left corner. Work as for Rows 1 and 2 of Center Panel Right Edging, turn.

Lay Right Side Panel and Center Panel on a flat surface and complete Row 3 of Right Side Panel, joining panels as follows:

Row 3: Sl st in ch-1 sp on Right Side Panel Edging, ch 4, sl st in ch-1 sp of ending ½ dc cluster on Center Panel Edging, dc in same ch-1 sp on Right Side Panel Edging (½ dc cluster complete), **dc in 2nd ch-1 sp of next dc cluster on Right Side Panel Edging, ch 1, dc in same sp, sl st in 2nd ch-1 sp of next dc cluster on Center Panel Edging, dc in same sp on Right Side Panel Edging, ch 1, dc in same sp (dc cluster made), rep from ** across, ending with dc in ch-1 sp of last ½ dc cluster on Right Side Panel Edging, sl st in ch-1 sp of last ½ dc cluster on Center Panel Edging, dc in same sp on Right Side Panel Edging, fasten off.

Weave in all ends.

Left Side Panel Left Edging

Row 1: With RS facing, join with a sl st in sc at upper left corner, work as for Right Side Panel Right Edging, fasten off.

Weave in all ends. Set aside.

Left Side Panel Right Edging

With RS facing, join with a sl st in sc at lower right corner.

Rows 1–3: Work as for Center Panel Right Edging.

Weave in all ends. Set aside.

Center Panel Left Edging & Joining

Rows 1 & 2: With RS facing, join with a sl st in sc at upper left corner, work as for Rows 1 and 2 of Center Panel Right Edging, turn.

Lay Center Panel and Left Side Panel on a flat surface and complete Row 3 of Center Panel, joining panels as follows:

Row 3: Sl st in ch-1 sp on Center Panel Edging, ch 4, sl st in ch-1 sp of ending ½ dc cluster on Left Side Panel Edging, dc in same ch-1 sp on Center Panel Edging (½ dc cluster complete), **dc in 2nd ch-1 sp of next dc cluster on

CHART A

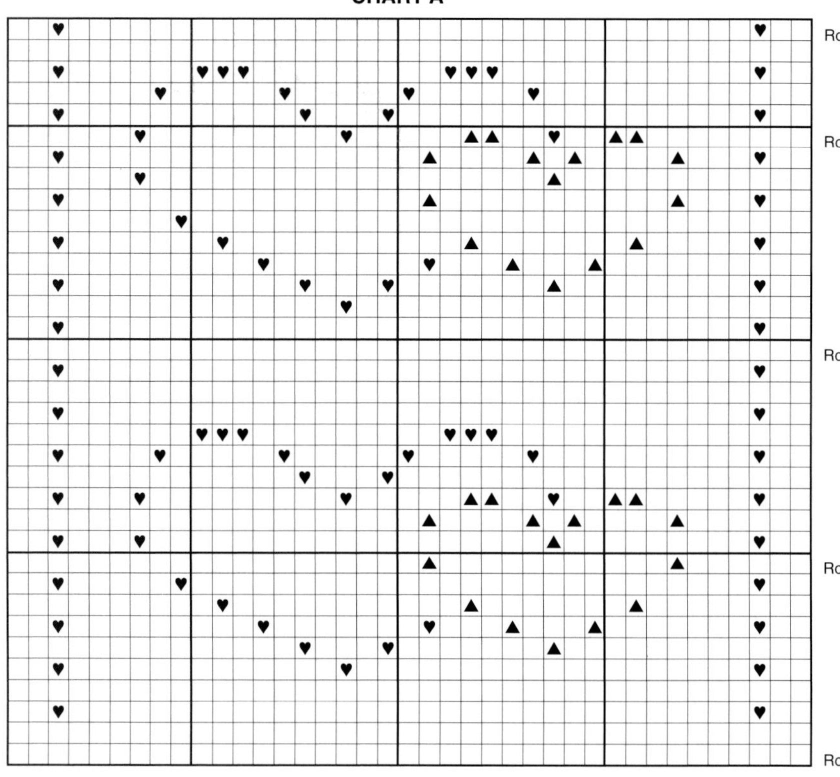

Center Panel Edging, ch 1, dc in same sp, sl st in 2nd ch-1 sp of next dc cluster on Left Side Panel Edging, dc in same sp on Center Panel Edging, ch 1, dc in same sp (dc cluster made), rep from ** across, ending with dc in ch-1 sp of last ½ dc cluster on Center Panel Edging, sl st in ch-1 sp of last ½ dc cluster on Left Side Panel Edging, dc in same sp on Center Panel Edging, fasten off.

Weave in all ends.

Fringe

Make triple knot fringe on both ends of afghan as follows:

Cut 22" strands; use 5 strands per knot. Tie 33 knots evenly sp across edges.

Block afghan according to manufacturer's instructions.

—Designed by Bobbi Hayward

CHART B

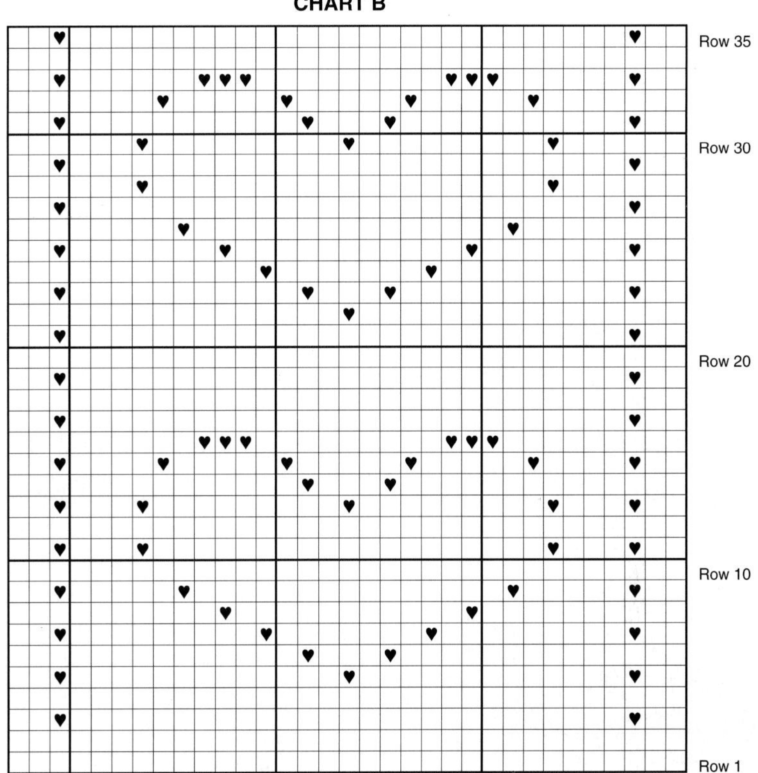

CHART C

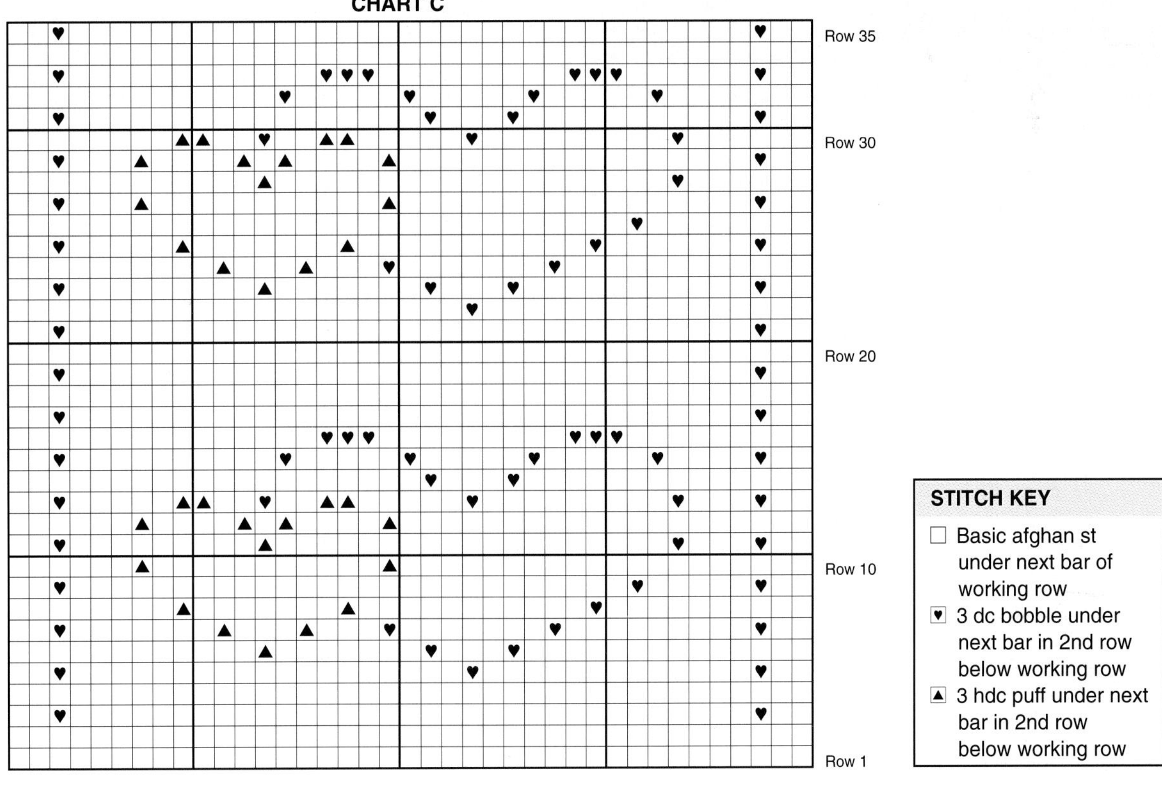

STITCH KEY

- ☐ Basic afghan st under next bar of working row
- ♥ 3 dc bobble under next bar in 2nd row below working row
- ▲ 3 hdc puff under next bar in 2nd row below working row

Heartstrings

Shown on page 8

Experience Level: Advanced beginner

Size: Approximately 48" x 61"

Materials

- Bernat® Berella "4"® worsted weight yarn (3.5 oz per skein): 10 skeins pale antique rose #8814
- Size F/5 crochet hook
- Size I/9 crochet hook or size needed to obtain gauge
- Yarn needle

Gauge: 3 shell rows = 2"; 1 lace panel of 4 shells = 4½" wide with size I hook

Heart motif = 1¾" with size F hook

To save time, take time to check gauge.

Afghan

Row 1: Beg at bottom edge with size I hook, loosely ch 147, sc in 2nd ch from hook and in each ch across, turn.

Row 2: Ch 3 (counts as first dc), sk 1 sc, shell of 2 dc, ch 1, 2 dc in next sc, [sk 2 sc, shell in next sc] 3 times (1 lace panel of 4 shells completed), *ch 12, sk 12 sc, shell of 2 dc, ch 1, 2 dc in next sc, [sk 2 sc, shell in next sc] 3 times, rep from * 5 times, sk next sc, dc in last sc, turn.

Rows 3 & 4: Ch 3 (counts as first dc), [shell in ch-1 sp of next shell] 4 times, *ch 12, [shell in ch-1 sp of next shell] 4 times, rep from * 5 times, dc in last dc, turn.

Row 5: Ch 3 (counts as first dc), [shell in ch-1 sp of next shell] 4 times, *ch 6, work 1 long sc around center of ch-12 sts of Rows 2, 3 and 4, ch 6, [shell in ch-1 sp of shell] 4 times, rep from * 5 times, dc in last dc, turn.

Rows 6–8: Rep Row 3.

Row 9: Rep Row 5.

Rows 10–89: Rep Rows 6–9.

Row 90: Rep Row 3.

Row 91: Ch 1, sc in each dc, ch-1 sp and ch across, fasten off.

Border

Rnd 1: With RS facing, attach yarn in 3rd ch of turning ch-3 in Row 90 on left side of afghan, ch 3, [dc, ch 1, 2 dc] in same sp, [sk next row, shell in top of next row] rep to bottom left corner, ending with last shell in top of Row 2, shell in corner (Row 1), working across opposite side of foundation ch, the bottom of the following 4 shells will be aligned with bottoms of 4 shells of Row 2 of afghan, [work shell in line with next shell] 4 times, *working across next 12 sts, [sk 2 sts, shell in next st] 3 times, [work shell in line with next shell] 4 times *, rep from * to * across, shell in corner (Row 1), working along right side of afghan, shell in top of next row, [sk next row, shell in top of next row] rep across to next corner, shell in dc at end of Row 90, working across top of afghan, [work shell in line with next shell of Row 90] 4 times, **working across area of next 12 sts between shells, [sk 2 sts, shell in next st] 3 times, [work shell in line with next shell of Row 90] 4 times **, rep from ** to ** across top edge, sl st to join in top of beg ch-3, sl st into next ch-1 sp of shell.

Rnd 2: Ch 3 (first dc), [dc, ch 1, 2 dc] in same sp, [shell in shell] rep around, working extra shells into corner sps where needed to keep corners flat, join in 3rd ch of beg ch-3, fasten off.

Heart Motif *(Make 132)*

With size F hook, ch 6, sl st in 2nd ch from hook, sc in next ch, hdc in next ch, dc in next ch, [3 tr, ch 1, sl st, ch 4, 2 tr] in last ch, working across opposite side of ch, dc in next ch, hdc in next ch, sc in next ch, sl st in each of next 2 chs, ending at bottom tip of heart, fasten off.

Finishing

Stitch a heart motif securely to center of each ch-12 group.

Note: *Stitch heart not only to long sc that encloses the ch-12s, but also to each of the chs on each side. This will secure the heart motif in a straight position on the ch group.*

—Designed by Wilma Pelley for Carol Alexander Designs, courtesy of Designs for America

Pansy Bouquet

Shown on page 9

Experience Level: Advanced beginner

Size: Approximately 51" x 62"

Materials

- Berna® Berella "4"® worsted weight yarn (3.5 oz/240 yds per skein): 10 skeins winter white #8941, 2 skeins deep sea green #8876 and 1 skein each medium damson #8855, pale damson #8853, navy #8965 and baby yellow #8945
- Size G/6 crochet hook
- Size I/9 crochet hook or size needed to obtain gauge

- 2 yds ¾"-wide medium blue velvet ribbon
- Sewing thread to match ribbon
- Tapestry needle

Gauge: 4 sc and 17 rows = 4"

To save time, take time to check gauge.

Pattern Notes: Horizontal stripes are worked into afghan in sc. Vertical stripes and stems of flowers are added later with ch st.

Pansies and leaves are crocheted separately and sewn on. Ribbon is sewn to afghan last.

Join rnds with a sl st unless otherwise stated.

Pattern Stitch

Bullion st: Referring to Fig. 2, bring ndl up at A, insert at B and bring up again at A, wrap yarn 10 times around ndl tip. Hold left thumb on coiled thread and pull ndl through; still holding the coiled thread, turn ndl back to B and insert in same place (A). Pull thread through until Bullion st lies flat.

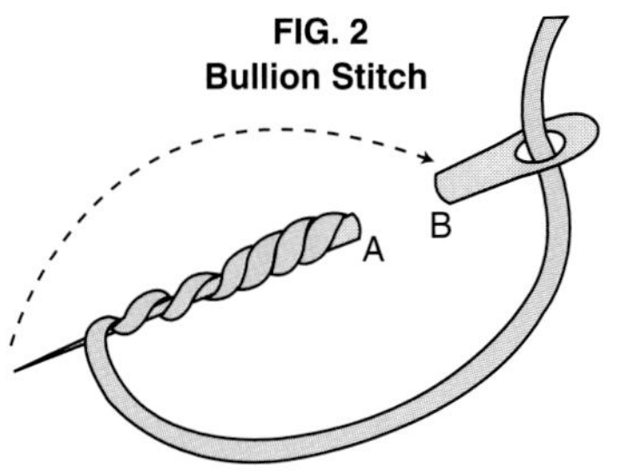

Bring needle up at A, wrap yarn around needle 10 times, take needle down at B, then back up at A.

Body

With larger hook and winter white, ch 159, sc in 2nd ch from hook and in each of next 11 chs, [ch 1, sk next ch, sc in next ch] twice, sc in each of next 7 chs, rep between [] twice, sc in each of next 104 chs, rep between [] twice, sc in each of next 7 chs, rep between [] twice, sc in each of rem 12 chs, turn. (158 sts)

Continue in pattern as set, working ch 1 at beg of each row, 1 sc in each sc, and 1 ch over each ch sp.

Work 13 more rows winter white, 2 rows each navy, winter white and baby yellow, 8 rows winter white, 2 rows each medium damson, winter white and pale damson; continue with winter white until body meas 48" from beg, ending with an even number of rows, rep stripes, reversing order of colors (beg with pale damson and end with navy), work 14 more rows winter white, cut winter white but do not fasten off, secure st for later use.

Vertical Stripes

With larger hook and double strand of yarn, hold yarn below afghan and hook above. Work 1 ch st into each ch sp from bottom of afghan to top. Work sts loosely so fabric does not pucker.

Beg 3¼" inside right-hand bottom edge of afghan, work 1 stripe each of navy, baby yellow, medium damson and pale damson, leaving approximately ¼" between navy and baby yellow, 2¼" between baby yellow and medium damson, and ¼" between medium damson and pale damson.

Rep on opposite side, reversing order of colors.

Weave in loose ends on wrong side of afghan.

Edging

(Multiple of 12 sts + 2)

Rnd 1 (RS): Attach deep sea green in last st of Body, ch 1, with RS facing, sc in each st across (158 sc), place a colored thread to mark corner, work 2 more sc in same place as last st, work 191 sc along side edge, mark corner, 2 sc in same st, sc in each rem lp of beg ch, mark corner, 2 sc in same st, 191 sc along side edge, mark corner, 2 sc in same place as first st of rnd, join in beg sc. (706 sc)

Rnd 2: Ch 1, 2 sc in same place as sl st, *[ch 2, sk next 2 sc, sc in each of next 2 sc] rep across to 1 st before marker, 2 sc in next sc, ch 2, sk corner sc, sc in each of next 2 sc, rep from * around, join in beg sc.

Rnd 3: Ch 1, sc in same place as sl st, sc in next sc, *[2 sc in next ch-2 sp, sc in each of next 2 sc] rep across to corner, 5 sc in ch-2 lp at corner, sc in each of next 2 sc, rep from * around, join in beg sc.

Rnd 4: Ch 1, sc in each of next 2 sc, *[ch 5, sk next 2 sc, sc in each of next 2 sc] rep across to corner, ch 5, sk next 2 sc, 2 sc in next sc, rep from * around, join in beg sc.

Rnd 5: Ch 1, *7 sc in each of next 2 ch-5 lps, 4 sc in next ch-5 lp, turn, [ch 5, sl st in 4th sc of next 7-sc group] twice, ch 1, turn, 7 sc in next ch-5 lp, 4 sc in next ch-5 lp, ch 5, turn, sl st in 4th sc of next 7-sc group, ch 1, turn, 7 sc in next ch-5 lp, 3 sc in each of next 2 ch-5 lps (these are the 2 ch-5 lps that each have only 4 sc sts), rep from * to corner, in corner work 7 sc in first ch-5 lp, 4 sc in next ch-5 lp, ch 5, turn, sl st in 4th sc of next 7-sc group, ch 1, turn, 7 sc in next ch-5 lp, 3 sc in next ch-5 lp (ch-5 lp that has only 4 sc sts), continue in patt from * around, join in beg sc, fasten off.

Pansies

Note: *Make 4 Combination 1 (A = medium damson/B = pale damson) and 3 Combination 2 (A = navy/B = medium damson)*

Rnd 1: With smaller hook and baby yellow, leaving 24" tail for sewing, ch 3, join to form a ring, ch 1, [sc in ring, ch 3] 5 times, fasten off baby yellow, attach A, join in beg sc.

Rnd 2: [Sl st in next lp, ch 2, 6 hdc in lp, sc in lp] 5 times.

Rnd 3: Ch 1, [2 sc around ch-2 of beg ch of previous rnd, ch 2, 2 dc in next hdc, hdc in each of next 4 hdc, 2 dc in next hdc, hdc in next sc, sl st in next sl st] twice, fasten off A, attach B, ch 1, [2 sc around beg ch-2 of previous rnd, ch 2, hdc in each of next 2 hdc, tr around baby yellow ch-5 lp between next 2 sts, sk next unworked st of Rnd 2, sc in each of next 3 hdc, hdc in next sc, sl st in next sl st] 3 times, fasten off.

Leaves *(Make 17)*

With larger hook and deep sea green, ch 10, sc in 2nd ch from hook, hdc in next ch, dc in each of next 3 chs, hdc in each of next 2 chs, sc in each of next 2 chs, working back along rem lp of beg ch, sc in each of first 2 chs, hdc in each of next 2 chs, dc in each of next 3 chs, hdc in next ch, sc in last ch, join in beg sc, fasten off, leaving tail for sewing.

Finishing

Arrange pansies on afghan as shown in Fig. 1. Sew to afghan with baby yellow yarn and 5 bullion sts (Fig. 2).

FIG. 1

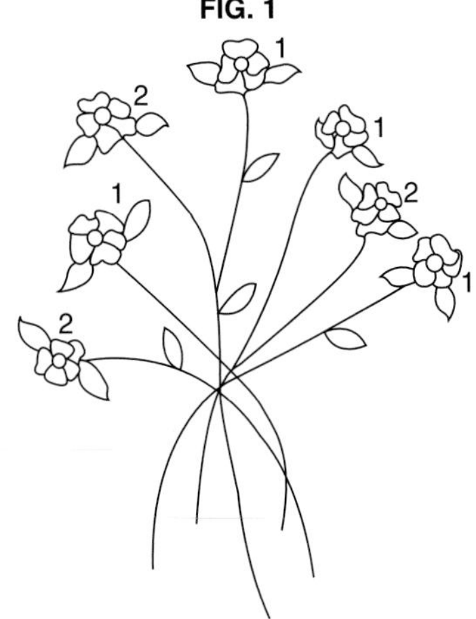

Using a single strand of deep green, ch-st stems.

Sew leaves in place (yarn tail is at base of leaf).

Tie ribbon into bow and pin to afghan (Fig. 3). Sew in place using matching thread and blind sts.

Weave in loose ends.

FIG. 3

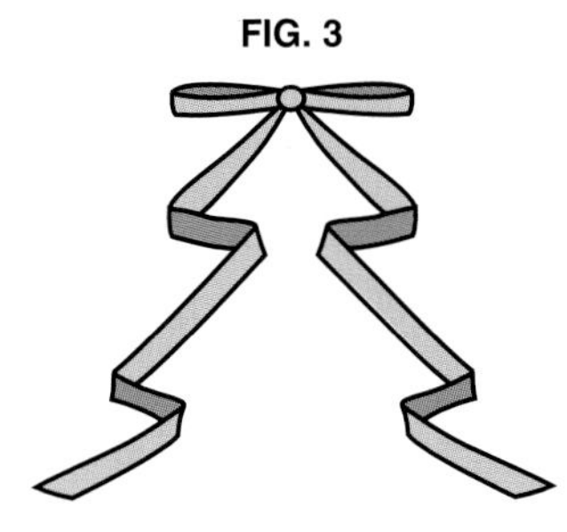

Note: *Pansies may be steamed open using damp pressing cloth and steam iron. Never touch iron to yarn or apply any pressure to work.*

—Designed by Maureen Egan Emlet, courtesy of Designs for America

White on White

Shown on page 9

Experience Level: Advanced beginner

Size: Approximately 41" x 51" without edging

Materials

- Caron Wintuk 4-ply yarn (3½ oz per skein): 14 skeins off-white #3002
- Size H/8 crochet hook
- Size I/9 crochet hook or size needed to obtain gauge
- Size 17 circular knitting needle or a broomstick or dowel of equal diameter
- Large-eyed, blunt-tipped tapestry needle

Gauge: 15 sts and 16 rows = 4" with larger hook over sc

To save time, take time to check gauge.

Pattern Notes: Afghan consists of 6 sc panels and 5 broomstick lace panels.

There will be some rippling between sc and broomstick lace panels. Gently steam-press, using a cool steam iron, before beginning edging.

Join rnds with a sl st unless otherwise stated.

Pattern Stitch

Puff st: [Yo, draw up a lp] 3 times in indicated st, yo and draw through all 7 lps on hook.

Afghan

Row 1: With larger hook, ch 153, sc in 2nd ch from hook and in each ch across, ch 1, turn. (152 sc)

Rows 2–15: Sc in each sc across, ch 1, turn, do not turn after Row 15.

Note: *Yarn will be on left side of work with RS facing.*

Lace pattern
Row 16: Sl lp from left side of work onto size 17 circular knitting ndl, sk first sc on left-hand side, draw up a lp from back lp of next sc and place on ndl, [draw up a lp from back lp of next sc on right and place on ndl] rep across until all sts are worked and there are 152 lps on ndl.

Row 17: Sl 4 lps off ndl, turn them tog to the right, draw up a lp through center of all 4 lps, ch 1, 4 sc in center of lps, [sl 4 lps off ndl, turn them to the right, 4 sc in center of all 4 lps] rep across, ch 1, turn.

Rows 18 & 19: Sc in each sc across, ch 1, turn, do not turn after Row 19.

Rows 20–31: Rep Rows 16–19.

Rows 32 & 33: Rep Rows 16 and 17.

Rows 34–49: Sc in each sc across, ch 1, turn.

[Rep Rows 16–49] 5 times, fasten off.

Edging
Rnd 1: With smaller hook, attach yarn at top right corner with RS facing, 3 sc in corner, sc in each sc across top, 3 sc in corner, sc in each row along left side of afghan, 3 sc in bottom corner, sc in each ch across bottom beg-ch edge, 3 sc in corner, sc in each row along right side of afghan, join in beg sc, ch 1, turn.

Rnd 2 (puff st rnd): With WS facing, sc in first sc, [puff st in next sc, sc in next sc] rep around, working 3 sc in middle sc of 3-sc group (corner), join in beg sc, ch 1, turn.

Rnd 3: With RS facing, sc in each st around, working 3 sc in corners, join in beg sc, ch 1, turn.

Tr shell edging
Rnd 4: With WS facing, sc in first sc, *sk 3 sc, [{tr, ch 1} 4 times, tr] in next sc, sk 3 sc, sc in next sc, rep from * around, adjusting patt to join in beg sc, turn.

Picot edging
Rnd 5: With RS facing, [ch 2, sl st in 2nd ch from hook, sk 1 st, sl st in next st] rep around, fasten off.

Trim
Rosettes *(Make 30)*
Rnd 1: With smaller hook, ch 3, join to form a ring, ch 4, [dc in ring, ch 1] 7 times, join in 3rd ch of beg ch-4, ch 1, turn.

Rnd 2 (WS): [Sc in dc, sc in ch-1 sp, puff st in same sp] rep around, join in beg sc, turn.

Rnd 3 (RS): [Ch 2, sl st in 2nd ch from hook, sk 1 st, sl st in next st] rep around, fasten off.

Vines *(Make 24)*
With smaller hook, ch 40, sl st in 2nd ch from hook, [ch 2, sl st in 2nd ch from hook, sk 1 ch, sl st in next ch] rep across, fasten off.

Finishing
With tapestry ndl, sew rosettes evenly sp on each sc panel. Using photo as a guide, wind vines over and under rosettes; sew in place.

—Designed by Michele Maks Thompson, courtesy of Designs for America

Snowflake Ripple

Shown on page 10

Experience Level: Advanced
Size: Approximately 44" x 56"
Materials

- Worsted weight yarn: 16 oz white
- Lion Brand Jiffy 2-ply brushed yarn: 40 oz mint green
- Size K/10½ hook

Gauge: 4 dc = 1"

To save time, take time to check gauge.

Afghan
Row 1: With mint green, ch 195, beg in 4th ch from hook, dc 2 tog over next 2 chs, *dc in each of next 5 chs, [2 dc, ch 1, 2 dc] in next ch, dc in each of next 5 chs, dc 5 tog over next 5 chs, rep from * across, ending last rep with dc in each of next 5 chs, dc rem 3 chs tog, ch 3, turn.

Row 2: Sk first st, bpdc 2 tog, *fpdc over each of next 5 sts, [2 dc, ch 1, 2 dc] in ch-1 sp, fpdc over each of next 5 sts, bpdc 5 tog, rep from * across, ending last rep with fpdc over each of next 5 sts, bpdc 3 tog, ch 3, turn.

Row 3: Sk first st, fpdc 2 tog, *bpdc over each of next 5 sts, [2 dc, ch 1, 2 dc] in ch-1 sp, bpdc over each of next 5 sts, fpdc 5 tog, rep from * across, ending last rep with bpdc over each of next 5 sts, fpdc 3 tog, ch 3, turn.

Row 4: Rep Row 2.

Row 5: Rep Row 3.

Row 6: Sk first st, bpdc 2 tog, *fpdc over each of next 5 sts, [2 dc, ch 1, 2 dc] in ch-1 sp, fpdc over each of next 5 sts, bpdc 5 tog, rep from * across, ending last rep with fpdc over each of next 5 sts, bpdc 3 tog, fasten off, attach white, ch 3, turn.

Row 7: Sk first st, fpdc 2 tog, [dc in next st, ch 1, sk 1 st] twice, dc in next dc, [2 dc, ch 1, 2 dc] in ch-1 sp, dc in next dc, [ch 1, sk 1 st, dc in next st] twice, fpdc 5 tog, rep from * across, ending last rep with dc in next dc, [ch 1, sk 1 st, dc in next st] twice, fpdc 3 tog, ch 3, turn.

Row 8: Sk first st, keeping last lp on hook, [bpdc over next st, dc in ch-1 sp], yo, draw through all 3 lps, *dc in next dc, ch 1, sk ch-1 sp, dc in next dc, ch 1, sk next dc, dc in next dc, [2 dc, ch 1, 2 dc] in ch-1 sp, dc in next dc, ch 1, sk next dc, dc in next dc, ch 1, sk ch-1 sp, dc in next dc, keeping last lp on hook, [dc in next ch-1 sp, bpdc over each of next 3 sts, dc in next ch-1 sp], yo, draw through all 6 lps, rep from * across, ending last rep with dc in next dc, ch 1, sk next dc, dc in next dc, ch 1, sk ch-1 sp, dc in next dc, keeping last lp on hook, [dc in ch-1 sp, bpdc over next 2 sts], yo, draw through all 4 lps on hook, ch 3, turn.

Row 9: Sk first st, keeping last lp on hook, [fpdc over next st, dc in ch-1 sp], yo, draw through all 3 lps, *dc in next dc, ch 1, sk ch-1 sp, dc in next dc, ch 1, sk next dc, dc in next dc, [2 dc, ch 1, 2 dc] in ch-1 sp, dc in next dc, ch 1, sk next dc, dc in next dc, ch 1, sk ch-1 sp, dc in next dc, keeping last lp on hook, [dc in next ch-1 sp, fpdc over each of next 3 sts, dc in next ch-1 sp], yo, draw through all 6 lps, rep from * across, ending last rep with dc in next dc, ch 1, sk next dc, dc in next dc, ch 1, sk ch-1 sp, dc in next dc, keeping last lp on hook, [dc in ch-1 sp, fpdc over next 2 sts], yo, draw through all 4 lps on hook, fasten off white, attach mint green, ch 3, turn.

Row 10: Sk first st, keeping last lp on hook, [bpdc over next st, dc in ch-1 sp], yo, draw through all 3 lps, *dc in each of next 5 sts, [2 dc, ch 1, 2 dc] in ch-1 sp, dc in each of next 5 sts, keeping last lp on hook, [dc in next ch-1 sp, bpdc over each of next 3 sts, dc in next ch-1 sp], yo, draw through all 6 lps, rep from * across, ending last rep with dc in each of next 5 sts, keeping last lp on hook, [dc in ch-1 sp, bpdc over next 2 sts], yo, draw through all 4 lps on hook, ch 3, turn.

Row 11: Rep Row 3.

Rep Rows 2–11 to make 9 (6-row) sections of mint green and 8 (3-row) sections of white.

Edging

Row 1: Attach white in corner, sc in each st around, working 3 sc in each point and sk 2 sc in each valley, turn.

Row 2: Rep Row 1, fasten off.

Row 3: Attach mint green, sl st in each st around, fasten off.

Make a tassel from mint green; attach to each point.

—Designed by Debby Caldwell

Butterflies in Flight

Shown on page 10

Experience Level: Advanced beginner

Size

Afghan: 48" x 74"

Each strip: 4½" x 74"

Materials

- Worsted weight brushed acrylic yarn (750 grams/2,025 yds per skein): 15 skeins lavender
- Size H/8 crochet hook
- Yarn needle

Gauge: Butterfly (Rows 2–7): 4½" wide x 3½" high

To save time, take time to check gauge.

Strip *(Make 10)*

Row 1: Ch 5, join with a sl st in beg ch to form a ring, ch 3, 2 dc, ch 2, 2 dc, ch 5, 2 dc, ch 2, 3 dc in ring, ch 5, turn.

Row 2: [3 dc, ch 2, 2 dc] in ch-2 sp, ch 10, sk next ch-5 sp, [2 dc, ch 2, 3 dc] in next ch-2 sp, ch 5, turn.

Row 3: [3 dc, ch 2, 2 dc] in ch-2 sp, ch 10, sk next ch-10 sp, [2 dc, ch 2, 3 dc] in ch-2 sp, ch 5, turn.

Row 4: [3 dc, ch 2, 2 dc] in ch-2 sp, ch 20, sk next ch-10 sp, [2 dc, ch 2, 3 dc] in next ch-2 sp, ch 5, turn.

Row 5: [3 dc, ch 2, 2 dc] in ch-2 sp, ch 2, wrap ch-20 down around first ch-5 to form a lp in back, 1 sc in first half of lp of ch-20, 1 sc in lp of ch-20, 1 sc in last half of lp of ch-20 (see Fig. 1), ch 2, 2 dc, ch 2, 3 dc in ch-2 sp, ch 5, turn.

FIG. 1

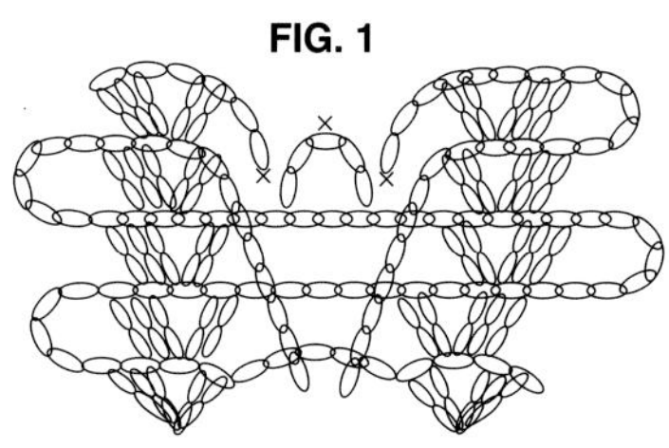

Row 6: [3 dc, ch 2, 2 dc] in first ch-2 sp, sk 2 ch-2 sps, [2 dc, ch 2, 3 dc] in last ch-2 sp, ch 5, turn.

Row 7: [3 dc, ch 2, 2 dc] in first ch-2 sp, ch 5, [2 dc, ch 2, 3 dc] in last ch-2 sp, ch 5, turn.

Rep Rows 2–7 for 18 butterflies, ending with Row 6.

Joining Strips

Join yarn with a sl st to 3rd ch of first ch-5 lp on first strip, *ch 5, sl st in same lp, ch 2, sl st in 3rd ch of next ch-5 lp on 2nd strip, ch 5, sl st in same lp, ch 2, sl st in 3rd ch of next ch-5 lp on first strip, rep from * to end of strips, fasten off.

Join rem strips in the same manner. Weave in all loose ends with yarn needle.

—Designed by Rhonda Semonis

Climbing Roses

Shown on page 11

Experience Level: Advanced

Size: Approximately 48" x 61"

Materials

- Caron Wintuk worsted weight yarn (3.5 oz per skein): 15 skeins oatmeal #3021, 3 skeins sunset apricot #3039 and 1 skein spring meadow #3046
- Size I/9 crochet hook or size needed to obtain gauge

Gauge: 3 dc = 1"; 3 dc rows = 2"

Pattern Notes: The cables formed by the bptr and fptr sts must be opened out around the puff sts which they enclose. To do this, grasp the 2 tr sts that surround each puff st and pull them outward away from the puff st into a circular shape. Slightly raise puff sts within the cables either by gently pulling from the front side or pushing from underneath.

Join rnds with a sl st unless otherwise stated.

Ch 3, turn at the end of afghan rows does not count as first dc of following row.

Pattern Stitches

Bobble st: [Yo, insert hook in st, yo, pull up lp loosely] 4 times, yo, pull through all 9 lps on hook.

Puff st: [Yo, insert hook in st, yo, pull up lp loosely] 5 times, yo, pull through all 11 lps on hook, ch 1 and draw tightly to close.

Back post treble crochet (bptr): Work tr around back of post of st indicated by inserting hook from right to left, unless indicated.

Front post treble crochet (fptr): Work tr around front of post of st by inserting hook from right to left.

Pattern

Row 1: [*Bptr around next st, puff st in next st, bptr around next st *, dc in next st] twice, rep from * to * once.

Row 2: [*Leaving last lp of each st on hook, work dc in next st, sk puff st, fptr around next tr, yo, draw through all 3 lps on hook, dc in top of sk puff st; leaving last lp of each st on hook, work fptr around tr just before same puff st, dc in top of tr just after puff st, yo, draw through all 3 lps on hook *, dc in next st] twice, rep from * to * once.

Row 3: [*Bptr by inserting hook from right to left under raised post of next tr previously worked on last row (the tr crossing above top of puff st), puff st in next st (directly aligned over puff st on previous row), bptr by inserting hook from left to right under raised post of same tr *, dc in next st] twice, rep from * to * once.

Afghan

Row 1: Beg at bottom edge with oatmeal, loosely ch 128, dc in 4th ch from hook and in each ch across, fasten off. (125 dc)

Row 2: Attach oatmeal in first dc of Row 1, dc in same st and in each st across, ch 3, turn. (125 dc)

Row 3: Dc in each of first 2 dc, work Row 1 of patt st, [dc in each of next 11 dc, work Row 1 of patt st] rep across, ending with dc in each of last 2 dc, ch 3, turn.

Row 4: Dc in each of first 2 dc, work Row 2 of patt st, [dc in each of next 11 dc, work Row 2 of patt st] rep across, ending with dc in each of last 2 dc, ch 3, turn.

Row 5: Dc in each of first 2 dc, work Row 3 of patt st, [dc in each of next 11 dc, work Row 3 of patt st] rep across, ending with dc in each of last 2 dc, ch 3, turn.

Rows 6–91: Rep Rows 4 and 5, ending with Row 5.

Row 92: Dc in each st across, sk each ch-1, fasten off. (125 dc)

Border

Rnd 1: Attach oatmeal at right corner on short side, ch 2, 2 hdc in same st, hdc evenly around, working 3 hdc in each rem corner, sl st in beg ch-2 and in next (corner) st.

Rnd 2: Ch 3, [dc, ch 2, 2 dc] in same st, ch 1, sk next st, {dc in next st, ch 1, sk next st} rep across to corner, *[2 dc, ch 2, 2 dc] in corner st, ch 1, sk next st, rep between {} to next corner, rep from * twice, join in 3rd ch of beg ch-3, fasten off.

Rnd 3: Attach oatmeal in first ch-1 sp to left of any corner group, ch 1, *[work bobble st around post of next dc by inserting hook from right to left around back of post, sc in next ch-1 sp] rep across to next corner group, work bobble st around post of each of next 2 dc of corner group, [sc, ch 2, sc] in corner ch-2 sp, work bobble st around post of each of next 2 dc of corner group, sc in next ch-1 sp, rep from * around, omitting last sc in ch-1 sp at end of last rep, join in beg ch-1.

Rnds 4 & 5: Ch 2, hdc in each st around, working [2 hdc, ch 2, 2 hdc] in each corner ch-2 sp, join in 2nd ch of beg ch-2, fasten off at end of Rnd 5.

Rnd 6: Attach oatmeal in any corner ch-2 sp, ch 3, *work bobble st in corner sp, ch 3, sk 1 st, sc in next st, [ch 3, sk next 2 sts, bobble st in next st, ch 3, sk next 2 sts, sc in next st] rep across side, ending 1 st away from next corner sp, rep from * 3 times, join in top of beg bobble st, fasten off.

Rose *(Make 48)*

Rnd 1: With sunset apricot, ch 5, join to form a ring, ch 1, [sc, 5 dc, sc] 3 times in ring (3 petals), join in beg sc.

Rnd 2: Working on backside of Rnd 1, in back of *posts* of sts, sl st to center of first petal, [ch 3, sl st in center st of next petal] twice, ch 3, join in first ch of beg ch-3 on first petal.

Rnd 3: [{Sc, hdc, 5 dc, hdc, sc} in next ch-3 sp] 3 times, join in beg sc.

Rnd 4: Rep Rnd 2, changing all ch-3 sts to ch-5.

Rnd 5: [{Sc, hdc, 7 dc, hdc, sc} in next ch-5 sp] 3 times, join in beg sc, fasten off.

Leaf *(Make 48)*

Rnd 1: With spring meadow, ch 17, beg in 2nd ch from hook, *sl st in next st, hdc in each of next 2 sts, dc in each of next 3 sts, hdc in next st, sl st in next st, sc in next st, hdc in next st, dc in each of next 3 sts, hdc in each of next 2 sts, sl st in next st *, ch 1, working along opposite side of foundation ch, rep from * to * once, fasten off.

With oatmeal, st leaf to back of rose; fasten off, leaving sewing length.

Finishing

With yarn ndl, sew 8 roses to each of the 6 cable sections, beg at bottom edge and sp evenly apart in a zigzag patt to top edge.

Note: *Alternate zigzag patt on cable section (i.e., on first cable section beg with first rose at bottom positioned at left outside edge of cables); on next cable section, beg with first rose at bottom positioned at right outside edge of cables, etc. Arrange roses so that leaves are not all positioned the same way.*

—Designed by Carol Alexander and Brenda Stratton, courtesy of Designs for America

Openwork Afghan

Shown on page 12

Experience Level: Advanced beginner

Size: 48" x 68"

Materials

- Aunt Lydia's 4-ply worsted weight yarn (3.5 oz per skein): 15 skeins dark classic rose #5247
- Size G/6 crochet hook

Gauge: 5 sc = 1¼"; 12 patt rows = 4"

To save time, take time to check gauge.

Pattern Note: Work loosely throughout.

Afghan

Row 1: Ch 242, sc in 2nd ch from hook and in each rem ch across, ch 1, turn. (241)

Row 2: Sc in each of first 3 sc, [ch 4, sk 3 sc, tr in next sc, ch 4, sk 3 sc, sc in each of next 5 sc] rep across, ending with ch 4, sk 3 sc, tr in next sc, ch 4, sk 3 sc, sc in each of last 3 sc, ch 3, turn.

Row 3: Sk first sc, dc in each of next 2 sc, [ch 3, sc in ch-4 lp, sc in tr, sc in next ch-4 lp, ch 3, sk 1 sc, dc in each of next 3 sc, sk next sc] rep across, ending with dc in each of last 3 sc, ch 3, turn.

Row 4: Sk first dc, dc in each of next 2 dc, [ch 4, sc in each of next 3 sc, ch 4, dc in each of next 3 dc] rep across, ending with dc in each of last 2 dc, dc in 3rd ch of ch-3, ch 1, turn.

Row 5: Sc in each of first 3 dc, [ch 3, tr in center sc of next 3-sc group, ch 3, sc in next ch lp, sc in each of next 3 dc, sc in next ch lp] rep across, ending with ch 3, tr, ch 3, sc in each of last 2 dc and top of turning ch, ch 1, turn.

Row 6: Sc in each sc, ch and tr across, ch 1, turn. (241)

Row 7: Sc in each sc across, ch 7, turn.

Row 8: Sk first 4 sc, [sc in each of next 5 sc (3rd is over tr below), ch 4, sk 3 sc, tr in next sc, ch 4, sk 3 sc] rep across, ending with ch 4, sk 3 sc, dc in last sc, ch 1, turn.

Row 9: Sc in first dc, sc in next ch lp, [ch 3, sk 1 sc, dc in each of next 3 sc, ch 3, sc in next ch lp, sc in tr, sc in next ch lp] rep across, ending with sc in ch-7 lp, sc in 3rd ch of ch-7, ch 1, turn.

Row 10: Sc in each of first 2 sc, [ch 4, dc in each of next 3 dc, ch 4, sc in each of next 3 sc] rep across, ending with ch 4, sc in each of last 2 sc, ch 6, turn.

Row 11: [Sc in ch lp, sc in each of next 3 dc, sc in ch lp, ch 3, tr in center sc of next 3-sc group, ch 3] rep across, ending with ch 3, dc in last sc, ch 1, turn.

Row 12: Sc in each sc, ch and tr across, ending with sc in each of next 4 chs of turning ch, ch 1, turn. (241 sc)

Row 13: Sc in each sc across, ch 1, turn.

[Rep Rows 2–13] 17 times.

[Rep Rows 2–6] once.

Edging

[Sc, ch 5, sc in 5th ch from hook (picot), sc] in first sc, *sc in each of next 5 sc, [sc, picot, sc] in next sc, rep from * across.

Note: *Picots should be over tr and center dc of 3-dc group in row below.*

Sc closely along long side, work picot edging along foundation ch, sc along other side. Join in beg sc, fasten off.

Notice that by pulling up or down on the center of motif patt, top and bottom will give the appearance of scallops to the edgings.

—Designed by Rose Pirrone

Dainty Rosebuds

Shown on page 13

Experience Level: Beginner

Size: 47" x 72"

Materials

- Lion Brand® Jiffy® 2-ply 100 percent acrylic yarn (3 oz/135 yds per skein): 15 skeins white #100 (MC), 7 skeins forest green #131 (B) and 3 skeins rose #140 (A)
- Size H/8 crochet hook or size needed to obtain gauge
- Yarn needle

Gauge

Large Motif: 6½" across

Small Motif: 3" across

Pattern Note: Join rnds with a sl st unless otherwise stated.

Large Motif *(Make 59)*

Rnd 1 (RS): With MC, ch 4, join to form a ring, ch 3 (counts as first dc throughout), 2 dc in ring, ch 2, [3 dc in ring, ch 2] 3 times, join in 3rd ch of beg ch-3, turn. (12 dc)

Rnd 2: Ch 3, [2 dc, ch 2, 3 dc] in ch-2 sp, ch 1, *[3 dc, ch 2, 3 dc] in next ch-2 sp, ch 1, rep from * around, join in 3rd ch of beg ch-3, turn.

Rnd 3: Ch 3, 2 dc in ch-1 sp, ch 1, [3 dc, ch 2, 3 dc] in ch-2 sp, ch 1, *3 dc in ch-1 sp, ch 1, [3 dc, ch 2, 3 dc] in ch-2 sp, ch 1, rep from * around, join in 3rd ch of beg ch-3, turn. (36 dc)

Rnd 4: Ch 3, 2 dc in ch-1 sp, ch 1, [3 dc, ch 2, 3 dc] in ch-2 sp, ch 1, *[3 dc in ch-1 sp, ch 1] twice, [3 dc, ch 2, 3 dc] in ch-2 sp, ch 1, rep from * around, ending with 3 dc in ch-1 sp, ch 1, join in 3rd ch of beg ch-3, turn.

Rnd 5: Ch 3, 2 dc in ch-1 sp, ch 1, 3 dc in next ch-1 sp, ch 1, [3 dc, ch 2, 3 dc] in ch-2 sp, ch 1, *[3 dc in ch-1 sp, ch 1] 3 times, [3 dc, ch 2, 3 dc] in ch-2 sp, ch 1, rep from * around, ending with 3 dc in ch-1 sp, ch 1, join in 3rd ch of beg ch-3, fasten off. (60 dc)

Rnd 6 (RS): Attach B in any ch-2 sp, ch 1, 3 sc in same sp, sc in each st and ch-1 sp across, 3 sc in corner, sc in each st and ch-1 sp across, rep from * around, join in beg sc, fasten off, leaving 12" length for sewing motifs tog.

Small Motif *(Make 20)*

Rnds 1 & 2: Rep Rnds 1 and 2 of Large Motif, fasten off.

Rnd 3: Rep Rnd 6 of Large Motif.

Roses *(Make 59)*

With A, ch 8, 5 sc in 2nd ch from hook, 5 sc in each of next 2 chs (mark last st worked), 5 hdc in each of next 4 chs, twist rose into shape, join in marked st, fasten off, leaving 12" length.

Leaves *(Make 118)*

With B, ch 7, sc in 3rd ch from hook, dc in each of next 2 chs, hdc in next ch, [sc, ch 1, sc] in last ch, working on opposite side of foundation ch, hdc in next ch, dc in each of next 2 chs, sc in next ch, join in next ch, fasten off, leaving 12" length.

Finishing

Weave in loose ends.

Sew 1 rose and 2 leaves to center of each large square, with leaves pointing toward opposite corners of squares.

FIG. 1

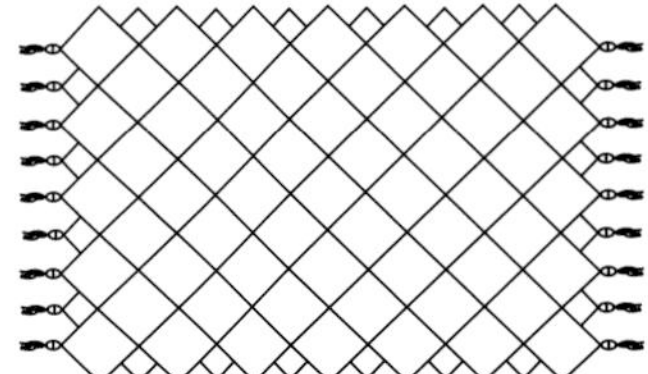

Sew squares tog as shown in Fig. 1, placing leaves parallel to shorter edges of afghan.

Add fringe to ends, if desired.

—Designed by Maggie Weldon, courtesy of Designs for America

Bedroom Comforts

Make your bedroom a beautiful sanctuary in which you can escape the everyday worries of life. Treat yourself to delicate crocheted accents throughout this room to yield simple loveliness and tranquillity of soul.

Capture the elegant beauty of the rose in this lovely Rose Filet Bedspread. Just as the rose has remained a treasured flower generation after generation, so this classic bedspread will remain a cherished heirloom in your family. Instructions begin on page 38.

Dress up a rich antique bureau with our Dresser Scarf, and, for bedtime reading, keep this delicate Lacy Bookmark close at hand to hold your place (below). Created at the turn of the century by Bertha Corbett, Sunbonnet Sue has become a popular motif for quilters. Stitched in a pretty filet pattern (inset right), she makes a charming throw pillow and is a sweet companion for the Hexagons & Squares bedspread (right). *Instructions on pages 39–42.*

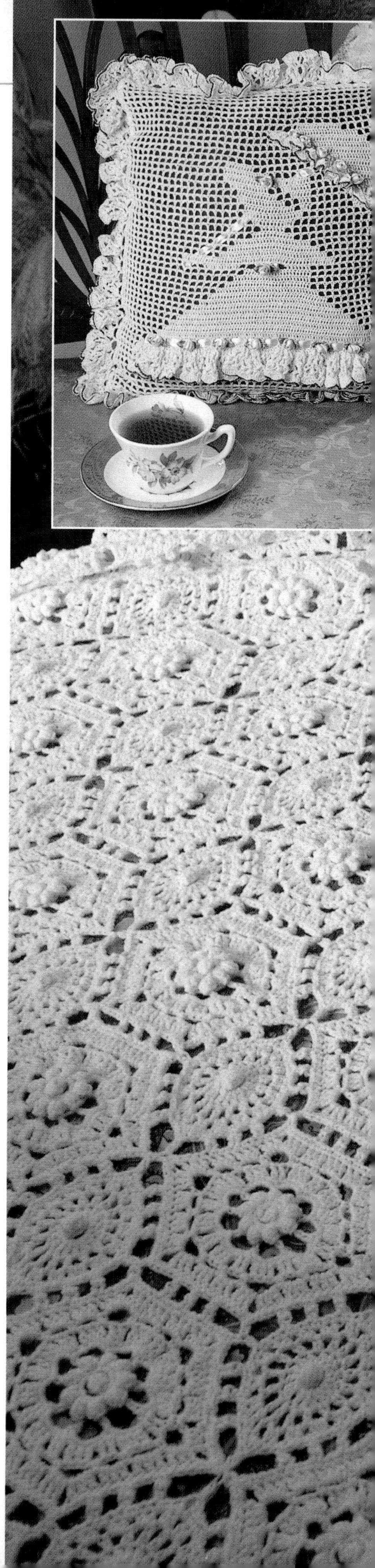

A GIRL OF THE
LIMBERLOST
FRECKLES
GENE STRATTON-PORTER

Frame a window overlooking a picturesque view with this lovely Fan Valance (below), hung on a handsome brass rod. Small accents, such as a Dainty Trinket Box (right) for holding jewelry, look especially pretty placed on a dresser next to antique perfume bottles. Colorful, scented Floral Sachets (right), tucked in your lingerie drawer, will bring you the sweet aromas of fresh flowers all year-round.

Instructions on pages 42–44.

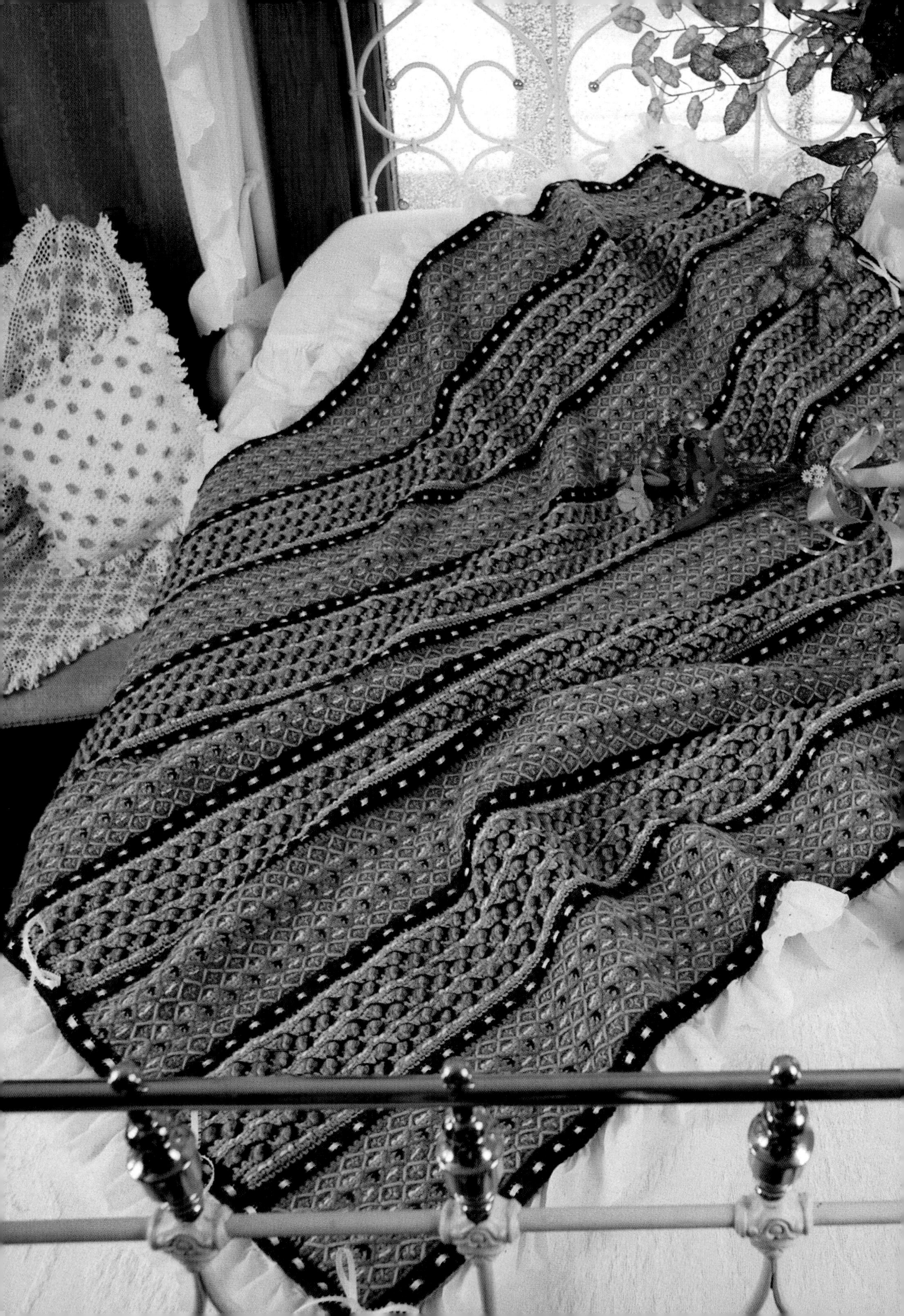

Exquisite embroidery worked on top of our Floral Bedspread (left) makes this pattern special. This bedspread is ideal for using during the cooler months. Instructions begin on page 47.

Rounds of pretty ruffles give this easy-to-crochet Garden Pillow (below) a frilly, feminine look. It makes a lovely throw pillow for the bed or an overstuffed armchair. Instructions begin on page 48.

Framed or hung against a solid-colored wall, a pretty filet picture, Bedtime Prayer (right), makes a refreshing and unusual accent piece for the bedroom. Instructions begin on page 51.

Butterflies, birds and blooms worked in an enchanting filet pattern grace the edges of a simple piece of ecru linen to make this lovely Butterflies & Blooms dresser scarf (below). Instructions begin on page 50.

Nine airy flowers, framed in a delicate border, form a lovely pillow top. Sewn to a satin pillow, it makes a pretty bedroom accent. *Instructions begin on page 56.*

Two pretty pairs of cozy slippers are a simple way to give yourself a special treat. Crochet Ladies' Moccasins (below left) or Warm & Wonderful Slippers (below right) with a soft, brushed yarn in your favorite colors to finish off your collection of bedroom comforts! *Instructions begin on page 53.*

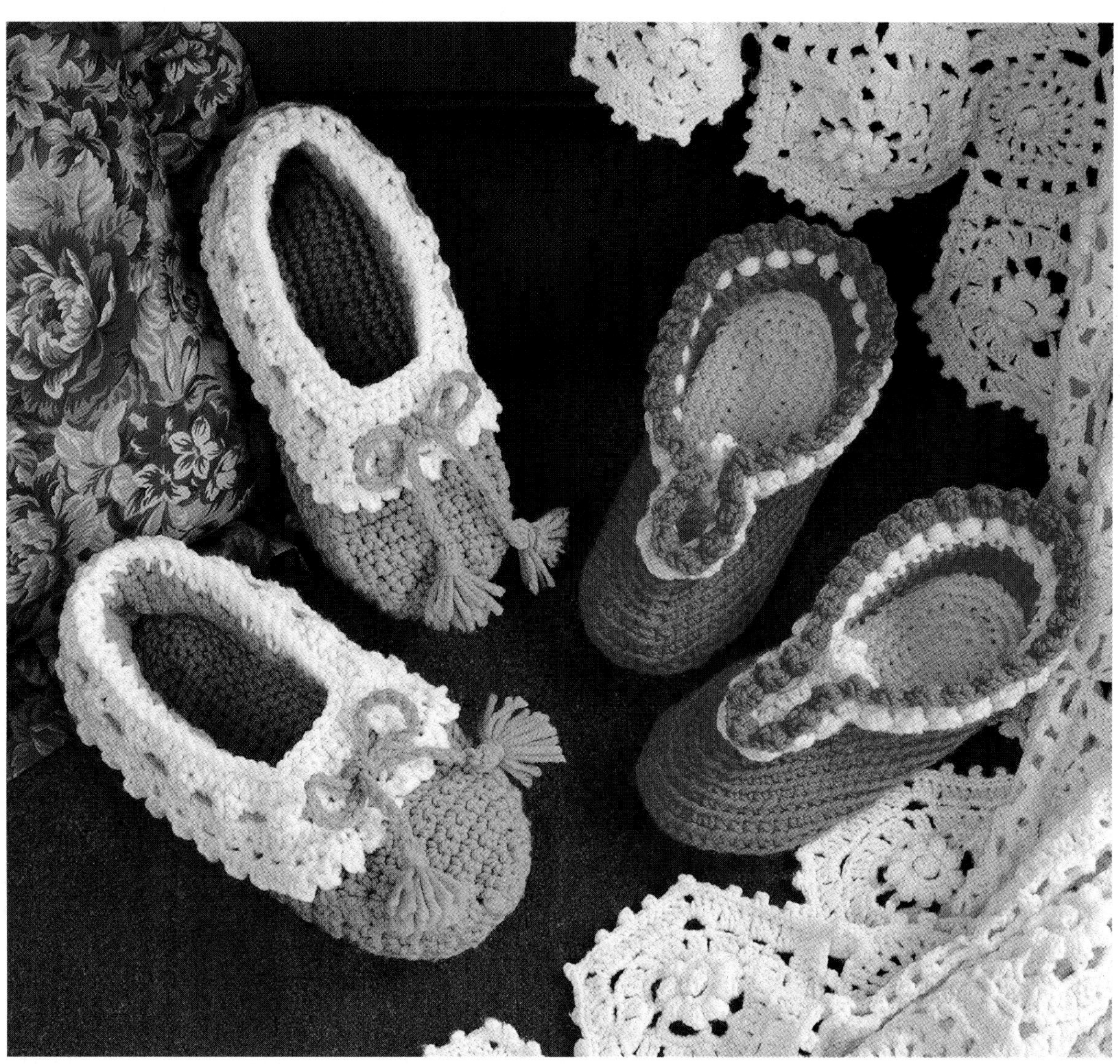

Rose Filet Bedspread

Shown on page 26

Experience Level: Intermediate

Size: Approximately 68" x 86"

Materials

- DMC Cebelia crochet cotton size 10 (50 grams per ball): 25 balls cream #712, 4 balls very light shell pink #224 and 3 balls very light fern green #524
- Size 7 steel crochet hook

Gauge: 11 sts and 4 rows = 1"

Motif: approximately 8½" x 9"

To save time, take time to check gauge.

Pattern Notes: Wind 2 bobbins of cream and 3 bobbins of green.

Join rnds with a sl st unless otherwise indicated.

Color change

A. Change colors within dc as follows: With first color, yo, insert hook in st, yo and draw through 2 lps, yo with 2nd color and draw through last 2 lps.

B. Work dc over dropped cotton, carrying it in the st to its next working area.

C. When a color is finished for the row, wrap over working cotton from RS to WS to position for next row.

D. To carry a dropped color through sps, wrap and form sp sts around the dropped cotton.

E. Carry cotton through 1–3 sps per row, attach new strand of color where desired.

Pattern Stitches

Block (bl): Dc in each of next 3 sts.

Bl over a bl: Dc in each of next 3 dc.

Bl over a sp: 2 dc in sp, dc in next dc.

Bl over a puff: 2 dc over puff, dc in next dc.

Sp: Ch 2, sk 2 sts, dc in next st.

Beg sp: Ch 5, sk 2 sts, dc in next st.

Sp over a bl: Ch 2, sk 2 dc, dc in next dc.

Sp over a sp: Ch 2, dc in next dc.

Sp over a puff: Ch 2, sk puff, dc in next dc.

Puff: [Yo, insert hook and draw lp through st/sp] 5 times, yo and draw through all lps on hook, ch 1 to close.

Beg puff: Ch 3, puff in indicated st/sp, dc in next dc.

Puff over a sp: Puff in ch-2 sp, dc in next dc.

Puff over a puff: Puff in top of puff, dc in next dc.

First Motif

Row 1 (RS): Ch 93, puff in 5th ch from hook, dc in next ch, sk 1 ch, puff in next ch, dc in next ch, *[ch 2, sk 2 chs, dc in next ch] twice, [sk 1 ch, puff in next ch, dc in next ch] twice, rep from * across.

Row 2: Beg puff over a puff, sp over a puff, [2 puffs over 2 sps, 2 sps over 2 puffs] rep across, ending with 2 puffs over 2 sps, sp over a puff, puff over a puff.

Rows 3–34: Follow Chart A, utilizing pattern stitches, do not fasten off.

With RS facing, working around entire piece, [ch 6, sc] in corner,

STITCH KEY

- ☐ Space; cream
- ⊡ Puff st; cream
- ⧄ Block; very light fern green
- ⦿ Block; light shell pink

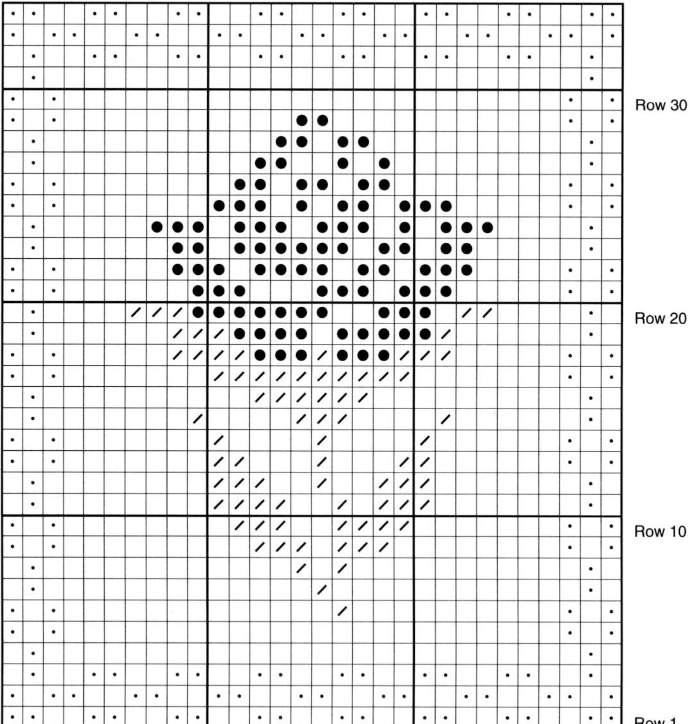

[ch 5, sk 5 sts, sc in next st] rep across top and lower edges, [ch 5, sk 1 row joining, sc in next row joining] rep along sides, working [sc, ch 5, sc] in each corner, fasten off.

Second & Subsequent Motifs *(Make 62)*
Rows 1–34: Rep Rows 1–34 of First Motif, attaching 2nd motif with ch 2, sl st in first motif's corresponding sp, [ch 2, sc] in designated st/row joining, working corners: sc in corner, [ch 2, sl st] in first motif's corresponding corner, [ch 2, sc] in 2nd motif's corner.

Join 9 rows of 7 motifs each.

Edging
Rnd 1 (RS): Attach cream in corner ch-5 sp, [ch 1, sc, ch 5, sc] in corner, [ch 5, sc in next ch-5 sp] rep along each side, working [sc, ch 5, sc] in each corner, join in beg sc.

Rnds 2–4: [Sl st, ch 1, sc, ch 5, sc] in corner ch-5 sp, [ch 5, sc in next ch-5 sp] rep along each side, working [sc, ch 5, sc] in each corner, join in beg sc.

Rnd 5: Sl st, ch 4 (counts as first tr), [ch 1, tr] 6 times in corner, *sc in next ch-5 sp, [{tr, ch 1} 4 times, tr] in next ch-5 sp, rep from * along each side, working [{tr, ch 1} 6 times, tr] in each corner, join in 4th ch of beg ch-4.

Rnd 6: Sl st in next ch-1 sp, ch 7, sl st in 3rd ch from hook (counts as dc, ch 1, picot), ch 1, dc in same ch-1 sp, [{dc, ch 1, picot, ch 1, dc} in next ch-1 sp] 5 times, *sl st in next sc, [{dc, ch 1, picot, ch 1, dc} in next ch-1 sp] 4 times, rep from * along each side, working [{dc, ch 1, picot, ch 1, dc} in next ch-1 sp] 6 times in each corner, join in 3rd ch of beg ch-7, fasten off.

—Designed by Nancy Hearne

Dresser Scarf

Shown on page 28

Experience Level: Intermediate
Size: Approximately 35" x 12"
Materials

- DMC Cebelia crochet cotton size 20 (405 yds per ball): 2 balls ecru
- Size 7 steel crochet hook

Gauge: Approximately 1" between ch-3 shell sps

Pattern Note: Join rnds with a sl st unless otherwise stated.

Dresser Scarf
Row 1: Ch 84, 2 dc in 4th ch from hook, ch 3, 3 dc in same ch, *[sk 1 ch, dc in next ch, ch 2] 3 times, sk 1 ch, dc in next ch, sk 1 ch, [3 dc, ch 3, 3 dc] in next ch, rep from * 7 times, ch 3, turn. (9 shells)

Row 2 & Subsequent Rows: *[3 dc, ch 3, 3 dc] in ch-3 sp of previous row, sk 3 dc of previous shell, dc in next dc, [ch 2, dc in next dc] 3 times, rep from * across, ch 3, turn.

Last Row: Sc in ch-3 sp, ch 3, sk 3 dc of previous shell, [dc in next dc, ch 2] 3 times, dc in next dc, *ch 3, sc in ch-3 sp, ch 3, sk 3 dc of previous shell, [dc in next dc, ch 2] 3 times, dc in next dc, rep from * across, ch 3, sc in ch-3 sp, ch 3, turning to the side, sl st in turning ch-3 of previous row.

Edging
Rnd 1: [Ch 3, 2 dc, ch 3, 3 dc] in ch-3 sp, *[ch 3, sc in next ch-3 sp, ch 3, shell in next ch-3 sp] rep to corner, ch 3 for corner, turn to work in foundation ch, shell in base of next shell, [ch 3, sc in center square, ch 3, shell in base of next shell] rep to next corner, ch 3 for corner, turn to work side, shell in first dc, rep from * around, working shells in ch-3 sp of shell across top, ending with ch 3, join in 3rd ch of beg ch-3.

Rnd 2: Sl st in each of next 2 dc and ch-3 sp, ch 3, [2 dc, ch 3, 3 dc] in ch-3, *[ch 3, sc in next sc, ch 3, shell in next shell] rep across, [ch 3, shell in corner ch-3 sp, ch 3, shell in shell] for corner, rep from * around, ending shell in corner ch-3 sp, ch 3, join in 3rd ch of beg ch-3.

Rnd 3: Sl st in each of next 2 dc and ch-3 sp, [ch 3, 2 dc, ch 5, sl st in 5th ch from hook (picot), 3 dc] in ch-3 sp, ch 3, *sc in sc, ch 3, [3 dc, picot, 3 dc] in next ch-3 sp, ch 3, rep from * around, making corners [shell, picot, shell, ch 3] 3 times, rep from * around, join in 3rd ch of beg ch-3, fasten off.

—Designed by Alice E. Heim

Lacy Bookmark

Shown on page 28

Experience Level: Beginner
Size: Approximately 1½" x 7"
Materials

- DMC Cebelia crochet cotton size 20 (50 grams per ball): 1 ball ecru
- Size 10 steel crochet hook
- 1" hairpin lace pin

Pattern Stitch

2-dc cluster (2-dc cl): Keeping last lp of each dc on hook, 2 dc in lp, yo and draw through all 3 lps on hook.

Bookmark

Work 1 strip of hairpin lace with 69 lps on each side, fasten off.

Working with 3 lps held tog (3-lp sp), attach with a sl st in 2nd 3-lp sp from bottom right, ch 3, dc in same sp, ch 4, sl st in 4th ch from hook (picot), 2-dc cl in same sp, *[2-dc cl, picot, 2-dc cl] in each 3-lp sp along side, [2-dc cl, picot, 2-dc cl, 2-dc cl, picot, 2-dc cl, picot, 2-dc cl] in next end 3-lp sp, [2-dc cl, picot, 2-dc cl, picot, 2-dc cl, 2-dc cl, picot, 2-dc cl] in next end 3-lp sp, rep from * once more, join in 3rd ch of beg ch-3, fasten off.

—Designed by Nancy Hearne

Sunbonnet Pillow

Shown on page 29

Experience Level: Advanced

Size: 14" square

Materials

- J. & P. Coats® South Maid® crochet cotton size 10 (225 yds per ball): 3 balls cream #430
- Size 5 steel crochet hook or size needed to obtain gauge
- Kreinik Fine (#8) Braid (33 yds per spool): 3 spools fuchsia #024HL
- 1 yd ⅜"-wide pink satin ribbon trim
- 14" pillow form
- 15" x 29" piece of burgundy satin fabric
- 14 ribbon roses
- Fabric glue (optional)

Gauge: 7 sps = 2"

To save time, take time to check gauge.

Front Panel

Row 1: With cream, ch 143, dc in 8th ch from hook, *ch 2, sk 2 chs, dc in next ch, rep from * across, turn.

Row 2: Ch 5 (counts as first dc, ch 2), dc in next dc of previous row, *ch 2, sk 2 chs, dc in next dc, rep from * across, turn.

Rows 3–7: Rep Row 2.

Row 8: Beg at bottom of skirt, ch 5 (counts as first dc, ch 2), dc in dc, *ch 2, sk 2 chs, dc in next dc, rep from * 4 times, dc in each of next 105 sts (35 squares filled in), [ch 2, sk 2 chs, dc in next dc] 5 times, turn. (6 open squares, 35 closed squares, 5 open squares)

Rows 9–48: Follow Chart A, ch 5 at beg of each row (counts as first dc, ch 2), turn at end of each row.

Rows 49–56: Rep Row 2.

Shell edging

At end of Row 56, do not turn, ch 3, 8 dc in last dc made, working in the rows on the side and in dc sts across the top and bottom, sc in next row, *[7 dc in next row, sc in next row] rep to corner, 9 dc in corner st, sc in next dc, [7 dc in next dc, sc in next dc] rep to corner, 9 dc in corner st, sc in next dc, rep from * around, join with a sl st in 3rd ch of beg ch-3, fasten off.

Back Panel

Row 1: Rep Row 1 of Front Panel.

Rows 2–56: Rep Row 2 of Front Panel.

Work shell edging same as for Front Panel.

Skirt Ruffle

Row 1: Beg at left side of skirt (top of Row 13), working in front lps only, attach cream with a sl st in first st, ch 6, sc in same st, *ch 6, sc in next st (going across skirt), rep from * across, ending with sc in last st, ch 3, dc in same st, turn.

Rows 2–4: *Ch 6, sc in top of next ch-6 lp, rep from * across, ending with ch 3, dc in last lp, turn.

Row 5: Sc in first ch-3 lp, ch 4, 6 tr in same lp, sc in 4th ch of next lp, *7 tr in 4th ch of next lp, sc in 4th ch of next lp, rep from * across, fasten off.

Row 6: Attach fuchsia braid with a sl st in top of ch-4 (beg of last row), sl st in back lp only of each st across, fasten off.

Parasol Ruffle

Row 1: With cream, working in front lps only, beg at left side of parasol (bottom left corner of sp where ribbon will be threaded), *[ch 6, sc] in same st, ch 6, sc in next st, rep from * down and across, following the patt, ending with ch 6, sc in same lp (the open sps for threading ribbon should be just above the ruffle), turn.

Row 2: Sc in first lp, *5 dc in next lp, sc in next lp, rep from * across, fasten off.

Row 3: Attach fuchsia braid with a sl st in 3rd ch of ch-3 (beg of last row), sl st in back lp only of each st across, fasten off.

Fold burgundy satin fabric in half, RS tog, so piece meas 14½" x 15"; sew 2 sides, using ½" seam allowance. Turn right side of fabric out. Insert pillow form;

stitch rem side closed.

Weave ribbon through grid patt as indicated on chart.

Joining Front & Back Panels

Note: *It helps to lightly spray-starch and press the front and back panels and ruffles before joining.*

Row 1: Holding Front and Back Panels tog with WS tog and working through both thicknesses around entire outer edge, beg at upper right corner, sc in center dc of first shell of both panels, *ch 7, sc in center of next shell (of both panels), rep from * around, inserting pillow after 3 sides are joined.

Rnd 2: [Sc, ch 7] 5 times in each lp around, in last lp, [sc, ch 7] 4 times, ch 3, tr in same lp.

Rnd 3: *Ch 7, sc in next lp, rep from * around, ending with ch 3, tr in tr.

Rnd 4: Rep Rnd 3.

Rnd 5: *7 tr in 4th ch of next lp, sc in 4th ch of next lp, rep from * around, ending with sl st in tr, fasten off.

Row 6: Attach fuchsia braid with a sl st in back lp only of any corner st, sl st in back lp only of each st around, fasten off.

Weave in loose ends. Secure ends of ribbon, ruffles and trim with thread or glue.

—Designed by Debby Caldwell

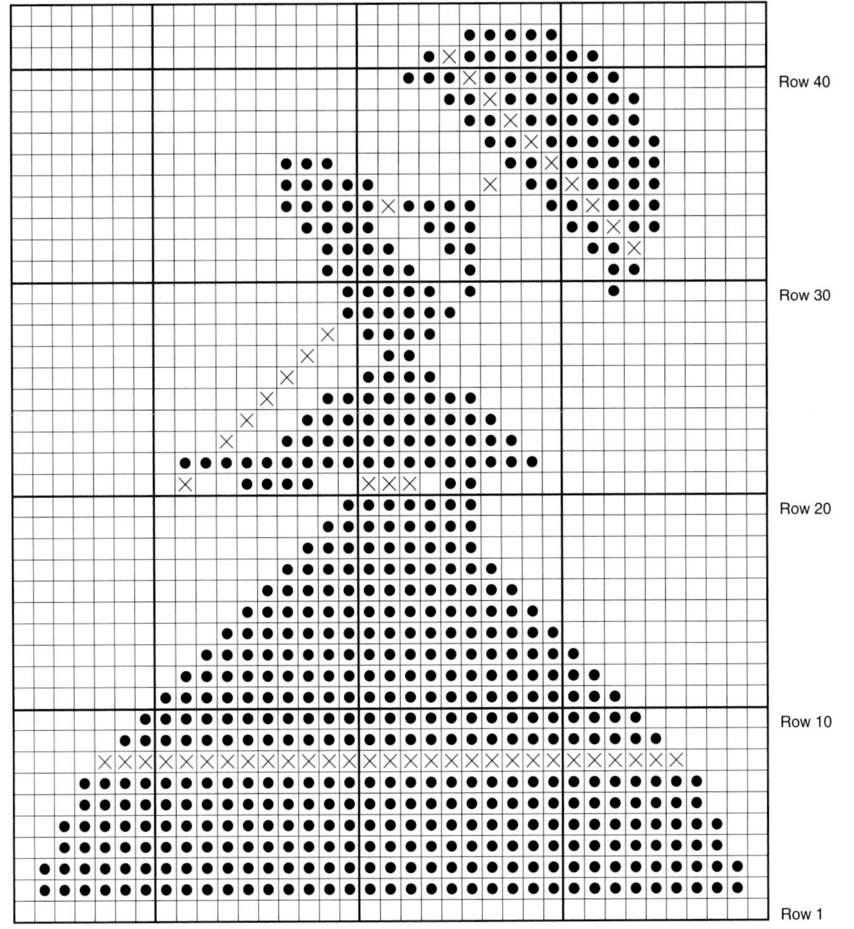

Hexagons & Squares

Shown on page 29

Shown on page 29

Experience Level: Intermediate

Size: Twin(full)(queen)(king)

Actual Measurements

68 x 100(81 x 100)(88 x 105)(100 x 110)"

Materials

- Lion Brand® Jamie® 85 percent acrylic/15 percent rayon baby weight yarn (1.75 oz/185 yds per skein): 43(51)(59)(70) skeins fisherman #299
- Size B/1 crochet hook
- Size E/4 crochet hook or size needed to obtain gauge

Gauge

Hexagon Motif: 6¼" at widest point across x 5¼" high

To save time, take time to check gauge.

Pattern Note: Join rnds with a sl st unless otherwise stated in pattern.

Pattern Stitches

Popcorn (pc): 5 dc in indicated st, drop lp from hook, insert hook in top of first dc of 5-dc group and draw dropped lp through.

Picot: Ch 3, sl st in top of sc just made.

Join picots: Ch 1, sl st in corresponding picot on adjoining motif, ch 1, sl st in top of indicated sc or dc.

First Hexagon Motif

Rnd 1: With smaller hook, ch 4, pc in first ch.

Rnd 2: Ch 1, sc in top of pc, ch 5, sc in bottom of pc, ch 5, join in beg sc.

Rnd 3: Ch 1, sc in same st as sl st, 8 sc in ch-5 lp, sc in next sc, 8 sc in next ch-5 lp, join in beg sc. (18 sc)

Rnd 4: Ch 3, 4 dc in same st as sl st, drop lp from hook, insert hook in 3rd ch of beg ch-3 and draw dropped lp through (starting pc made), [ch 2, sk 1 sc, pc in next sc] rep around, ending with ch 2, join in top of first pc. (9 pcs)

Rnd 5: With larger hook, ch 6, [hdc in top of next pc, ch 4] rep around, join in 2nd ch of beg ch-6. (9 ch-4 sps)

Rnd 6: Ch 1, [7 sc in ch-4 sp, sk next hdc] rep around, join in beg sc.

Rnd 7: Ch 4 (counts as first dc, ch 1), [sk next sc, dc in each of next 3 sc, ch 1, sk next sc, dc in each of next 2 sc, ch 1] rep around, ending with sk next sc, dc in last sc, join in 3rd ch of beg ch-4.

Rnd 8: Ch 1, *sc in next ch sp, [ch 3, sc in next sp] twice, ch 5, rep from * around, join in beg sc.

Rnd 9: Sl st in first ch-3 sp, ch 3, 2 dc in same sp, 3 dc in next ch-3 sp, *[3 dc, ch 2, 3 dc] in next ch-5 lp **, [3 dc in next ch-3 sp] twice, rep from * 4 times, rep from * to ** once, join in 3rd ch of beg ch-3.

Rnd 10: Ch 1, sc in same st, sc in each of next 2 dc, [picot, sc in each of next 3 dc] twice, *[2 sc, picot, 2 sc] in next ch-2 sp, [sc in each of next 3 dc, picot] 3 times, sc in each of next 3 dc, rep from * around, ending last rep with sc in each of next 3 dc, picot, join in beg sc, fasten off.

Second Hexagon Motif

Rnds 1–9: Rep Rnds 1–9 of First Hexagon Motif.

Rnd 10: Ch 1, sc in same st as sl st, sc in each of next 2 dc, [picot, sc in each of next 3 dc] twice, [2 sc, join picots to corresponding picot of first motif, 2 sc] in next ch-2 sp, [sc in each of next 3 dc, join picots] 3 times, sc in each of next 3 dc, work corner as before, joining picots (5 picots joined), complete rnd as for first motif.

Continue joining hexagons in this manner until strip is 19(19)(20)(21) motifs long. Beg in 2nd strip and, at same time, join to first strip at side points of hexagons. Join a total of 11(13)(14)(16) strips.

Fill-In Motif

Rnd 1: With smaller hook, ch 4, pc in first ch, change to larger hook, ch 1, sc in top of pc, ch 4, sc in bottom of pc, ch 4, join in beg sc.

Rnd 2: Ch 3 (counts as first dc), 7 dc in ch-4 sp, dc in next sc, 7 dc in next ch-4 sp, join in 3rd ch of beg ch-3. (16 dc)

Rnd 3: Ch 4 (counts as first hdc, ch 2), [hdc in next dc, ch 2] 15 times, join in 2nd ch of beg ch-4.

Rnd 4: Sl st in first ch-2 sp, ch 2 (counts as first hdc), hdc in same ch-2 sp, ch 1, [2 hdc in next ch-2 sp, ch 1] 15 times, join in 2nd ch of beg ch-2.

Rnd 5: Ch 1, sc in same st as sl st, hdc in next hdc, dc in next ch sp, place motif inside opening formed by hexagons at top left corner of bedspread, join picots in joining of hexagons at top of diamond-shaped opening, hdc in next hdc, sc in next hdc and ch sp, join picots, *[sc in each of next 2 hdc and ch sp, join picots] twice, sc in each of next 2 hdc and ch sp, join picots in next joining of hexagons, rep between [] 3 times **, sc in next hdc, hdc in next hdc, dc in next ch sp, join picots at bottom of diamond, hdc in next hdc, sc in next hdc and ch sp, join picots, rep from * to ** once, join in beg sc, fasten off.

Rep for all rem openings. Weave in loose ends.

—Designed by Maureen Egan Emlet, courtesy Designs for America

Fan Valance

Shown on page 30

Experience Level: Intermediate

Size: 10" x 30"

Materials

- Crochet cotton size 10: 500 yds blue
- Size 7 steel crochet hook or size needed to obtain gauge

Gauge: 8 dc and 8 rows = 2" in filet crochet

To save time take time to check gauge.

Pattern Notes: Valance is worked in both directions.

Turning ch-5 of each row counts as first dc, ch 2 of following row.

Pattern Stitch

Shell: [3 dc, ch 2, 3 dc] in indicated st.

Valance

Row 1: Ch 304, dc in 7th ch

from hook, [ch 2, sk 2 chs, dc] 3 times, [sk 2 chs, shell in next ch, sk 2 chs, dc in next ch, *ch 2, sk 2 chs, dc in next ch, rep from * 7 times] 9 times, ending with sk 2 chs, shell in next ch, sk 2 chs, dc in next ch, **ch 2, sk 2 chs, dc in next ch, rep from ** 3 times, ch 5, turn.

Row 2: Dc in dc, *ch 2, dc in dc, rep from * twice, **shell in ch-2 sp, sk 3 dc, dc in dc, [ch 2, dc in dc] 8 times, rep from ** 8 times, ending with shell in ch-2 sp, sk 3 dc, dc in dc, [ch 2, dc in dc] 3 times, ch 2, dc in 3rd ch of turning ch-5, ch 5, turn.

Rows 3–24: Rep Row 2.

Row 25: Dc in dc, [ch 2, dc in dc] twice, [{ch 2, 3 dc} 4 times in ch-2 sp of shell, sk next 4 dc and ch-2 sp, ch 2, dc in dc, {ch 2, dc in dc} 6 times] 9 times, [ch 2, 3 dc] 4 times in 2nd ch-2 sp, ch 2, sk 4 dc and ch-2 sp, dc in dc, [ch 2, dc in dc] twice, ch 2, dc in 3rd ch of turning ch-5, turn.

Row 26: [Dc in dc, ch 2] twice, [shell in 3rd ch-2 sp, {dc, ch 1, dc, ch 1, dc} in next ch-2 sp, shell in next ch-2 sp, ch 2, sk first dc, dc in dc, {ch 2, dc} 4 times, ch 2] 9 times, ending with shell in 3rd ch-2 sp, [dc, ch 1, dc, ch 1, dc] in next ch-2 sp, shell in next ch-2 sp, ch 2, sk 4 dc and 2 ch-2 sps, dc in next dc, ch 2, dc, ch 2, dc in 3rd ch of turning ch-5, ch 5, turn.

Row 27: Dc in dc, ch 2, dc in dc, [shell in 2nd ch-2 sp, sk 3 dc, {dc, ch 1, dc in next dc, ch 1} twice, dc, ch 1, dc in next dc, shell in next ch-2 sp, sk 3 dc and ch-2 sp, dc in dc, {ch 2, dc in dc} 4 times] 9 times, shell in 2nd ch-2 sp, sk 3 dc, {dc, ch 1, dc in next dc, ch 1} twice, dc, ch 1, dc in next dc, shell in next ch-2 sp, sk 3 dc and ch-2 sp, dc in dc, ch 2, dc in dc, ch 2, dc in 3rd ch of turning ch-5, ch 5, turn.

Row 28: Dc in dc, [shell in 2nd ch-2 sp, sk 3 dc, {dc in next dc, ch 2} 3 times, dc in next ch, ch 2, {dc in next dc, ch 2} twice, dc in next dc, shell in next ch-2 sp, sk 4 dc and ch-2 sp, {dc in dc, ch 2} twice, dc in dc] 9 times, shell in 2nd ch-2 sp, sk 3 dc, {dc in dc, ch 2} 3 times, dc in next ch, ch 2, {dc in dc, ch 2} twice, dc in dc, shell in next ch-2 sp, sk 4 dc and ch-2 sp, dc in dc, ch 2, dc in 3rd ch of turning ch-5, ch 3, turn.

Row 29: [Sk first ch-2 sp, shell in ch-2 sp, sk 4 dc, shell in next dc, {sk 1 dc, shell in dc} twice, sk 1 dc, shell in ch-2 sp, sk 4 dc and ch-2 sp, dc in next dc] 10 times, ending with dc in 3rd ch of turning ch-5, fasten off.

Right Top Edge

Row 1: With RS facing, working in the opposite side of starting ch, sl st in dc, ch 3, dc in each st across. (301 dc)

Row 2: Ch 3, turn, dc in each of next 2 dc, [ch 5, sk 5 dc, dc in each of next 5 dc] rep across, ending with dc in each of last 3 dc, ch 3, turn.

Row 3: Dc in each st across, ch 5, turn.

Row 4: Sk 3 sts, [dc in dc, ch 2, sk 2 dc] 3 times, dc in dc, [sk 2 dc, shell in dc, sk 2 dc, dc in dc, {ch 2, sk 2 dc, dc in dc} 8 times] 9 times, ending with sk 2 dc, shell in dc, [sk 2 dc, dc in dc, ch 2] 3 times, sk 2 dc, dc in 3rd ch of turning ch-3, ch 5, turn.

Row 5: Dc in dc, [ch 2, dc in dc] 3 times, [shell in ch-2 sp, sk 3 dc, dc in dc, {ch 2, dc in dc} 8 times] 9 times, ending with shell in ch-2 sp, sk 3 dc, [dc in dc, ch 2] 4 times, dc in 3rd ch of turning ch-5, fasten off.

Weave in loose ends.

—Designed by Rhonda Semonis

Dainty Trinket Box

Shown on page 31

Experience Level: Beginner

Size: 4" x 2⅛" x 1½"

Materials

- Anchor® pearl cotton size 12 (12 grams per ball): 1 ball each pink #050 and green #0228
- Size 10 steel crochet hook or size needed to obtain gauge
- 4" oval ivory-colored box
- 1 yd light ecru prepleated lace
- Low-temp glue gun
- Sewing needle

Gauge: 12 dc = 1"

To save time, take time to check gauge.

Rosebud *(Make 5)*

Row 1: Ch 32, 2 dc in 3rd ch from hook, *3 dc in next ch, rep from * across, fasten off, leaving 6" tail.

Twist into shape of a rosebud; secure into shape using sewing ndl and 6" tail.

Leaf *(Make 5)*

Row 1: Ch 10, sc in 2nd ch from hook, hdc in next ch, [2 dc in next ch] 5 times, hdc in next ch, 2 sc in next ch, working on opposite side of ch, hdc in next ch, [2 dc in next ch] 5 times, hdc in next ch, sc in last ch, join with a sl st in beg sc, fasten off.

Assembly

Beg on outer edge, glue lace to box lid, working toward the center until all lace is used.

Using photo as guide, glue leaves in place over lace; glue rosebuds over leaves.

—Designed by Nazanin S. Fard

Floral Sachets

Shown on page 31

Experience Level: Intermediate

Sizes

Chrysanthemum Sachet: 7" square

Forget-Me-Not Sachet: 8" tall x 7" wide

Pansy Sachet: 7" in diameter

Materials

- DMC Cebelia crochet cotton size 10 (50 grams per ball): 3 balls white
- DMC pearl cotton size 5 (10 grams/49 yds per skein): 1 skein each dark blue #931, light blue #932, rose #3688, deep rose #3687, lavender #340 and purple #333, 7 yds yellow #744 and 2 yds green #320
- Size 7 steel crochet hook
- 9" x 18" piece blue satin polyester fabric
- 9" x 15" piece rose satin polyester fabric
- 9" x 18" piece purple satin polyester fabric
- Matching sewing thread
- Sewing needle
- Tapestry needle
- Paper for pattern
- Polyester fiberfill
- 1 yd 3/16"-wide blue ribbon
- 8" 1/4"-wide rose ribbon
- 48" 1/8"-wide purple ribbon
- 57 (5mm) pearl beads
- Washable fabric glue
- Potpourri oil

Gauges

Chrysanthemum Sachet: 20 dc and 7 rows = 2"

Forget-Me-Not Sachet: 7 rows = 2"

Pansy Sachet: Rnds 1–3 of doily = 1¾" in diameter; yellow center of pansy = 1"

To save time, take time to check gauge.

Pattern Note: Join rnds with a sl st unless otherwise stated.

Pattern Stitches

Popcorn (pc): 5 (or indicated number) dc in ring, remove hook, insert hook under top 2 lps of first dc in group, pick up working lp and draw through, pull cluster tog, ch 1 to secure popcorn.

2-dc cluster (2-dc cl): Keeping last lp of each dc on hook, 2 dc in indicated st, yo and draw through all 3 lps.

3-dc cluster (3-dc cl): Keeping last lp of each dc on hook, 3 dc in indicated st, yo and draw through all 4 lps.

Chrysanthemum Sachet

Square Doily

Row 1: With white size 10 crochet cotton, ch 51, dc in 12th ch from hook, dc in next ch, ch 4, sk 4 chs, dc in next ch, [ch 4, sk 4 chs, dc in each of next 2 chs, ch 4, sk 4 chs, dc in next ch] 3 times, turn.

Row 2: Ch 5, sk 2 chs, dc in each of next 2 chs, dc in each of next 2 dc, dc in each of next 2 chs, ch 2, dc in dc, [ch 2, sk 2 chs, dc in each of next 2 chs, dc in each of next 2 dc, dc in each of next 2 chs, ch 2, dc in dc] 3 times, turn.

Row 3: Ch 4 (counts as dc, ch 1), sk 1 ch, dc in next ch, dc in each of next 6 dc, dc in next ch, ch 1, dc in dc, [ch 1, sk 1 ch, dc in next ch, dc in each of next 6 dc, dc in next ch, ch 1, dc in dc] 3 times, turn.

Row 4: Ch 5 (counts as dc, ch 2), sk 1 ch and 1 dc, dc in each of next 6 dc, ch 2, sk dc and ch-1, dc in next dc, [ch 2, sk 1 ch and 1 dc, dc in each of next 6 dc, ch 2, sk dc and ch-1, dc in dc] 3 times, turn.

Row 5: Ch 7 (counts as dc, ch 4), sk 1 sp and 2 dc, dc in each of next 2 dc, ch 4, sk 2 dc and 1 sp, dc in next dc, [ch 4, sk 1 sp and 2 dc, dc in each of next 2 dc, ch 4, sk 2 dc and 1 sp, dc in next dc] 3 times, turn.

Rows 6–17: Rep Rows 2–5, do not fasten off, do not turn.

Edging

Rnd 1: Ch 5, [dc, ch 2, dc, ch 2, dc] in corner dc just made, *working down side, [ch 3, sk next row, dc, ch 3, dc in next row] 7 times, ch 3, 4 dc with ch 2 between each dc in corner st, working across in base of dc sts, [{ch 3, dc in next dc} 3 times, ch 3, dc in same dc] 3 times, [ch 3, dc in next dc] twice, ch 3, 4 dc with ch 2 between each dc in corner st, rep from * around, join in 3rd ch of beg ch-5.

Rnd 2: Sl st in sp, ch 3, 2-dc cl

in same sp, ch 4, sl st in top of cl (picot), *[{ch 3, 3-dc cl, picot} in next sp] twice, [ch 3, sc in next sp, ch 3, 3-dc cl, picot in next sp] 7 times, ch 3, [3-dc cl, picot] in next sp, rep from * around, join in top of beg cl, fasten off.

Chrysanthemum

Rnd 1: With light blue pearl cotton, ch 6, join to form a ring, ch 3, 4-dc popcorn in ring, [ch 2, 5-dc pc in ring] 7 times, ch 2, join in top of first pc, fasten off.

Rnd 2: Attach dark blue with a sc in ch-1 sp of any pc, [hdc, 3 dc, hdc in ch-2 sp, sc in ch-1 sp of pc] rep around, hdc, 3 dc, hdc in ch-2 sp, join in beg sc.

Rnd 3: Ch 1, sc in same sc as sl st, working behind petals, [ch 3, sc in next sc] rep around, ch 3, join in beg sc.

Rnd 4: Ch 1, sc in same sc as sl st, [hdc, dc, 3 tr, dc, hdc in sp, sc in sc] rep around, hdc, 3 tr, dc, hdc in sp, join in beg sc.

Rnd 5: Ch 1, sc in same sc as sl st, working behind petals, [ch 5, sc in next sc] rep around, ch 5, join in beg sc.

Rnd 6: Ch 1, sc in same sc as sl st, [hdc, 2 dc, 5 tr, 2 dc, hdc in sp, sc in sc] rep around, hdc, 2 dc, 5 tr, 2 dc, hdc in sp, join in beg sc, fasten off.

Rnd 7: Attach light blue with sc in any sc, [ch 3, sk 1 st, sc in next st] rep around, ch 3, join in beg sc, fasten off.

Sew flower to center of white doily.

Pillow

Trace doily onto paper around outside of picots. Cut out pattern, adding ½" all around.

Cut 2 blue satin fabric pieces from fabric. Stitch with RS tog, using ¼" seam allowance and leaving opening for stuffing. Turn and stuff. Add potpourri oil to stuffing; whipstitch opening closed.

Finishing

Sew doily to pillow, positioning points of doily in center of each side of pillow.

Cut blue ribbon into 4 (9") lengths. Slip each piece through a corner st of doily; tie in a bow.

Glue 1 pearl bead into sp below each cluster of doily edging; glue 1 pearl bead in flower center.

Forget-Me-Not Sachet

Heart Doily

Row 1: With white size 10 crochet cotton, ch 5, 3 dc in 5th ch from hook, ch 1, dc in same ch, turn.

Row 2: Ch 4, 3 dc in first sp, ch 1, 3 dc in end sp, ch 1, dc in same sp, turn.

Row 3: Ch 4, 3 dc in first sp, ch 1, 3 dc in next sp, ch 1, 3 dc in end sp, ch 1, dc in same sp, turn.

Row 4: Ch 4, 3 dc in first sp, [ch 1, 3 dc in next sp] twice, ch 1, 3 dc in end sp, ch 1, dc in same sp, turn.

Row 5: Ch 4, 3 dc in first sp, [ch 1, 3 dc] in each sp to end sp, ch 1, 3 dc in end sp, ch 1, dc in same sp, turn.

Rows 6–9: Rep Row 5.

Row 10: Ch 3, dc in first sp, [ch 1, 3 dc] in each sp to end sp, ch 1, 2 dc in end sp, turn. (8 groups of 3-dc)

Row 11: Ch 4, [3 dc, ch 1] in each sp across, dc in 3rd ch of turning ch-3, turn. (9 3-dc groups)

Rows 12 & 13: Rep Rows 10 and 11.

Row 14: Ch 3, dc in first sp, [ch 1, 3 dc in next sp] 4 times, turn.

Row 15: Ch 3, [3 dc, ch 1 in next sp] 3 times, 3 dc in end sp, dc in 3rd ch of turning ch-3, turn.

Row 16: Ch 3, [3 dc, ch 1] in each of next 2 ch-1 sps, 3 dc in next ch-1 sp, dc in 3rd ch of turning ch-3, turn.

Row 17: Ch 3, 3 dc in each of next 2 ch-1 sps, dc in 3rd ch of turning ch-3, fasten off.

Attach white size 10 crochet cotton with a sl st in first ch sp at outside edge of heart on Row 13, Rep Rows 14–17, do not fasten off, do not turn.

Edging

Rnd 1: Ch 1, 3 sc in each sp to point of heart, sc, ch 2, sc in point, 3 sc in each sp to and including sp of top row of heart, sc in each of next 6 dc, 3 sc in each of next 4 sps, sc in center dc of heart, 3 sc in each of next 4 sps, sc in each of next 6 dc, join in beg sc.

Rnd 2: Ch 1, sc in same sc as sl st, [ch 4, sk 2 sc, sc in next sc] 17 times, ch 4, sk ch-2 sp, sc in next sc, [ch 4, sk 2 sc, sc in next sc] 22 times, ch 4, sk 3 sc, sc in next sc (center sc of heart), ch 4, sk 3 sc, sc in next sc, [ch 4, sk 2 sc, sc in next sc] 4 times, ch 4, join in beg sc.

Rnd 3: Sl st in each of next 2 chs, sc in sp, [ch 4, sc in next sp] 39 times, sk 2 ch-4 sps at center of heart, sc in next sp, [ch 4, sc in next sp] 4 times, ch 4, join in beg sc.

Rnd 4: Sl st in each of next 2 chs, sc in sp, [ch 5, sc in next sp] 38 times, sc in next sp, [ch 5, sc in next sp] 4 times, ch 2, dc in beg sc.

Rnd 5: Sc in sp over dc just made, [ch 3, 2 dc in next sp, {ch 4, sl st in 4th ch from hook} 3 times, sl st in last dc made to complete triple picot, 2 dc in same sp, ch 3, sc in next sp] 19 times, [ch 3, sc in next sp, ch 3, 2 dc, triple picot, 2 dc in next sp] twice, ch 3, join in beg sc, fasten off.

Forget-Me-Nots *(Make 7 rose & 5 deep rose)*
With size 5 pearl cotton, ch 5, join to form a ring, [ch 3, 2-dc cl in ring, ch 3, sl st in ring] 5 times, fasten off.

Sew flowers to heart, forming a spray. Wrap 2 strands of yellow once around tapestry ndl to make French knot in center of each flower.

Pillow
With rose satin fabric, make pillow in same manner as for Chrysanthemum Sachet.

Finishing
Center doily over pillow; stitch in place.

Tie 8" length of rose ribbon into bow through center top of doily.

Glue 1 pearl bead in center of each triple picot around outer edge of doily.

Pansy Sachet

Six-Pointed Doily

Rnd 1: With white size 10 crochet cotton, ch 5, join to form a ring, ch 6, [dc in ring, ch 3] 5 times, join in 3rd ch of beg ch-6. (6 sps)

Rnd 2: Ch 5, dc in same st as sl st, *ch 2, [dc, ch 2, dc] in next dc, rep from * around, ch 2, join in 3rd ch of beg ch-5.

Rnd 3: Ch 3, [3 dc in next sp, dc in next dc, ch 3, dc in next dc] rep around, ending last rep with ch 3, join in 3rd ch of beg ch-3.

Rnd 4: Ch 3, dc in next dc, [3 dc in next dc, dc in each of next 2 dc, ch 3, dc in each of next 2 dc] rep around, ending last rep with ch 3, join in 3rd ch of beg ch-3.

Rnd 5: Ch 3, dc in same st as sl st, [dc in each of next 2 dc, 3 dc in next dc, dc in each of next 2 dc, 2 dc in next dc, ch 3, 2 dc in next dc] rep around, ending last rep with ch 3, join in 3rd ch of beg ch-3.

Rnd 6: Ch 3, dc in each of next 2 dc, [ch 3, sk 2 dc, sc in next dc, ch 4, sl st in sc (picot), ch 3, sk 2 dc, dc in each of next 3 dc, ch 5, dc in each of next 3 dc] rep around, ending last rep with ch 5, join in 3rd ch of beg ch-3.

Individual petals

Rnd 7: Ch 1, sc in same st as sl st, sc in each of next 2 dc, ch 5, sc in each of next 3 dc, turn, ch 3, 2-dc cl over 2 sc, 5 dc in ch-5 sp, 3-dc cl over 3 sc, turn, sc in cl, hdc in next dc, dc in each of next 3 dc, hdc in next dc, sc in cl, fasten off.

Attach white with a sl st in first dc of next 3-dc group, rep Rnd 7 for 5 more petals.

Rnd 8 (Underlayer): Holding petal forward, attach white with a sc in picot of Rnd 6, [ch 7, 3 sc in ch-5 sp, ch 7, sc in next picot (holding petal forward so chs and sc are in back of petals)] rep around, ending last rep before sc, join in beg sc.

Individual points

Row 9: Ch 3, dc in same sc as sl st, ch 3, sc in sp, ch 3, sc in next sc, [ch 3, sc in next sc] twice, ch 3, sc in sp, ch 3, 2 dc in sc (mark this sc with a colored thread), turn.

Row 10: Ch 3, dc in dc, ch 3, sk sp, [sc in next sp, ch 3] 4 times, sk sp, dc in each of next 2 dc, turn.

Row 11: Ch 3, dc in dc, ch 3, sk sp, [sc in next sp, ch 3] 3 times, sk sp, dc in each of next 2 dc, turn.

Row 12: Ch 3, dc in dc, ch 3, sk sp, [sc in next sp, ch 3] twice, sk sp, dc in each of next 2 dc, turn.

Row 13: Ch 3, dc in dc, ch 3, sk sp, sc in next sp, ch 3, sk sp, dc in each of next 2 dc, turn.

Row 14: Ch 3, dc in dc, sk 2 sps, dc in each of next 2 dc, turn, sc in dc, ch 3, sl st in next dc, fasten off.

Attach white with a sl st in marked sc, rep Rows 9–14 for 5 more points.

Pansy

Rnd 1: With yellow pearl cotton, ch 5, join to form a ring, [ch 3, 2-dc cl in ring, ch 3, sl st in ring] 5 times, fasten off. (5 petals)

Rnd 2: Attach lavender pearl cotton with a sl st in sl st between 2 petals, [ch 3, sc in top of cluster, ch 3, sl st in sl st between next 2 petals] 4 times, ch 3, sc in top of next cluster, dc in sl st between last 2 petals.

Rnd 3: [Ch 5, sc in sc on top of next petal] 4 times, ch 5, sl st in dc of last petal.

Rnd 4: [Ch 1, dc, ch 1, tr, ch 1, 7 dtr with ch 1 between each dtr, {ch 1, tr, ch 1, tr, ch 1, dc} in ch-5 sp, ch 1, sl st in sc] twice, [ch 3, 11 dc in ch-5 sp, ch 3, sl st in sc] 3 times, fasten off.

Large petal edging
Attach purple pearl cotton with sl st in first ch-1 sp of Rnd 4, *ch 3, sc in same sp, [sc in next st, ch 3, sc in next sp] 13 times *, sc in first ch-1 sp of next large petal, rep from * to * once, ending ch 3, sc in same sp, fasten off.

Leaves
With green pearl cotton, ch 8, dc in 3rd ch from hook, [ch 1, dc in next ch] 3 times, ch 1, hdc in next ch, ch 1, sc in end ch, ch 2, sc in same ch, working on opposite side, ch 1, hdc in next ch, [ch 1, dc in next ch] 4 times, fasten off.

Pillow
With purple satin fabric, make pillow in same manner as Chrysanthemum Sachet.

Finishing
Sew pansy and leaves to white doily; sew doily to top of sachet, matching points of doily to points of sachet.

Cut purple ribbon into 8" lengths; tie into bows and sew or glue to each point of doily. Trim ends of bows.

Glue pearl bead in center of each doily point and in center of pansy.

—Designed by Lucille LaFlamme

Floral Bedspread

Shown on page 32

Experience Level: Intermediate

Size: Approximately 55" wide x 61" long

Materials
- Caron Wintuk 4-ply yarn (3.5 oz per skein): 8 skeins each sage #3149 and pure pink #3085, 7 skeins golden wheat #3054, 6 skeins dark sage #3194 and 1 skein white #3001
- Size G/6 crochet hook
- Size I/9 crochet hook or size needed to obtain gauge
- 30 yds 3/16"-wide picot-edged satin ribbon
- 8 yds 3"-wide gathered eyelet edging
- 4 yds 45"-wide coordinating fabric
- Sewing needle and thread

Gauge: 4 sc and 4 rows = 1" with larger hook

To save time, take time to check gauge.

Pattern Notes: Take care to maintain 243 sc sts across rows.

Embroidery stitches on charts are all backstitch.

Join rnds with a sl st unless otherwise indicated.

Pattern Stitches
Cluster (cl): [Yo, draw up a lp in indicated st, yo, draw through 2 lps] 3 times, yo, draw through all lps on hook, sk next sc, ch 1, dc in next st, ch 1, sk next st.

Bicolor puff (bp): Carrying colors under work, change to pure pink in last lp of last sc made, yo, insert hook in st, yo, draw up a lp with pure pink, change to golden wheat, yo, insert hook in st, yo, draw up a lp with golden wheat, change to pure pink, yo, insert hook in st, yo, draw up a lp with pure pink, change to sage, yo and draw through all lps on hook.

Afghan
Row 1: With larger hook and pure pink, ch 244, sc in 2nd ch from hook and in each ch across, ch 1, turn. (243 sc)

Rows 2–4: Sc in each sc across, ch 1, turn, fasten off at end of Row 4, attach golden wheat, ch 1, turn.

Rows 5–8: Sc in each sc across, ch 1, turn, fasten off at end of Row 8, attach pure pink, ch 1, turn.

Rows 9–12: Sc in each sc across, ch 1, turn, fasten off at end of Row 12, attach golden wheat, ch 1, turn.

Rows 13–16: Rep Rows 5–8.

Rows 17–20: Rep Rows 9–12, attach dark sage at end of Row 20, ch 1, turn.

Row 21: Sc in each sc across, turn.

Row 22: Ch 3 (counts as first dc), sk first 2 sc, [cl in next sc, ch 1, sk next sc, dc in next sc, ch 1, sk next sc] rep across, ending with dc in last sc, ch 1, turn.

Row 23: Sc in each dc, ch-1 sp and cl across, ch 1, turn, fasten off, attach sage at right-hand side of work, RS facing. (243 sc)

Rows 24–26: Sc in each sc across, ch 1, turn.

Row 27 (WS): Sc in each of first 3 sc, [bp in next st, sc in each of next 3 sc] rep across, fasten off, turn.

Row 28 (RS): Attach dark sage, ch 1, sc in each st across, fasten off, turn.

Row 29 (WS): Attach sage, ch 1, sc in first sc, [bp in next st, sc in each of next 3 sts] rep across, ending sc in last sc, ch 1, turn.

Rows 30–32: Sc in each st across, ch 1, turn.

Rows 33–44: [Rep Rows 27–32] twice, fasten off sage at

end of Row 44, attach dark sage.

Rows 45–47: Rep Rows 21–23, do not attach sage at end of Row 47.

[Rep Rows 1–47] 4 times.

Next Row: Attach pure pink, sc in each st across. (243 sc)

Rep Rows 2–20, do not attach golden wheat.

Embroidery

Following Chart A, embroider on sc panels. Work lazy-daisy sts around puffs with dark sage. Following Chart B, embroider on puff sections.

CHART A

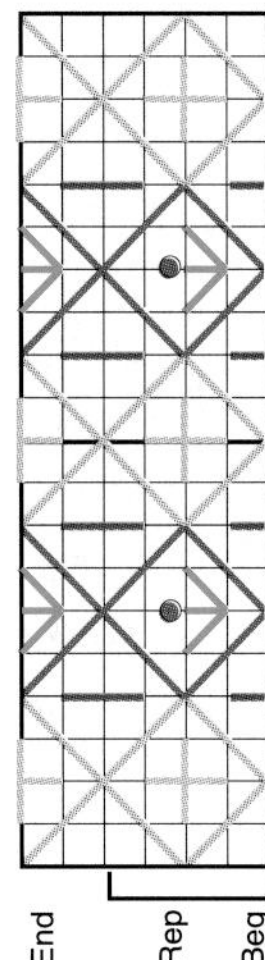

CHART B

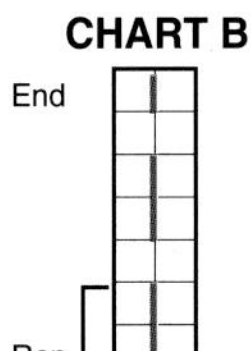

Work after 2nd WS row before popcorns and on 2nd WS row after popcorns.

Outside Edging

Rnd 1: With smaller hook and dark sage, attach yarn at side edge, sc in each row and each st around afghan, working 3 sc in each corner, with RS facing, join in beg sc, turn.

Rnd 2: Ch 3 (counts as first dc), sk first sc, [cl in next sc, ch 1, sk next sc, dc in next sc, ch 1, sk next sc] rep around, working 3 sts in each corner, join in 3rd ch of beg ch-3.

Rnd 3: Sc in each st and sp around, working 3 sc in corners, join in beg sc, fasten off.

Finishing

Weave ribbon under cls and over dc of cl rows.

Sew eyelet on underside of outside edging.

Cut fabric for backing in half; sew selvage edges tog.

Pin backing along 1 edge of afghan on back; sew with sewing ndl and thread. Continue pinning backing to afghan, easing to fit, and sewing 1 side at a time.

Make 12 small bows from rem ribbon. Sew at even intervals along top and bottom edges, using photo as a guide.

—Designed by Michele Maks Thompson, courtesy of Designs for America

Garden Pillow

Shown on page 33

Experience Level: Intermediate

Size: 15" square with ruffle

Materials

- Coats & Clark Red Heart knitting worsted weight yarn: 5 oz each off-white #3 and new berry #760, and 3½ oz each light berry #761, paddy green #686 and pale rose #755
- Size H/8 crochet hook or size needed to obtain gauge
- 11" square pillow form
- Tapestry needle

Gauge: Rnds 1 and 2 = 2½"
To save time, take time to check gauge.

Pattern Note: Join rnds with a sl st unless otherwise stated.

Back

Rnd 1: With off-white, ch 7, join to form a ring, sl st in ring, ch 2 (counts as first hdc throughout for back), 2 hdc in ring, ch 2, [3 hdc in ring, ch 2] 3 times, join in 2nd ch of beg ch-2, fasten off.

Rnd 2: Attach new berry with a sl st in any ch-2 sp, ch 2, 2 hdc, ch 2, 3 hdc in same sp for corner, ch 2, [3 hdc, ch 2, 3 hdc, ch 2 in next ch-2 sp] 3 times, join in 2nd ch of beg ch-2, fasten off.

Rnd 3: Attach off-white with a sl st in any corner ch-2 sp, ch 2, 2 hdc, ch 2, 3 dc in same sp, *ch 2, 3 hdc in next ch-2 sp, ch 2, [3 hdc, ch 2, 3 hdc] in corner, rep from * twice, ch 2, 3 hdc in next ch-2 sp, ch 2, join in 2nd ch of beg ch-2, fasten off.

Rnd 4: Attach new berry with a sl st in any corner ch-2 sp, ch 2, 2 hdc, ch 2, 3 hdc in same sp, *ch 2, [3 hdc in next ch-2 sp, ch 2] twice, [3 hdc, ch 2, 3 hdc] in corner, rep from * twice, ch 2, [3 hdc in next ch-2 sp, ch 2] twice, join in 2nd ch of beg ch-2, fasten off.

Rnd 5: Attach off-white with sl st in any corner ch-2 sp, ch 2, 2 hdc, ch 2, 3 hdc in same sp, *ch 2, [3 hdc in next ch-2 sp, ch 2] 3 times, [3 hdc, ch 2, 3 hdc] in corner, rep from * twice, ch 2, [3 hdc in next ch-2 sp, ch 2] 3 times, join in 2nd ch of beg ch-2, fasten off.

Rnd 6: Attach new berry with a sl st in any corner ch-2 sp, ch 2, 2 hdc, ch 2, 3 hdc in same sp, *ch 2, [3 hdc in next ch-2 sp, ch 2] 4 times, [3 hdc, ch 2, 3 hdc] in corner, rep from * twice, ch 2, [3 hdc in next ch-2 sp, ch 2] 4 times, join in 2nd ch of beg ch-2, fasten off.

Rnd 7: Attach off-white with a sl st in any corner ch-2 sp, ch 2, 2 hdc, ch 2, 3 hdc in same sp, *ch 2, [3 hdc in next ch-2 sp, ch 2] 5 times, [3 hdc, ch 2, 3 hdc] in corner, rep from * twice, ch 2, [3 hdc in next ch-2 sp, ch 2] 5 times, join in 2nd ch of beg ch-2, fasten off.

Rnd 8: Attach new berry with a sl st in any corner ch-2 sp, ch 2, 2 hdc, ch 2, 3 hdc in same sp, *ch 2, [3 hdc in next ch-2 sp, ch 2] 6 times, [3 hdc, ch 2, 3 hdc] in corner, rep from * twice, ch 2, [3 hdc in next ch-2 sp, ch 2] 6 times, join in 2nd ch of beg ch-2, fasten off.

Rnd 9: Attach off-white with a sl st in any corner ch-2 sp, ch 2, 2 hdc, ch 2, 3 hdc in same sp, *ch 2, [3 hdc in next ch-2 sp, ch 2] 7 times, [3 hdc, ch 2, 3 hdc] in corner, rep from * twice, ch 2, [3 hdc in next ch-2 sp, ch 2] 7 times, join in 2nd ch of beg ch-2, fasten off.

Rnd 10: Attach new berry with a sl st in any corner ch-2 sp, ch 2, 2 hdc, ch 2, 3 hdc in same sp, *ch 2, [3 hdc in next ch-2 sp, ch 2] 8 times, [3 hdc, ch 2, 3 hdc] in corner, rep from * twice, ch 2, [3 hdc in next ch-2 sp, ch 2] 8 times, join in 2nd ch of beg ch-2, fasten off.

Rnd 11: Attach off-white with a sl st in any corner ch-2 sp, ch 2, 2 hdc, ch 2, 3 hdc in same sp, *ch 2, [3 hdc in next ch-2 sp, ch 2] 9 times, [3 hdc, ch 2, 3 hdc] in corner, rep from * twice, ch 2, [3 hdc in next ch-2 sp, ch 2] 9 times, join in 2nd ch of beg ch-2, fasten off.

Front

Rnds 1–11: Rep Rnds 1–11 of Back.

Rnd 12: With RS facing, attach pale rose with a sl st to top of any sk hdc of Rnd 1, ch 3 (counts as first dc), 4 dc in same st, 5 dc in each sk hdc of Rnd 1, join in 3rd ch of beg ch-3, fasten off.

Rnd 13: Attach light berry with a sl st between any 2 sts of Rnd 12, [ch 2, sl st between next 2 sts] rep around, ch 2, join in beg sl st, fasten off.

Rnd 14: Attach paddy green with a sc in center hdc of any 3-hdc group of Rnd 3, *[ch 4, sc in same st] twice, ch 4, sc in center hdc of next 3-hdc group, rep from * around, ch 4, join in beg sc, fasten off.

Rnd 15: Attach light berry with a sc in center hdc of any 3-hdc group of Rnd 5, *[ch 3, sc in same st] 3 times, ch 5, sc in center hdc of next 3-hdc group, rep from * around, ch 5, join in beg sc, fasten off.

Rnd 16: Attach green with a sc in center hdc of any 3-hdc group of Rnd 7, rep Rnd 14.

Border/Joining

Rnd 1: With back and front held tog, WS to inside and front facing, attach pale rose through ch-2 sps of both pieces at any corner, ch 2, 2 hdc, ch 2, 3 hdc in same sp, working through ch-2 sps of front and back throughout to join, *[ch 2, 3 hdc in next ch-2 sp] 10 times, ch 2, [3 hdc, ch 2, 3 hdc] in corner ch-2 sp, rep from * twice, [ch 2, 3 hdc in next ch-2 sp] 10 times, ch 2, join, fasten off.

Rnd 2: Attach new berry with sc in any ch-2 corner sp, ch 3, sc in same sp, [*ch 3, 3 sc over ch-2 sp of Rnd 1 and into center hdc of Rnd 11, rep from * across to next corner, ch 3, {sc, ch 3, sc} in corner] 3 times, rep from * to * once, ch 3, join in beg sc, fasten off.

Rnd 3: Attach paddy green with a sc in any corner ch-3 sp, ch 5, sc in same sp, ch 5, [*sc over next ch-3 sp of Rnd 2 and in center hdc of next 3-hdc group, ch 5 **, rep from * across to corner, {sc, ch 5, sc} in corner, ch 5] 3 times, rep from * to **, join in beg sc, fasten off.

Rnd 4: Attach light berry with a sl st in any corner ch-5 sp, ch 4, [dc, ch 1] 6 times in same sp, ch 1, sc in next ch-5 sp, *[ch 5, sc in next ch-5 sp] rep across to corner, ch 1, [dc, ch 1] 7 times in corner ch-5 sp, rep from * twice, [ch 5, sc in next ch-5 sp] rep across to next corner, ch 1, join in 3rd ch of beg ch-4, fasten off.

Rnd 5: Attach pale rose with a sl st in first ch-1 sp at any corner, *[ch 2, sl st in next ch sp] 7 times, [ch 5, sl st in next ch sp] 13 times, rep from * 3 times, ending last rep with ch 5, join in beg sl st, fasten off.

—Designed by Ruth G. Shepherd

Butterflies & Blooms

Shown on page 34

Experience Level: Intermediate

Size: 31" x 11"

Materials

- DMC Cebelia crochet cotton size 20 (405 yds per ball): 2 balls ecru
- Size 10 steel crochet hook
- 8" x 30" piece linen

Gauge: 6 squares and 5 rows = 1" To save time, take time to check gauge.

Pattern Note: Edging may be adjusted to fit desired measurements.

Part 1

Row 1: Ch 68, dc in 8th ch from hook, *ch 2, sk 2 chs, dc in next ch, rep from * across for 21 squares, ch 5, turn.

Row 2: Dc in dc, ch 2, dc in dc, dc in sp, dc in dc, *ch 2, dc in dc, rep from * across to next-to-last square, dc in sp, dc in dc, ch 2, dc in 3rd ch of turning ch-5, ch 5, turn, following Chart A, rep design 2 more times, then rows 1–18 or more for desired length across front.

Part 2

Ch 5, working along side of crochet, follow Chart B, at end of first row, ch 3, turn, sk 2 dc,

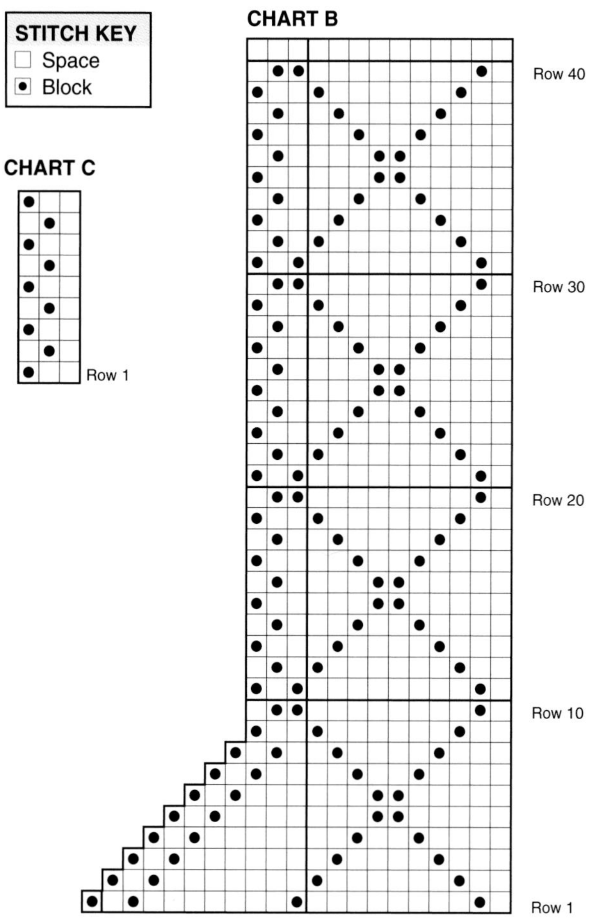

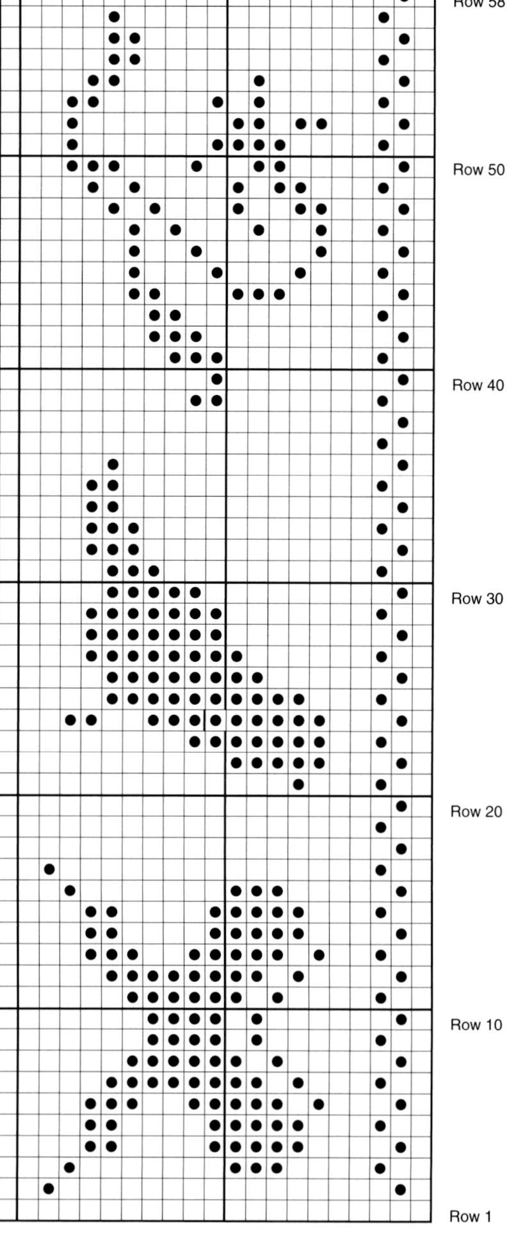

dc in 3rd dc, dc in sp, dc in dc.

Use this method of turning on this edge only for next 7 rows, follow Chart B, fasten off. For opposite end, with RS facing, attach in end of foundation ch, work Chart B in reverse, ch 5, turn to the side.

Part 3

Work along side of Part 2, work Chart C across for back of scarf lace, fasten off, sew ending to other end.

Finishing

Wash linen and lace to preshrink before sewing edging to linen.

Make a narrow hem in linen and join edging as follows:

Sc in corner sp, 3 dc in same sp, *ch 3, sl st in first ch (picot), 3 dc in next sp, sc in next sp, 3 dc in next sp, rep from * around working [3 dc, sc, 3 dc] in each corner.

—Designed by Alice Heim

Bedtime Prayer

Shown on page 35

Experience Level: Intermediate

Size: 15½" x 36"

Materials

- Coats & Clark® Big Ball® 100 percent crochet cotton size 20 (400 yds per ball): 3 balls white
- Size 10 steel crochet hook or size needed to obtain gauge
- 17" ⅛"-diameter white metal or wooden rod

Gauge: 16 sts and 12½ rows = 4" over filet patt

To save time, take time to check gauge.

Pattern Notes: Work wall hanging from hem up, following instructions and Chart A.

Chart is read right to left for odd-numbered rows, and left to right for even-numbered rows.

Each square on chart represents 3 sts, with 1 additional st at end of each row.

For each dot on chart, work 2 dc in ch-2 sp.

Hem

Row 1 (RS): Working sideways, beg at narrow end, ch 12, [3 dc, ch 2, 3 dc] in 5th ch from hook (shell), ch 3, sk each of next 3 chs, sc in next ch, sk next 2 chs, shell in next ch, ch 4, turn.

Row 2: Shell in ch-2 sp of next shell (shell in shell made), ch 3, sc in first dc of next shell, shell in same shell, ch 4, turn.

Row 3: Shell in next shell, ch 3, sc in first dc of next shell, shell in same shell, ch 4, turn.

Row 4: Shell in next shell, ch 3, sc in first dc of next shell, shell in same shell, ch 2, sk next 2 dc of same shell, dc in next dc, ch 5, turn.

Row 5: Dc in first dc of next shell, ch 2, shell in same shell, ch 3, sc in first dc of next shell, shell in same shell, ch 4, turn.

Row 6: Shell in next shell, ch 3, sc in first dc of next shell, shell in same shell, ch 2, sk 3 dc of same shell, dc in next dc, ch 2, dc in 3rd ch of turning ch-5, ch 5, turn.

Row 7: Dc in first dc, ch 2, dc in next dc, ch 2, dc in first dc of next shell, ch 2, shell in same shell, ch 3, sc in first dc of next shell, shell in same shell, ch 4, turn.

Row 8: Shell in next shell, ch 3, sc in first dc of next shell, shell in same shell, sk next 3 dc of same shell, [ch 2, dc in next dc] 3 times, ch 2, dc in 3rd ch of turning ch-5, ch 5, turn.

Row 9: Dc in first dc, [ch 2, dc in next dc] 3 times, ch 2, dc in first dc of next shell, ch 2, shell in same shell, ch 3, sc in first dc of next shell, shell in same shell, ch 4, turn.

Row 10: Shell in next shell, ch 3, sc in first dc of next shell, shell in same shell, ch 1, *sk next ch-2 sp, [3 dc, ch 3, 3 dc] in next ch-2 sp, rep from * twice, working along next side in sps formed by edge dc, **sk next sp, [3 dc, ch 3, 3 dc] in next sp, rep from ** once, sk next sp, sc in last dc of shell at end of next row, ch 1, turn.

Row 11: 9 dc in each of next 2 ch-3 lps, 10 dc in next ch-3 lp, 9 dc in each of next 2 ch-3 lps, ch 1, sc in next ch-1 sp, ch 2, shell in next shell, ch 3, sc in first dc of next shell, shell in same shell, ch 4, turn.

Row 12: Shell in next shell, ch 3, sc in first dc of next shell, shell in same shell, ch 4, turn.

[Rep Rows 3–12] 3 times, ending last row with ch-3 instead of ch-4, turn, sc in ch-2 sp, ch 5, sc in next ch-2 lp, ch 3, sc in 4th ch of beg ch of previous row, turn hem to work across long, straight edge of shells.

Body

Row 1: Ch 5 (counts as first dc, ch 2), ch 2, dc in same st as last sc, *ch 2, dc in first ch of ch-4, ch 2, tr in ch-2 lp between shells, ch 2, dc in 4th ch of ch-4, rep from * across, ending with

CHART A

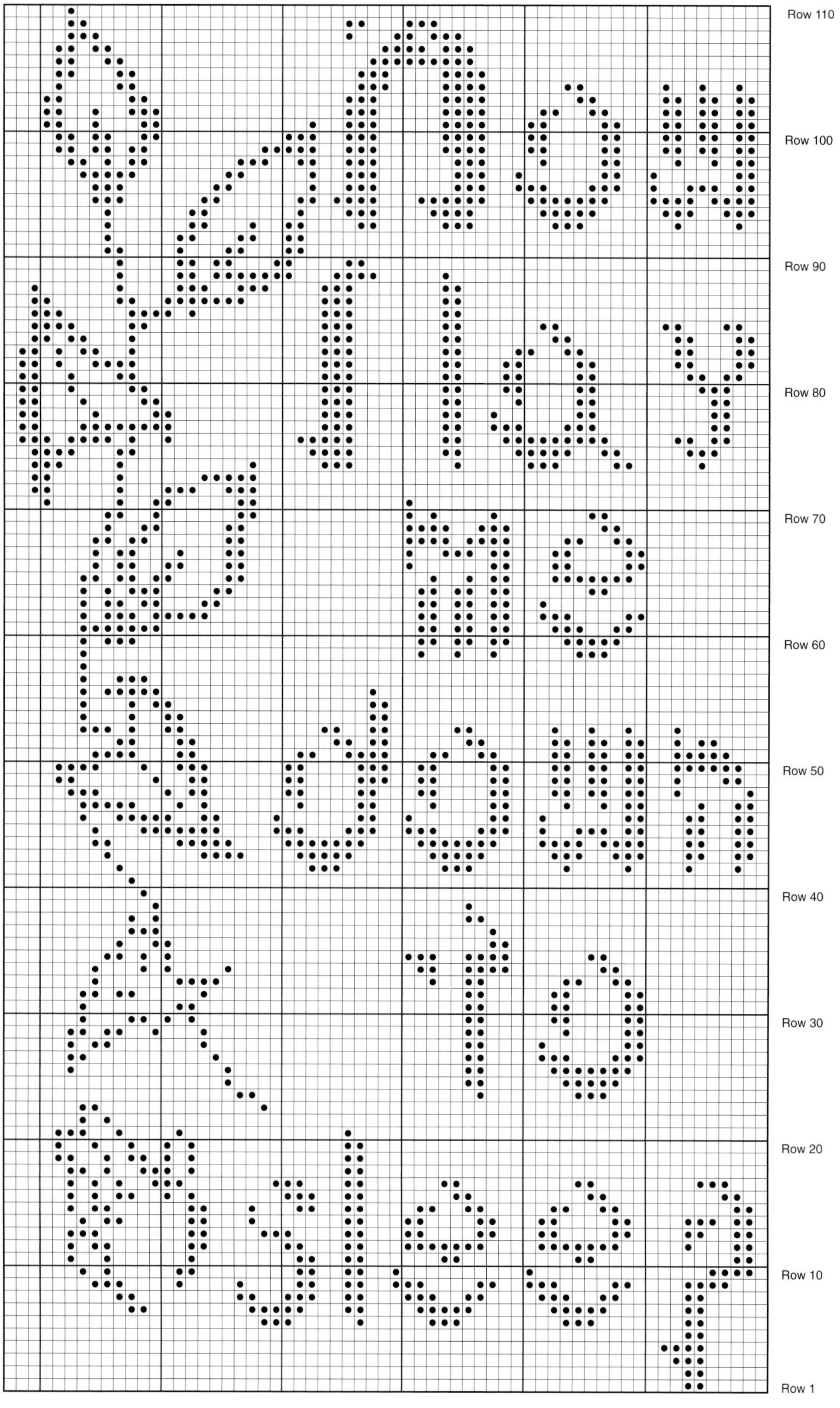

Row 110
Row 100
Row 90
Row 80
Row 70
Row 60
Row 50
Row 40
Row 30
Row 20
Row 10
Row 1

STITCH KEY

- □ Space
- ● Dc block

ch 2, dc in top of first dc of beg shell, ch 2, dc in same st, turn. (63 ch-2 sps)

Row 2: Ch 5 (counts as first dc, ch 2), *dc in next dc, ch 2, rep from * across, dc in 3rd ch of beg ch-5.

Work Rows 1–110 from Chart A in filet crochet, work 2 more rows of sps, ch 1, turn at end of last row.

Top Edging

Row 1 (RS): Sc in first dc, 9 dc in next ch-2 sp, sk next dc and ch-2 sp, sc in next dc, *sk next ch-2 sp and dc, 9 dc in next ch-2 sp, sk next dc and ch-2 sp, sc in next dc, rep from * across, ending last sc in 3rd ch of turning ch.

Turn to work along side edge of wall hanging, rep from * to end of Row 1, sk post at end of first row above hem, fasten off.

Attach cotton on opposite side of hanging at top of first row of filet, work edging as for opposite side to end of row, join in first sc of top edge, fasten off.

Weave in loose ends.

Finishing

Press with steam iron on WS of fabric. Insert rod across top of hanging, weaving through ch-2 sps below each 9-dc shell and sk 3 dc between.

Cord

Cut 5 lengths of thread 2 yds each. Holding threads tog, tie 1 end to a pencil and the other end to a doorknob. Turn pencil clockwise until threads are tightly twisted. Fold twist in half and allow cord to twist back on itself. Secure 1 end to each end of rod. Trim ends of cord to ½"; untwist ends.

—Designed by Maureen Egan Emlet

Cozy Slippers

Shown on page 36

Experience Level: Advanced beginner

Size: Ladies' small (medium) (large) Instructions are given for smallest size, with larger sizes in parentheses. When only 1 number is given, it applies to all sizes.

Finished Measurements

Ladies' Moccasins: 7½(9)(10)" sole

Warm & Wonderful Slippers: 8½–9(9½–10)(10½–11)" sole

Ladies' Moccasins

Materials

- Coats & Clark® Red Heart Super Saver® worsted weight yarn: 6 oz mint green and 2 oz cream
- Size F/5 crochet hook
- Size H/8 crochet hook or size needed to obtain gauge
- 26(28)(30)" ⅛"-wide white elastic
- Sewing needle
- White thread
- 1½" strip cardboard

Gauge: 6 sc and 6 sc rows = 2" To save time, take time to check gauge.

Pattern Note: Use size H hook unless otherwise stated.

Sole *(Make 4)*

Note: *Do not join at end of rnds. Mark beg st of each rnd.*

Rnd 1: With mint green, ch 15(19)(23), 2 sc in 2nd ch from hook, sc in each of next 5(7)(9) chs, hdc in next 1(2)(3) ch, dc in each of next 4(5)(6) chs, 2 dc in next ch, hdc in next ch, 6 sc in last ch (toe), working along opposite side of beg ch, hdc in next ch, 2 dc in next ch, dc in each of next 4(5)(6) chs, hdc in 1(2)(3) ch, sc in each of next 5(7)(9) chs, 2 sc in next ch. (35, 43, 51 sts)

Rnd 2: 2 sc in first sc, 2 sc in next sc, sc in each of next 13(17)(21) sc, [2 sc in next st, sc in next st] twice, 2 sc in next st, sc in each of next 13(17)(21) sts, 2 sc in each of next 2 sts. (42, 50, 58 sts)

Rnd 3: Sc in first sc, 2 sc in next sc, sc in each of next 14(18)(22) sc, [2 sc in next sc, sc in each of next 2 sc] 3 times, 2 sc in next sc, sc in each of next 14(18)(22) sc, 2 sc in next sc, sc in last sc. (48, 56, 64 sts)

Rnd 4: Sc in first sc, 2 sc in next sc, sc in each of next 17(21)(25) sc, [2 sc in next sc, sc in each of next 2 sc] 3 times, 2 sc in next sc, sc in each of next 17(21)(25) sc, 2 sc in next sc, sc in last sc. (54, 62, 70 sts)

Rnd 5: Sc in first sc, sc in each of next 23(27)(31) sc, 2 sc in next sc, sc in each of next 4 sc, 2 sc in next sc, sc in each of next 23(27)(31) sc, sc in last sc, fasten off, leaving a long end for sewing. (56, 64, 72 sts)

Set aside sole pieces.

Slipper Sides *(Make 8)*

Row 1: With mint green, ch 4, sc in 2nd ch from hook, sc in each ch across, ch 1, turn.

Rows 2–7(9)(11): Sc in each sc across, ch 1, turn.

Row 8(10)(12): Sc in each sc across, 2 sc in last sc, ch 1, turn. (4 sts)

Row 9(11)(13): Sc in each sc across, ch 1, turn.

Rows 10–12(12–14)(14–16): Rep Rows 8 and 2 alternately, ending with Row 8.

Rows 13–15(15–19)(17–21): Sc in each sc across, ch 1, turn.

Row 16(20)(22): Sc in each sc across (for sizes medium and large, 2 sc in last sc), ch 1, turn.

Rows 17–21(21–25)(23–29): Rep Row 2.

Row 22(26)(30): Rep Row 8.

Rows 23–28(27–32)(31–36): Sc in each sc across, fasten off, leaving an end for sewing.

Instep *(Make 2)*

Row 1: Beg at toe with mint green, ch 3(4)(4), 2 sc in 2nd ch from hook, sc in next 0(1)(1) ch, 2 sc in last ch, ch 1, turn. (4, 5, 5 sts)

Row 2: 2 sc in first sc, sc in each of next 2(3)(3) sc, 2 sc in last sc, ch 1, turn. (6, 7, 7 sts)

Row 3: 2 sc in first sc, sc in each of next 4(5)(5) sc, 2 sc in last sc, ch 1, turn. (8, 9, 9 sts)

Row 4: Sc in each sc across, ch 1, turn.

Row 5: 2 sc in first sc, sc across to last sc, 2 sc in last sc, ch 1, turn. (10, 11, 11 sts)

Row 6(6 & 7)(6–8): Sc in each sc across, ch 1, turn.

Row 7(8)(9): Rep Row 5, ch 1, turn. (12, 13, 13 sts)

Rows 8 & 9(9 & 10)(10–12): Sc in each sc across, ch 1, turn.

Rows 10–13(11–14)(13–16): Sc first 2 sc tog as 1, sc across, sc last 2 sc tog as 1, ch 1, turn, fasten off, leaving a long end for sewing. (4, 5, 5 sts)

Assembly

Sew 2 sections of side pieces tog at toe and heel. Sew 2nd 2 pieces tog in same way. Turn so that wrong sides face; pin to hold.

Place 1 sole in place on bottom of slipper, centering at heel and toe seams. Sew sole in place, easing to fit where necessary.

Place 2nd sole over first sole; sew in place.

Sew Row 1 and ends of rows on instep to opening on front of slipper.

Slipper Top & Cuff

Cut elastic in half. Overlap ends of each piece ½"; sew securely with sewing ndl and white thread.

Rnd 1: With right side of slipper facing, working through both thicknesses of upper slipper and elastic at the same time, attach cream with a sl st at center heel, ch 1, sc in same st, sc in each st around, matching sts carefully, join with a sl st in beg sc, turn.

Rnd 2: Working in back lps only for this rnd, ch 2, hdc in each st to front corner, 3 hdc in corner, hdc in 4(5)(5) sts across instep, 3 hdc in corner st, hdc in each st to end, join with a sl st in 2nd ch of beg ch-2.

Rnds 3 & 4: Ch 2, hdc in each hdc to corner hdc, 3 hdc in corner hdc, hdc in each hdc across instep, 3 hdc in corner hdc, hdc in each hdc to last hdc, join with a sl st in 2nd ch of beg ch-2.

Rnd 5: *Ch 3, sc in 3rd ch from hook (picot), sk next st, sc in next st, rep from * to corner 3 hdc, do not sk st for these 3 sts, but work picot in each st, continue in patt to next corner, work same as first corner, continue in patt around, join, fasten off.

Trim Around Top Opening

Attach cream with a sl st in any st of rem lps of Rnd 1 of cuff, ch 1, sl st evenly in each st around, join with a sl st in beg sc, fasten off.

Cord *(Make 2)*

With smaller hook and mint green, ch 100, fasten off.

Tassel *(Make 4)*

Wind mint green around 1½" piece of cardboard 15 times. Thread an 8" piece of yarn into yarn ndl; insert under strands at 1 edge. Tie firmly. Remove yarn from cardboard, holding tassel firmly. Wind 10" piece of yarn approximately ½" from top; fasten off. Cut lps at bottom; trim evenly.

Finishing

Weave crocheted cord through every 2nd hole of Rnd 2 of cuff, bringing ends out at front. Fasten 2 tassels to ends of cord. Tie in a bow, pulling slightly to gather.

— Designed by Colleen Sullivan

Warm & Wonderful Slippers

Materials

- 4-ply worsted weight yarn: 5(7)9) oz each cream and coral
- Size G/6(H/8)(I/9) crochet hook or size needed to obtain gauge
- Tapestry needle

Gauge: 4 sts and 4 sc rnds = 1" with size G hook (for size small)

7 sts = 2"; 3 sc rnds = 1" with size H hook (for medium)

3 sts = 1"; 5 sc rnds = 2" with size I hook (for size large)

To save time, take time to check gauge.

Pattern Note: Join rnds with a sl st unless otherwise stated.

Sole *(Make 2)*
Rnd 1: With coral, ch 20, hdc in 3rd ch from hook, 2 hdc in next ch, hdc in each of next 14 chs, 2 hdc in next ch, 3 hdc in next ch, working on opposite side of foundation ch, 2 hdc in next ch, hdc in each of next 14 chs, 2 hdc in next ch, hdc at base of beg ch-2, join in 2nd ch of beg ch-2. (42 sts)

Rnd 2: Ch 2, hdc in joining st, 2 hdc in each of next 2 sts, hdc in each of next 4 sts, sc in each of next 10 sts, hdc in each of next 2 sts, 2 hdc in each of next 5 sts, hdc in each of next 2 sts, sc in each of next 10 sts, hdc in each of next 4 sts, 2 hdc in each of next 2 sts, join in 2nd ch of beg ch-2. (52 sts)

Rnd 3: Ch 2, hdc in joining st, 2 hdc in each of next 4 sts, hdc in each of next 8 sts, sc in each of next 10 sts, [2 sc in next st, sc in next st] twice, [sc in next st, 2 sc in next st] twice, sc in each of next 10 sts, hdc in each of next 8 sts, 2 hdc in each of next 3 sts, join in 2nd ch of beg ch-2. (64 sts)

Rnd 4: Ch 2, hdc in joining st, 2 hdc in each of next 6 sts, hdc in each of next 5 sts, sc in each of next 20 sts, 2 sc in each of next 6 sts, sc in each of next 20 sts, hdc in each of next 5 sts, 2 hdc in next st, join in 2nd ch of beg ch-2, fasten off. (78 sts)

Sides *(Make 2)*
Note: *Mark center front and back st.*

Rnd 1: With RS facing, join coral with sc in back lp of center back st, working in back lps only, sc in each st around, join in beg sc. (78)

Rnd 2: Ch 1, working in back lp of each st, sc in each st around, dec 1 st on each side of center st at toe, join in beg sc. (76)

Rnds 3 & 4: Rep Rnd 2. (72)

Rnds 5–8: Ch 1, working in back lp of each st, sc in each st around, dec 1 st on each side of center st at toe and heel, fasten off at end of last rnd. (56 sc)

Cuff *(Make 2)*
Rnd 1: Join cream with sc at center back, [ch 1, sk 1 st, sc in next st] rep around, join in beg sc. (28 ch-1 sps)

Rnd 2: Ch 3 (counts as first hdc, ch 1), [hdc in next sc, ch 1] rep around, join in 2nd ch of beg ch-3.

Rnd 3: Ch 2, 3 hdc around vertical post of first hdc, ch 1, [4 hdc around vertical post of next hdc, ch 1] rep around, join in 2nd ch of beg ch-2, fasten off.

Rnd 4: Join coral with sc in center back ch-1 sp of Rnd 2, 2 hdc, sc in same sp, [sc, 2 hdc, sc] in each ch-1 sp around, join in beg sc, fasten off.

Insole *(Make 2)*
With cream, rep Rnds 1–4 of sole. Place inside slipper; tack in place.

Tie *(Make 2)*
With cream, ch 40, fasten off. Loop through 3rd ch-1 sp on each side of center front of Rnd 1 of Cuff. Tie ends in a bow.

—Designed by Ruth Shepherd

Dye-Lot Alert!

If you've been crocheting for any length of time, you've heard how important it is to buy yarn for big projects all at the same time, and to be sure that each skein is from the same dye lot.

Some yarns don't have a dye lot, but most have a dye-lot number on the label. Buying the same dye lot will ensure each skein will match perfectly. Each dye lot can vary in color—even blacks and whites—so don't take any chances. Even if you have to purchase a few extra skeins it will be worth it. If you've ever run short before, you'll know how true this is!

If you get into a bind and have to purchase yarn from different dye lots, color differences won't be as obvious if you're able to separate the different lots with another color, such as you might do for a striped afghan. Planning correctly, though, by purchasing enough of one dye lot is the best way of making sure your project will look its best!

—By Jocelyn Sass

Floral Pillow

Shown on page 37

Experience Level: Intermediate

Size: Approximately 12" square

Materials

- J. & P. Coats® Knit-Cro-Sheen® 100 percent cotton crochet cotton size 10 (225 yds per ball): 1 ball white #001
- Size 7 steel crochet hook
- 12" square pillow insert
- 2 (13") square pieces pink satin fabric
- Pink sewing thread
- Sewing needle
- Fabric stiffener

Gauge: 9 sc = 1"

To save time, take time to check gauge.

Pattern Note: Join rnds with a sl st unless otherwise stated.

Pattern Stitches

5-tr cluster (5-tr cl): [Yo twice, insert hook in next dc, draw up a lp, {yo, draw through 2 lps} twice, leave last lp on hook] 5 times, yo, draw through all lps on hook.

2-dc cluster (2-dc cl): Keeping last lp of each dc on hook, 2 dc in same st, yo and draw through all 3 lps on hook.

3-dc cluster (3-dc cl): Keeping last lp of each dc on hook, 3 dc in same st, yo and draw through all 4 lps on hook.

First Motif

Rnd 1: Ch 8, join to form a ring, ch 6 (counts as first dc, ch 3), [dc in ring, ch 3] 7 times, join in 3rd ch of beg ch-6.

Rnd 2: Sl st in next ch sp, ch 3 (counts as first dc), 4 dc in same ch sp, [ch 3, 5 dc in next ch sp] rep around, ending with ch 3, join in 3rd ch of beg ch-3.

Rnd 3: Ch 4, 4-tr cluster over next 4 dc, [ch 9, sl st in 2nd ch of ch-3 sp, ch 9, 5-tr cluster over next 5 dc] rep around, ending with ch 9, sl st in 2nd ch of ch-3 sp, ch 9, join in top of beg cluster.

Rnd 4: Sl st in each of next 5 chs, *ch 11, sl st in 5th ch of ch-9 lp, [ch 7, sl st in 5th ch of ch-9 lp] 3 times, rep from * around, join in first ch of beg ch-11.

Rnd 5: Ch 1, *6 sc in next ch sp, ch 3, 6 sc in same ch sp, [3 sc, ch 3, 3 sc in next ch sp] 3 times, rep from * around, join in beg sc, fasten off.

Second & Subsequent Motifs *(Make 8)*

Rnds 1–4: Rep Rnds 1–4 of First Motif.

Rnd 5: Rep Rnd 5 of First Motif, except replace center st of ch-3 lps with sl st worked in corresponding ch lp of adjacent motif.

Border

Rnd 1: Attach thread to any corner ch-3 lp, [ch 9, sl st in next ch-3 lp] rep around, join in beg corner lp.

Rnd 2: Ch 4 (counts as first dc, ch 1), working in chs and sl sts, [sk 1 ch, dc in next st, ch 1] rep around, join in 3rd ch of beg ch-4.

Rnd 3: Ch 3, 2 dc in same dc, *[ch 1, sk next dc, 3 dc in next dc] 30 times, ch 1, 3 dc in same dc, rep from * around, ending with ch 1, join in 3rd ch of beg ch-3.

Rnd 4: Ch 3, 2-dc cl in same dc, [ch 5, sk next dc, 3-dc cl in next dc, ch 5, sk 1 ch, 3-dc cl in next dc] rep around, ending with ch 5, join in 3rd ch of beg ch-3, fasten off.

Finishing

With RS tog and ½" seam allowance, sew 3 sides of fabric squares; turn. Place pillow insert inside. Stitch closed.

Stiffen crocheted cover and block to size. Place cover on pillow and st 2nd rnd of border to sides of the pillow.

—Designed by Nazanin S. Fard

Tips for Better Crocheting

You will be able to see your crochet work better if you use a light-colored hook when crocheting with dark yarn and a dark-colored hook when crocheting with a light yarn.

When crocheting with black yarn or other dark colors, it will be easier to see your work if you lay a light-colored cloth (like a purchased cloth napkin) over your lap when crocheting.

When making crochet rugs that will lie on a bare floor, use a latex backing in brush-on or spray form. This can be found in most craft stores.

Instructions for Filet Crochet

Filet crochet is a method of forming designs with solid and openwork squares called blocks (bl) and spaces (sp).

A bl will appear to have 4 dc; the first dc of the bl is the dc that defines the sp preceding the bl. A group of 3 bls will have 9 dc plus 1 dc of sp preceding bl.

A foundation chain is 3 times the number of sps in the first row plus 5 if the row begins with a sp (dc in 8th ch from hook) or plus 3 if row begins with a bl (dc in 4th ch from hook and next 2 chs). On following rows ch 5 if next row begins with a sp or ch 3 if row begins with bl.

Bl: Dc in each of next 3 sts.

Beg bl: Ch 3, dc in each of next 3 sts.

Sp: Ch 2, sk 2 sts, dc in indicated st.

Beg sp: Ch 5, sk 2 sts, dc in next st/dc.

Bl over a bl: Dc in each of next 3 dc.

Bl over a sp: 2 dc in sp, dc in next dc.

Sp over a bl: Ch 2, sk 2 dc, dc in next dc.

Sp over a sp: Ch 2, dc in next dc.

Sp inc at the beginning of a row: Ch 7, dc in first dc of previous row; to add several sps, ch 3 times the number of sps plus 4, dc in 8th ch from hook for first sp, *ch 2, sk 2 chs, dc in next ch, rep from *, dc of last sp inc will be in first dc of previous row.

Sp inc at the end of a row: Ch 2, yo 3 times, draw up lp in turning ch where last dc was worked, [yo and draw through 2 lps] 4 times (dtr made for 1 sp). For additional sps, *ch 2, yo 3 times, draw up lp in middle of last dtr, [yo and draw through 2 lps] 4 times, rep from * as many times as needed.

Bl inc at the beginning of a row: Ch 5, ch 3 more for each additional bl inc, dc in 4th ch from hook, dc in next ch (1 bl inc), dc in each of next 3 chs for each additional bl inc.

Bl inc at the end of a row: Yo, draw up lp in top of turning ch where last dc was worked, yo and draw through 1 lp on hook (base st), [yo and draw through 2 lps on hook] twice (dc), *yo, draw up lp in base st, yo and draw through 1 lp on hook for next base st, [yo and draw through 2 lps on hook] twice, rep from * once for 1 bl inc, rep from * 3 times for each additional bl inc.

Sp or bl dec at the beginning of a row: Ch 1, sl st in each of next 3 sts across for each sp or bl dec, sl st in next dc, ch 5, sk next 2 sts, dc in next dc if row starts with a sp or ch 3, dc in next 2 sts if row starts with a bl.

Sp or bl dec at the end of a row: Leave 3 sts of each sp or bl unworked.

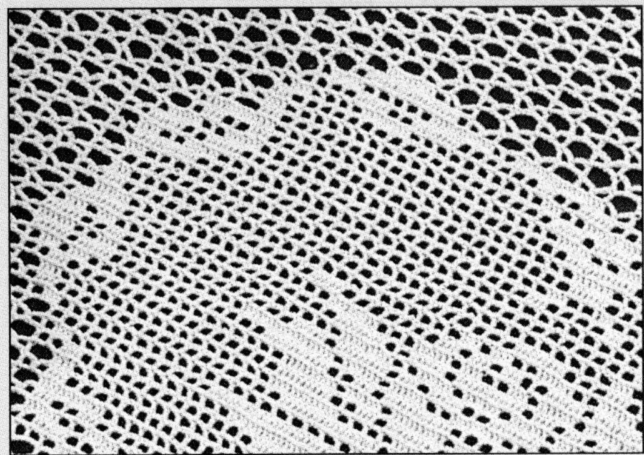

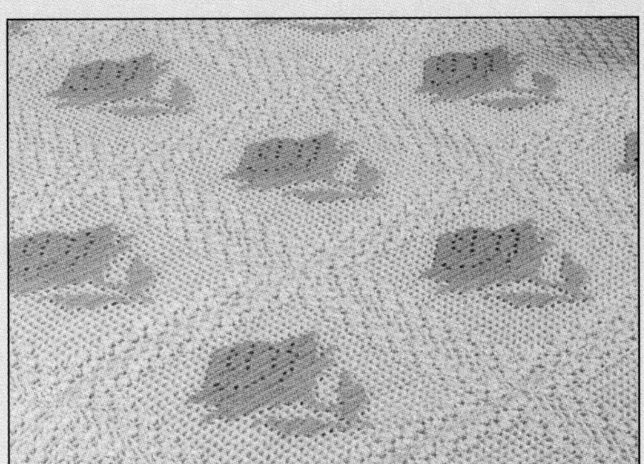

Notice the fine detail on these exquisite examples of filet crochet.

Dining Elegance

Add an elegant dimension to your entertaining by crocheting a variety of beautiful tablecloths, centerpieces and runners to grace your table and buffet. Lacy motifs, monogrammed designs and floral patterns will bring a time-honored, classic look to your dining room.

Crochet your family's initials into this handsome Monogram Set to create a family heirloom to be treasured for years. Worked with size 20 crochet cotton and embellished with pearls, the complete ensemble includes a centerpiece, place mat and envelope napkin holder. Instructions begin on page 68.

Showcase each of these three enchanting pieces by placing them atop a rich, solid-colored tablecloth. Favorite Runner (below) combines small, intricate motifs into a lovely runner. Floral Centerpiece (right) is a striking square filet piece perfect for setting off a bouquet of fresh flowers, and lacy Flower Basket, filled with silk flowers, is quick to stitch and makes a lovely permanent decoration for the main table, buffet or side table. Instructions on pages 71–74..

Few crocheted pieces require as much dedication as a delicate tablecloth, and few bring as much satisfaction when complete! Create this heirloom Roses Tablecloth (left) with all the care and attention to detail Grandmother put into everything she did. A smaller, yet equally lovely piece, Queen Anne runner (above), is ideal for special dining occasions during which you serve a buffet. Cutlery, linen napkins or small dishes can be artfully arranged on this elegant runner. Instructions on pages 75–78.

Two classic tablecloths, Nostalgia (below) and Snowflakes (right), can be worked to fit any size table. Nostalgia is simply named in honor of days gone by when life was somewhat slower and when friends and neighbors spent more time with each other sharing food and fellowship. Snowflakes will remind you of the peaceful calm that settles on the earth after a soft snowfall. Crochet both tablecloths to treasure and share with loved ones. Instructions on pages 78 and 79.

If your preference is for cheerful flowers and a dining room bathed in sunlight, these patterns will be the perfect accent pieces for you. Flowers Everywhere (below) can be worked in white as shown or, for a refreshing change, in a variety of your favorite colors. My Dahlia Delight (left) makes a pretty topper for a small round side table. Instructions on pages 79–81.

Monogram Set

Shown on page 58

Experience Level: Intermediate

Size

Envelope Napkin Holder: 5" x 7" folded

Place Mat: 10½" x 16"

Centerpiece: 13" x 13½"

Materials

- DMC® Cebelia® crochet cotton size 20 (50 grams per ball): 4 balls white
- Size 10 steel crochet hook
- 150 (3mm) white pearls

Gauge: 15 sts and 5 rows = 1" To save time, take time to check gauge.

Pattern Note: Beg ch-3 counts as first dc throughout.

Pattern Stitches: See Instructions for Filet Crochet on page 57.

Bar: Ch 5, sk 5 sts, dc in next st/dc.

2 bls over a bar: Dc in each of next 5 chs, dc in next st/dc.

Sp over a bar: Ch 2, sk 2 chs, dc in next st/dc.

Lacet: Ch 3, sk 2 sts, sc in next st, ch 3, sk 2 sts, dc in next dc.

Popcorn: 5 dc in indicated st/sp, remove hook from lp and insert in top of first dc, pull lp through dc and form popcorn on RS of work, ch 1 to close.

Popcorn over a sp: Popcorn in next ch, dc in next dc.

Popcorn over a popcorn: Popcorn in top of popcorn, dc in next dc.

Sp over a popcorn: Ch 2, sk popcorn, dc in next dc.

Pearlwork (pearls are worked within a sp): Sl pearl forward on

CHART A
Napkin Holder

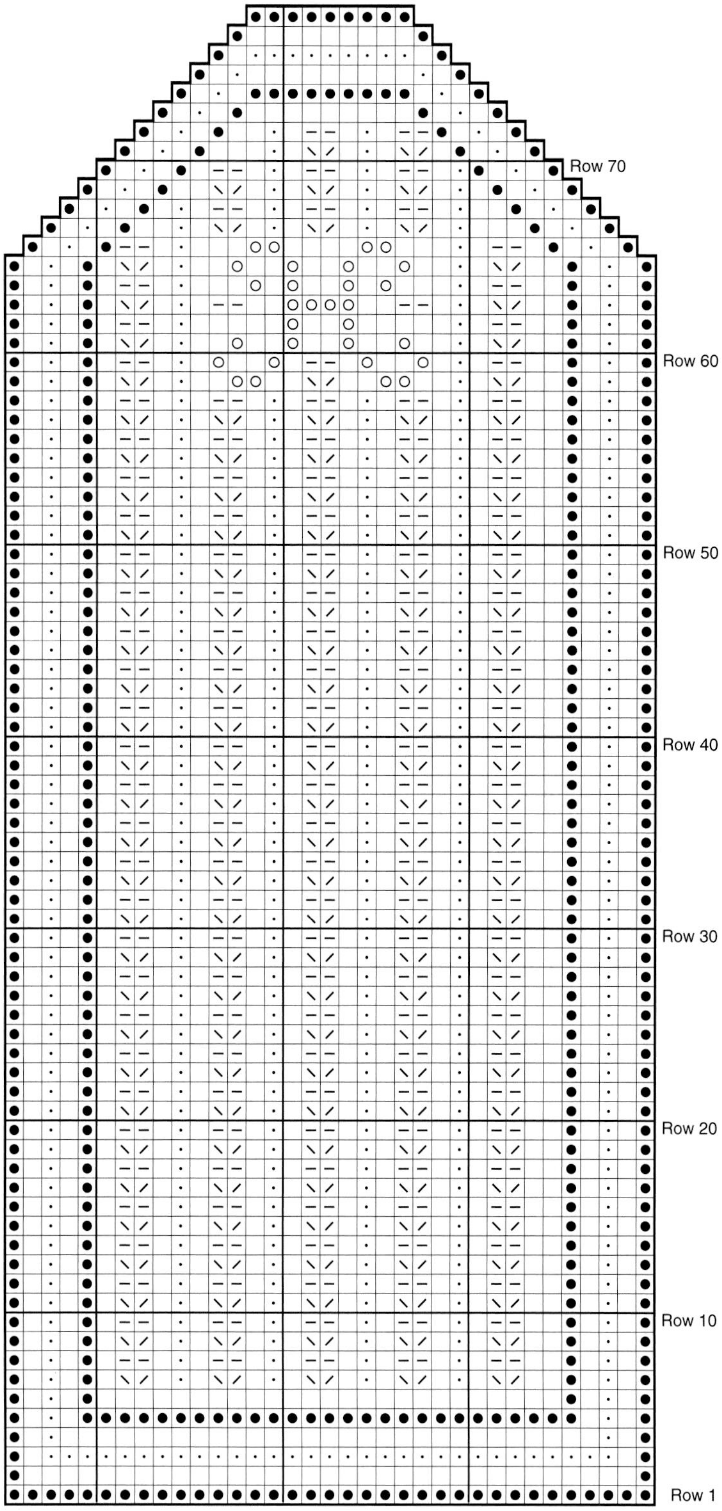

Row 70
Row 60
Row 50
Row 40
Row 30
Row 20
Row 10
Row 1

cotton, finish ch at top of pearl, ch 1, dc in next dc.

Sp over a pearl: Ch 2, sk pearl, dc in next dc.

Bl inc between short-row sections: Bl inc at end of row technique working last added dc as follows: yo, insert in base of dc just made, yo and through base, insert hook in desired st on next section, yo and draw through st and first lp on hook, [yo and draw through 2 lps] twice.

Envelope Napkin Holder

Row 1 (RS): Thread 30 pearls onto cotton, ch 108, dc in 4th ch from hook and in each ch across.

CHART B
Centerpiece

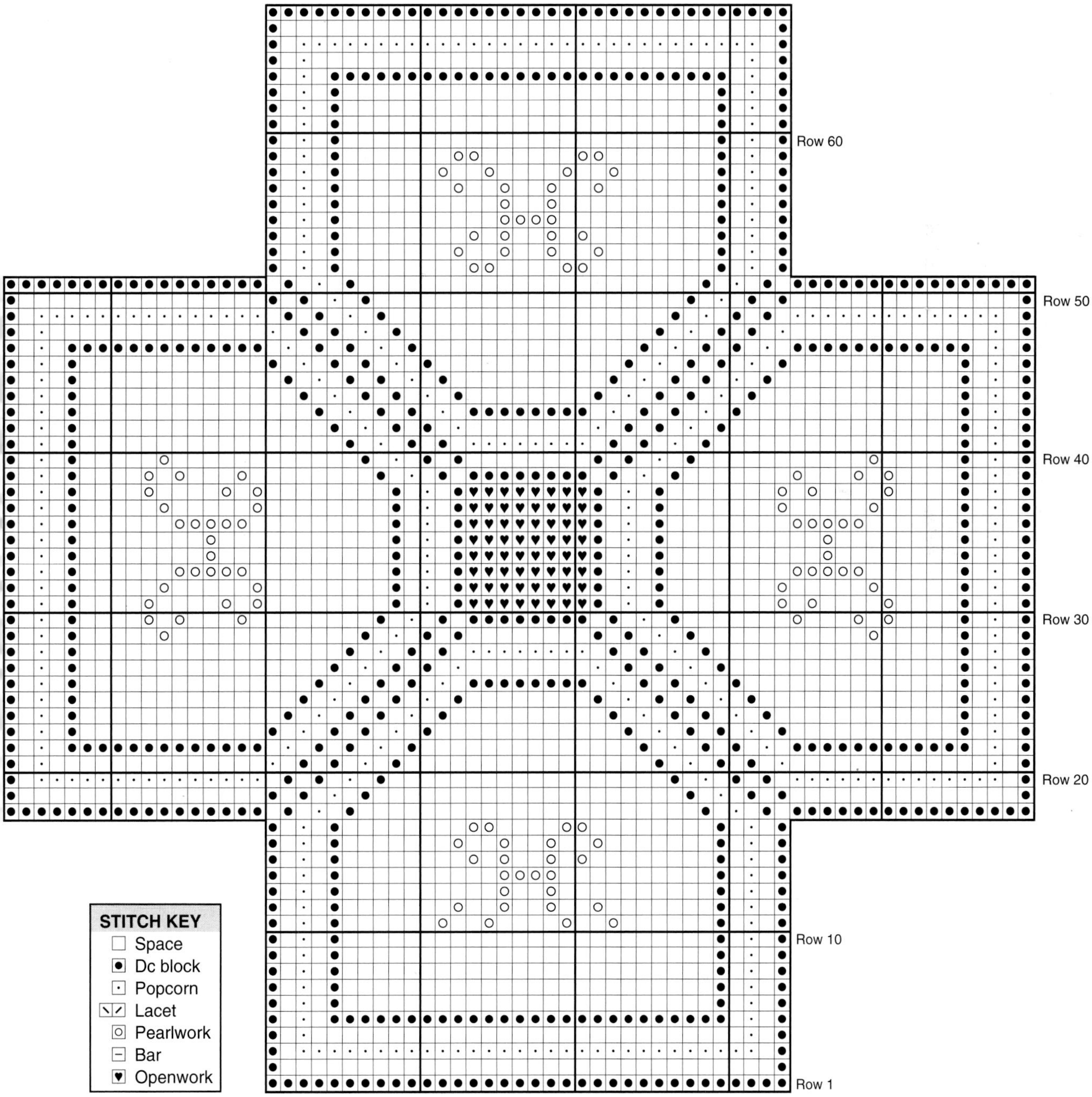

Row 60

Row 50

Row 40

Row 30

Row 20

Row 10

Row 1

STITCH KEY

- Space
- Dc block
- Popcorn
- Lacet
- Pearlwork
- Bar
- Openwork

CHART C
Place Mat

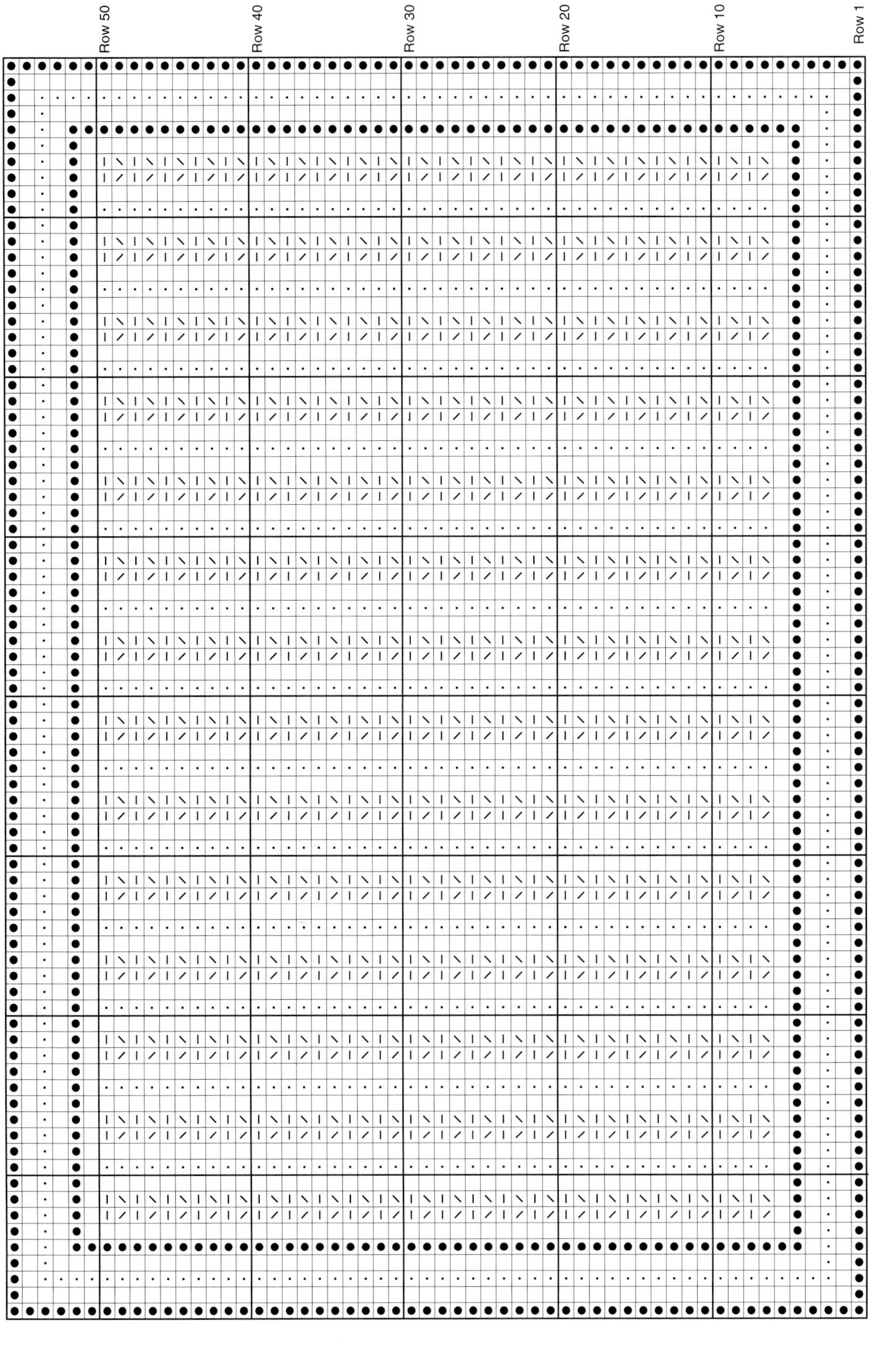

Row 50 · Row 40 · Row 30 · Row 20 · Row 10 · Row 1

ALPHABET

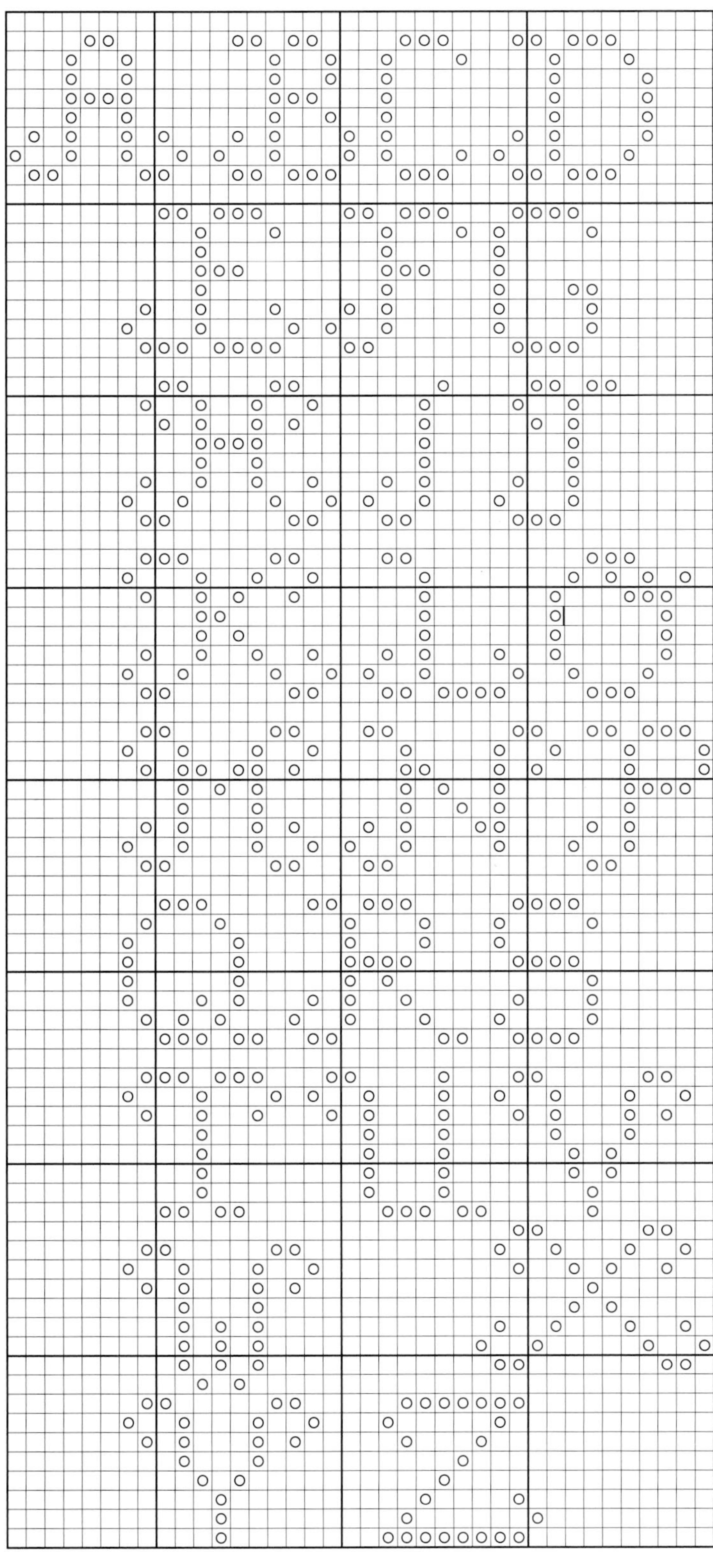

Row 2: Ch 3, dc in each of next 3 dc, *[ch 2, sk 2 dc, dc] in next dc, rep from * 32 times, dc in each of last 3 dc.

Row 3: Beg bl over a bl, sp over a sp, 31 popcorns over 31 sps, sp over a sp, bl over a bl.

Rows 4–78: Follow Chart A, utilizing Pattern Stitches, fasten off at end of Row 78.

Finishing

Fold lower edge of envelope (RS facing) to match Row 54. Sew side seams.

Centerpiece

Row 1 (RS): Ch 105, dc in 4th ch from hook and in each ch across.

Row 2: Beg bl over a bl, 32 sps over 32 bls, bl over a bl.

Rows 3–68: Follow Chart B, utilizing Pattern Stitches, fasten off at end of Row 68.

Place Mat

Row 1 (RS): Ch 240, dc in 4th ch from hook and in each ch across.

Row 2: Beg bl over a bl, 77 sps over 77 bls, bl over a bl.

Rows 3–56: Follow Chart C, utilizing Pattern Stitches, fasten off at end of Row 56.

—Designed by Nancy Hearne courtesy of DMC

Favorite Runner

Shown on page 60

Experience Level: Intermediate

Size

Runner: 14" wide x 41" long

Motif: 2½" square

Materials
- Coats & Clark South Maid® mercerized crochet cotton size 10: 750 yds white
- Size 6 steel crochet hook
- Rustproof pins

Pattern Notes: Join rnds with a sl st unless otherwise stated.

Join 5 rows of 15 motifs each for runner.

Pattern Stitch
Picot: [Sc, ch 3, 2 dc in 3rd ch from hook, sc] in indicated lp.

First Motif
Rnd 1: Ch 4, 11 dc in first ch, join in 4th ch of beg ch-4. (12 dc)

Rnd 2: Ch 3, dc in same st, [2 dc in next st] rep around, join in 3rd ch of beg ch-3. (24 dc)

Rnd 3: Ch 1, sc in same st, *[ch 5, sk 1 dc, sc in next dc] twice, ch 7, sk 1 dc, sc in next dc, rep from * around, ending with ch 4, dc in beg sc.

Rnd 4: Ch 3, 2 dc in same lp, *[3 dc in next lp] twice, [3 dc, ch 3, 3 dc] in next lp, rep from * twice, [3 dc in next lp] 3 times, ch 1, hdc in beg ch-3.

Rnd 5: Ch 1, sc in sp just made, *[ch 7, sk 3 dc, sc between next 2 dc] 3 times, ch 7, 3 sc in corner sp, rep from * 3 times, ending with 2 sc in same corner sp as beg sc, join in beg sc, fasten off.

Second & Subsequent Motifs
(Make 74)

Rnds 1–4: Rep Rnds 1–4 of First Motif.

Rnd 5: Ch 1, sc in lp just made, *[ch 3, sl st in next ch-7 lp of adjacent motif, ch 3, sk 3 dc on working motif, sc between next 2 dc] 3 times, ch 3, sl st in next ch-7 lp of adjacent motif, ch 3, 3 sc in corner sp, rep from * across 2nd side if needed, or finish as Rnd 5 of First Motif.

Border
Rnd 1: Attach thread in first free lp of any side motif, ch 1, sc in same lp, *[ch 7, sc in next lp] 3 times, ch 6, sk next ch-3 lp, sc in joining, ch 3, sc in same sp, ch 6, sk next ch-3 lp, sc in next ch-7 lp, rep from * across to corner, ch 3, [sc, ch 3, sc] in center sc of corner, ch 3, sc in next ch-7 lp, rep from first * around, join in beg sc.

Rnd 2: Sl st to center of next ch-7 lp, ch 1, sc in same lp, [ch 10, picot in next lp, ch 10, sc in next lp, ch 7, sk next lp, picot in ch-3 lp, ch 7, sk next lp, sc in ch-7 lp] rep around, join in beg sc, fasten off.

Finishing
Mist lightly with water or spray starch. Pin to size; press with cool iron through pressing cloth.

—Designed by Angela Tate

Flower Basket

Shown on page 61

Experience Level: Intermediate

Size: Approximately 8½" long x 7" tall

Materials
- Coats & Clark South Maid® crochet cotton size 10 (350 yds per ball): 1 ball cream #430
- Size 5 steel crochet hook or size needed to obtain gauge
- Fabric stiffener
- 3½ yds ⅜"-wide rose-colored feather-edged satin ribbon
- Hot-glue gun
- 3" plastic foam ball, cut in half
- 15" x 6" scrap of white tulle
- 10 (1½"- to 2"-diameter) cream-colored artificial roses
- 9 small sprays ¾"-diameter rose-colored silk flowers
- 9 small sprays dried baby's breath

Gauge: Rnds 1 and 2 = 2" across
To save time, take time to check gauge.

Pattern Note: Join rnds with a sl st unless otherwise stated.

Pattern Stitches
Sc picot: Sc in indicated st, ch 3, sl st in sc just made.

Shell: [2 dc, ch 2, 2 dc] in same sp.

Basket
Rnd 1: Ch 4, join to form a ring, ch 3 (counts as first dc), 19 dc in ring, join in 3rd ch of beg ch-3. (20 dc)

Rnd 2: Ch 6 (counts as first tr, ch 2), [tr, ch 2] in each st around, join in 4th ch of beg ch-6.

Rnd 3: Sl st to first ch of next ch-2 sp, ch 4 (counts as first tr), tr in next ch, [ch 3, sk next tr, tr in each of next 2 chs] rep around, ch 3, join in 4th ch of beg ch-4.

Rnd 4: Sl st to center of ch-3 sp, sc in same sp, ch 7, [sc in next ch-3 sp, ch 5, sc in next ch-3 sp, ch 7] rep around 9 times, sc in next ch-3 sp, ch 5, join in beg sc.

Rnd 5: Sl st to first ch of ch-7 sp, sc in same st, *ch 3, sk 1 ch, sc in next ch, ch 5, sk 1 ch, sc in next ch, ch 3, sk 1 ch, sc in next ch, [ch 1, sc, ch 1] in ch-5 sp

**, sc in first ch of ch-7 sp, rep from * around, ending last rep at **, join in beg sc.

Rnd 6: *[Sc in next ch, 2 sc in next ch, sc in next ch, sl st in next sc, [sc, 2 sc, sc, 2 sc, sc] in next 5 chs, sl st in sc, [sc, 2 sc, sc] in next 3 chs, sl st in sc, sc in ch-1 sp, sc picot in next sc, sc in next ch-1 sp, sl st in next sc, rep from * around, join in beg sc.

Rnd 7: Sl st to 3rd sc of ch-5 sp, ch 13, working in back lps only, [{sc, ch 13} in 3rd sc of ch-5 sp] rep around, join in beg sc.

Rnd 8: Sl st to 2nd ch of ch-13 lp, ch 3 (counts as first dc), dc in same st, *[ch 2, sk 2 chs, 2 dc in next ch] 3 times, ch 2 **, 2 dc in 2nd ch of next ch-13 lp, rep from * around, ending last rep at **, join in 3rd ch of beg ch-3.

Rnd 9: Sl st to next ch-2 sp, [ch 3 (counts as first dc), dc, ch 2, 2 dc] in same sp, *[ch 2, sc, ch 2] in next ch-2 sp, shell in next ch-2 sp, [ch 1, sc, ch 1] in next ch-2 sp **, shell in next ch-2 sp, rep from * around, ending last rep at **, join in 3rd ch of beg ch-3.

Rnd 10: Sl st to ch-2 sp of shell, ch 1, sc in same sp, [ch 9, sc in next shell, ch 5 *, sc in next shell] rep around, ending last rep at *, join in beg sc.

Rnd 11: Ch 1, sc in same st, *[ch 3, sk 1 ch, sc in next ch] twice, ch 5, sk 1 ch, sc in next ch, ch 3, sk 1 ch, sc in next ch, ch 3, sk 1 ch, sc in next sc, [ch 1, sc, ch 1] in next ch-5 sp, sc in next sc, rep from * around, join in beg sc.

Rnd 12: *[{Sc, 2 sc, sc} in next 3 chs, sl st in next sc] twice **, [sc, 2 sc, sc, 2 sc, sc] in each of next 5 chs, sl st in next sc, rep from * to ** twice, sc in ch-1 sp, sc picot in sc, sc in ch-1 sp, sl st in next sc, rep from * around, ending last rep with sc in ch-1 sp, join in beg sc, fasten off.

Handle

Row 1: Ch 89, dc in 8th ch from hook, ch 2, [sk 2 chs, dc in next ch, ch 2] rep across, ending with dc in last ch.

Rnd 2: 2 sc in same sp as dc just made, 3 sc over side of dc just made, 2 sc in first ch of foundation ch, sc in each ch across to last dc, [sc in each of next 2 chs, 2 sc in next ch, 3 sc in next ch-2 sp, 2 sc in next ch, sc in each of last 2 chs] around ch-7 sp, sc in dc and in each rem st, join in beg sc, fasten off.

Finishing

Stiffen handle; lay flat to dry.

Stiffen basket; shape over cereal bowl to dry. Before bowl is completely dry, remove and bend in sides slightly.

Weave length of ribbon through handle; trim ends. Shape handle over center of basket; glue to each side of basket.

Weave length of ribbon through beading row of basket (refer to photo), beg and ending at 1 side. Trim ends; secure with glue.

Cut rem ribbon into 4 equal lengths. Tie 2 lengths into double bow; rep for rem 2 lengths. Glue 1 bow to each side of ribbon where handle joins. Trim ends to desired length.

Glue plastic foam ball in bottom of basket, flat side down. Arrange tulle around and over ball.

Insert roses into ball through tulle, filling spaces with small sprays of silk flowers and baby's breath.

—Designed by Jo Ann Maxwell

Floral Centerpiece

Shown on page 61

Experience Level: Beginner

Size: Approximately 13¾" x 15" before blocking

Materials

- DMC® Cebelia® crochet cotton size 20 (50 grams per ball): 1 ball cream #712
- Size 10 steel crochet hook

Gauge: 14 sts and 5 rows = 1"

Pattern Stitches: See Instructions for Filet Crochet on page 57.

Centerpiece

Row 1 (RS): Ch 210, dc in 4th ch from hook and in each ch across, turn.

Row 2: Ch 3, dc in each of next 3 dc, *[ch 2, sk 2 dc, dc in next dc] 3 times, dc in each of next 3 dc, rep from * across, ending with dc in each of last 3 dc, turn.

Row 3: Beg bl over a bl, [sp over each of next 3 sps, bl over a bl] rep across, ending with bl over a bl, turn.

Rows 4–69: Following chart on next page, utilize Pattern Stitches, fasten off at end of Row 69.

—Designed by Nancy Hearne courtesy of DMC

Easy Tip for Counting Rows

To keep count of rows while crocheting, use a round knitting row counter on the end of your crochet hook.

STITCH KEY

- ☐ Space
- ◙ Dc block

CHART A
Floral Centerpiece

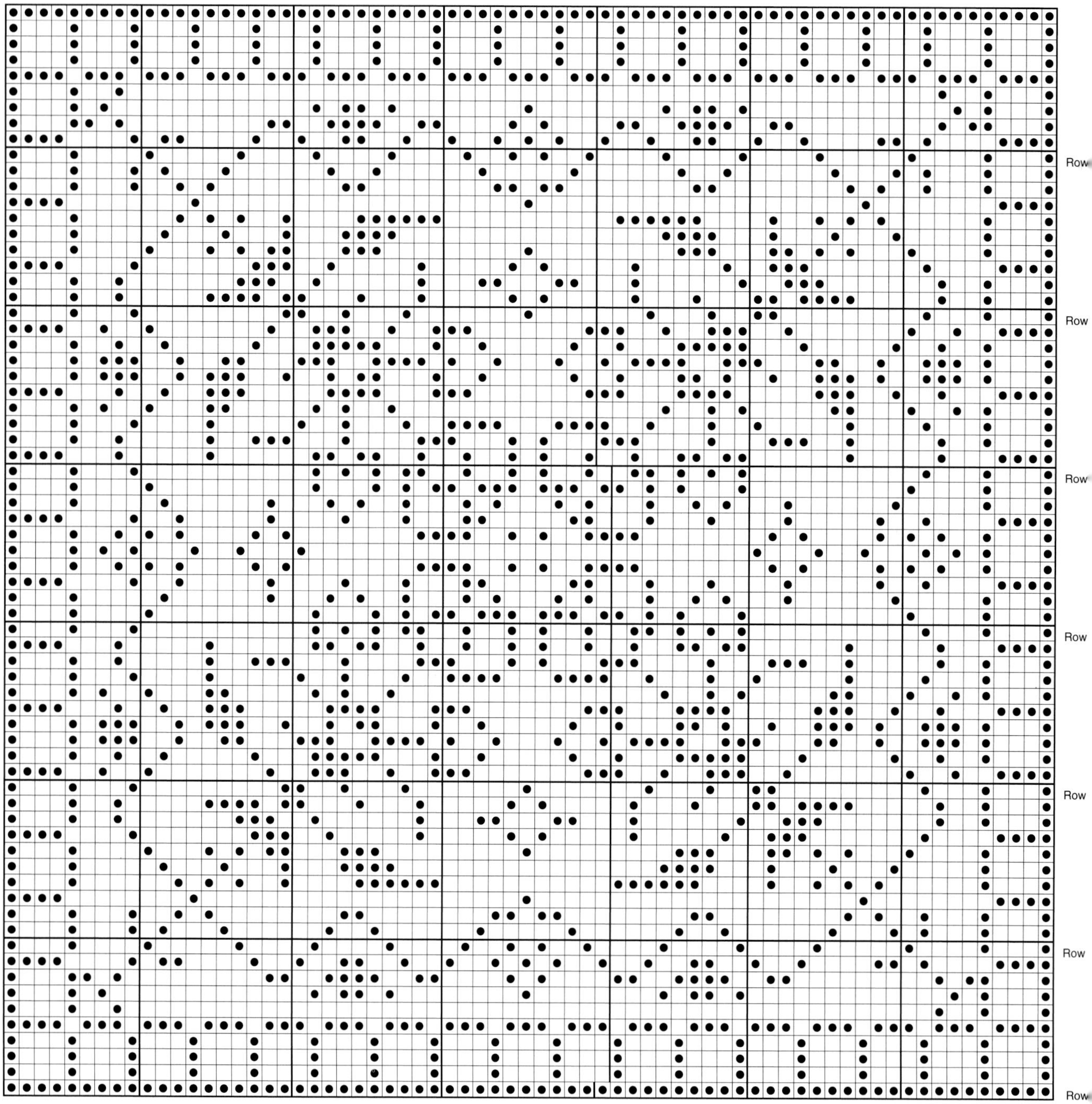

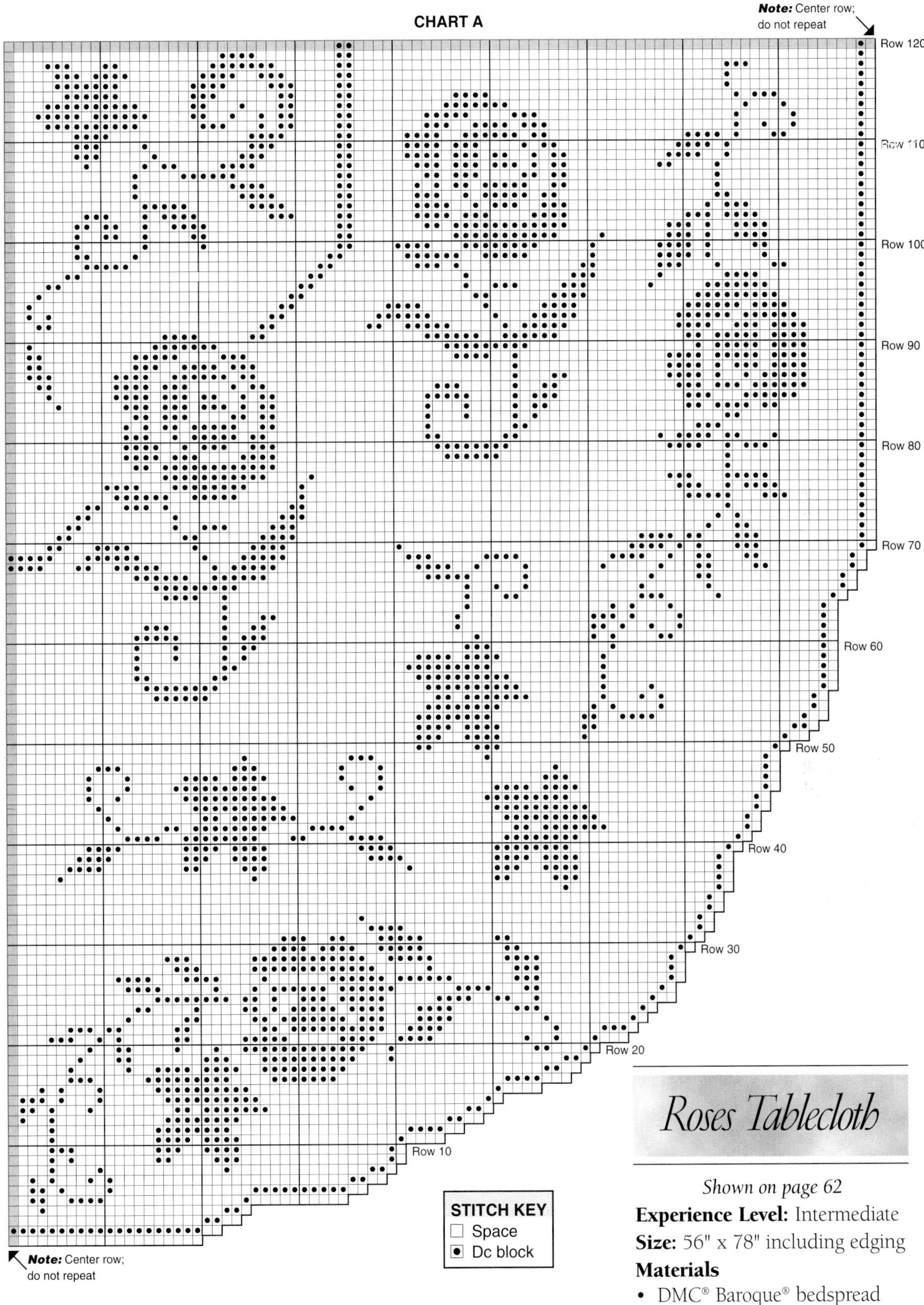

Roses Tablecloth

Shown on page 62

Experience Level: Intermediate

Size: 56" x 78" including edging

Materials

- DMC® Baroque® bedspread

weight crochet cotton (400 yds per skein): 12 skeins ecru naturel

- Size 8 steel crochet hook

Gauge: 13 rows and 13 sps = 4" To save time take time to check gauge.

Pattern Notes

Do not rep center sp or center row of chart. After working center sp, rep row from center sp back to beg of row. After working center row, work chart in reverse back to Row 1.

To inc at end of row, ch 2, yo 4 times, insert hook in same st as last dc, then complete a trtr (this inc 1 sp), *ch 2, yo 4 times, insert hook in middle of post of trtr just made, complete trtr for an inc of a 2nd sp, rep from * for as many inc as needed to be made as indicated in chart.

Body

Row 1: Ch 122, dc in 8th ch from hook, [ch 2, sk 2 chs, dc in next ch] 38 times. (39 sps)

Row 2: Ch 10 for inc of 2 sps to beg row, dc in 8th ch from hook, ch 2, sk 2 chs, dc in dc, [2 dc in sp, dc in dc] 39 times, inc 2 sps (see Pattern Notes).

Beg with Row 3, continue to follow Chart A, inc and dec as indicated. Do not fasten off after last row and do not turn.

Edging

Work ch-7 sps evenly around, sk 2–3 sps or rows as follows:

Rnd 1: Ch 3, dc in corner sp, ch 7, [sk 2–3 sps or rows, 2 dc in next sp or st, ch 7] rep around, join in 3rd ch of beg ch-3.

Rnd 2: Sl st in dc, sl st in each of next 4 chs, ch 3, dc in same ch as last sl st, ch 7, [2 dc in 4th ch of next ch-7, ch 7] rep around, join in 3rd ch of beg ch-3.

Rnd 3: Sl st in dc, sl st in each of next 4 chs, ch 3, dc in same ch as last sl st, ch 4, sl st in 4th ch from hook (picot), 2 dc in same ch as last dc, ch 6, [sc in next ch-7 sp, ch 6, {2 dc, picot, 2 dc} in 4th ch of next ch-7 sp, ch 6] rep around, join in 3rd ch of beg ch-3, fasten off.

—Designed by Lucille LaFlamme

Queen Anne

Shown on page 63

Experience Level: Advanced

Size: Approximately 18" x 69"

Materials

- Coats & Clark South Maid® crochet cotton size 10 (350 yds per ball): 5 balls cream #430
- Size 6 steel crochet hook or size needed to obtain gauge

Gauge: Whorl Motif = 4½" in diameter

Pattern Note: Runner consists of 3 whorl motif strips and 4 lace strips.

Whorl strips consist of 15 whorl motifs. Each whorl motif is made of eight segments.

Each lace strip consists of 120 segments.

Length of runner can be changed by inc or dec number of motifs and segments in strips.

Join rnds with a sl st unless otherwise stated.

Whorl Motif Strip

First Whorl Motif

First segment

Ch 9, join to form base ring.

Row 1 (RS): Ch 3 (counts as first dc), [dc in ring, ch 6, dc in top of dc just made, dc in ring] 3 times, dc in ring, ch 2, 10 dc in ring, turn.

Row 2: Ch 5, sl st in 5th ch from hook (picot), sk first dc, sc in each of next 9 dc, turn.

Second segment

Ch 1, sc in first sc, ch 3, sk next sc, sc in next sc, ch 9, turn, join in beg sc to complete adjoining base ring, turn.

Row 1: Rep Rnd 1 of first segment, do not turn.

Row 2: Ch 2, sc in picot of previous segment, ch 3, turn, sl st in first ch of beg ch-2 to complete picot, sk first dc, sc in each of next 9 dc, turn.

Third–seventh segments

Rep 2nd segment.

Eighth segment

Work as for 2nd segment, joining to first segment in 2nd row as follows: Ch 2, sc in picot of 7th segment, ch 1, sc in picot of first segment, ch 2, turn, join in first ch of beg ch-2 to complete picot, sk first dc, sc in each of next 6 dc, sl st to first segment in first ch of beg ch-3 of Row 1, sc in each of next 3 dc, sl st to first segment in 3rd ch of beg ch-3, fasten off.

Second Whorl Motif

First segment

Work as for first segment of First Whorl Motif.

Second segment (join to First Whorl Motif)

Row 1: Ch 1, sc in first sc, ch 3, sk next sc, sc in next sc, ch 9, turn, join in beg sc to complete adjoining base ring, turn, ch 3 (counts as first dc), dc in ring, ch 6, dc in top of dc just made,

2 dc in ring, ch 3, sl st in corresponding center ch-6 of First Whorl Motif, ch 3, dc in top of dc just made, 2 dc in ring, ch 3], sl st in next corresponding ch-6 of First Whorl Motif, ch 3, dc in top of dc just made, 2 dc in ring, ch 2, 10 dc in ring, do not turn.

Row 2: Rep Row 2 of 2nd segment of First Whorl Motif.

Third segment
Ch 1, sc in first sc, ch 3, sk next sc, sc in next sc, ch 9, turn, join in beg sc to complete adjoining base ring, turn.

Row 1: Ch 3 (counts as first dc), [dc in ring, ch 3, sl st in next corresponding ch-6 of First Whorl Motif, ch 3, dc in top of dc just made, dc in ring] twice, dc in ring, ch 6, dc in picot of dc just made, 2 dc in ring, ch 2, 10 dc in ring, turn.

Row 2: Work as for Rnd 2 of 2nd segment.

Fourth–seventh segments
Work as for 2nd segment of First Whorl Motif.

Eighth segment
Work as for 8th segment of First Whorl Motif.

Continue joining motifs in this manner until strip is 15 motifs long.

First Lace Strip

First segment
Row 1: Ch 9, join to form a ring, ch 3 (counts as first dc), 13 dc in ring, ch 1, turn.

Row 2: Sc in each of first 2 dc, [ch 4, sc in each of next 2 dc] 6 times, ch 6, turn. (6 ch-4 lps)

Second segment
Row 1: Sl st in first free ch-4 lp of segment just completed, ch 3, turn, 13 dc in ch-6 sp, sl st in first sc of Row 2 of previous segment, ch 1, turn.

Row 2: Sc in each of first 2 dc, [ch 4, sc in each of next 2 dc] 6 times, sl st in next free ch-4 lp of previous segment, ch 6, turn.

Third segment
Row 1: Sl st in first free ch-4 lp of segment just completed, ch 3, turn, 13 dc in ch-6 sp, sl st in next free ch-4 lp of first segment, ch 1, turn.

Row 2: Sc in each of first 2 dc, [ch 4, sc in each of next 2 dc] twice, ch 2, sl st in middle ch-6 lp at top of right edge of Whorl Motif, ch 2, sc in each of next 2 sc of Lace Strip, ch 2, sl st in next ch-6 lp of whorl motif, ch 2, sc in each of next 2 sc of lace strip, [ch 4, sc in each of next 2 dc] 2 times, sl st in next free ch-4 lp of previous segment, ch 6, turn.

Fourth segment
Row 1: Sl st in first free ch-4 lp of segment just completed, ch 3, turn, 13 dc in ch-6 sp, sl st in first free ch-4 lp of 2 segments back, ch 1, turn.

Row 2: Sc in each of first 2 dc, [ch 4, sc in each of next 2 dc] 6 times, sl st in next free ch-4 lp of previous segment, ch 6, turn.

Fifth segment
Row 1: Sl st in first free ch-4 lp of segment just completed, ch 3, turn, 13 dc in ch-6 sp, sl st in next free ch-4 lp of 2 segments back, ch 1, turn.

Row 2: Sc in each of first 2 dc, [ch 4, sc in each of next 2 dc] twice, ch 2, sl st in first ch-6 lp of next segment of whorl motif, ch 2, sc in each of next 2 sc of lace strip, ch 2, sc in next ch-6 lp of whorl motif, ch 2, sc in each of next 2 sc of lace strip, [ch 4, sc in each of next 2 dc] 2 times, sl st in next free ch-4 lp of previous segment, ch 6, turn.

Sixth–10th segments
Rep 4th segment 5 times.

Rep 3rd–10th segments 13 times.

Rep 3rd–8th segments once, omitting final ch-6, fasten off.

Joining Second Lace Strip to First & Second Whorl Strips

First & second segments
Ch 9, join to form a ring. Work as for first and 2nd segments of first lace strip.

Third segment
Work as for 3rd segment of first lace strip, joining to 2nd whorl strip.

Fourth segment
Rep 3rd segment of first lace strip, joining to first whorl strip.

Fifth segment
Work as for 5th segment of first lace strip, joining to 2nd whorl strip.

Sixth segment
Rep 5th segment, joining to first whorl strip.

Seventh–10th segments
Row 1: Sl st in first free ch-4 lp of segment just completed, ch 3, turn, 13 dc in ch-6 sp, sl st in first free ch-4 lp of 2 segments, ch 1, turn.

Row 2: Sc in each of first 2 dc, [ch 4, sc in each of next 2 dc] 6 times, sl st in next free ch-4 lp of previous segment, ch 6, turn.

Rep 3rd–10th segments 13 times.

Rep 3rd–8th segments once, fasten off.

Join 3rd lace strip and 3rd whorl strip in same manner.

Work 4th lace strip as for first lace strip, joining to whorl strip in 4th segment of lace strip instead of 3rd.

Finishing

Weave in all loose ends. Press with steam iron on cotton setting.

—Designed by Maureen Egan Emlet

Nostalgia Tablecloth

Shown on page 64

Experience Level: Advanced beginner

Size

Tablecloth: 60" in diameter; 68" diagonally

Motif: 3¼" in diameter

Materials

- Talon® Aunt Lydia's Crochet Cotton® size 10 (1,000 yds per ball): 2,750 yds white
- Size 7 steel crochet hook
- Spray starch

Gauge: 4 sc = ½"
Motif = 3¼" in diameter

To save time, take time to check gauge.

Pattern Notes: Join motifs on Rnd 3 around 2, 4, 6 or 8 ch-5 lps as work progresses.

Motifs are joined in 10 rnds, with 10 motifs per side on last rnd.

Mark first and last motif of each rnd as rnds are worked.

Join rnds with a sl st unless otherwise stated.

Weave in loose ends as work progresses.

First Motif

Rnd 1: Ch 10, join to form ring, ch 4 (counts as first tr), 23 tr in ring, join in 4th ch of beg ch-4. (24 tr)

Rnd 2: Ch 4 (counts as first tr), tr in next st, ch 5, [tr in each of next 2 tr, ch 5] 11 times, join in beg tr. (12 lps)

Rnd 3: Sl st in first lp, ch 1, [4 sc, ch 5, 4 sc] in each lp around, join in beg sc, fasten off.

Remaining Motifs *(Make 270)*

Rnds 1 & 2: Rep Rnds 1 and 2 of First Motif.

Joining motifs

Rnd 3: Sl st in first lp, ch 1, *[4 sc in ch-5 lp, ch 2, sl st in corresponding ch-5 lp of adjacent motif, ch 2, 4 sc in same ch-5 lp of working motif, sk 2 tr] twice, rep from * across to join adjacent motifs, work in basic patt around rem of motif, join in beg sc, fasten off.

Border

Rnd 1: With RS facing, attach cotton in any free ch-5 lp, ch 4 (counts as first tr), tr in same lp, ch 7, [2 tr in next free ch-5 lp, ch 7] rep around, join in 4th ch of beg ch-4.

Rnd 2: Sl st to center of ch-7 lp, ch 4 (counts as first tr), tr in same lp, ch 10, [2 tr in next lp, ch 10] rep around, join in 4th ch of beg ch-4.

Rnd 3: Sl st to center of ch-10 lp, ch 4 (counts as first tr), tr in same lp, ch 13, [2 tr in next lp, ch 13] rep around, join in 4th ch of beg ch-4.

Rnd 4: Ch 1, [8 sc, ch 5, 8 sc] in each lp around, join in beg sc, fasten off.

Finishing

Mist tablecloth lightly with spray starch. Press with warm iron through pressing cloth.

—Designed by Angela Tate

Snowflakes Tablecloth

Shown on page 65

Experience Level: Advanced beginner

Size: Approximately 48" square

Materials

- Patons Opera® crochet cotton size 10 (50 grams per ball): 16 balls champagne #503
- Size 3 steel crochet hook

Gauge: Snowflake motif = 5" in diameter

To save time, take time to check gauge.

Pattern Notes: Tablecloth consists of 100 snowflake motifs.

Size of tablecloth can be changed by inc or dec number of rows of motifs. For each additional 6 motifs, add 1 ball of crochet cotton.

Join rnds with a sl st unless otherwise indicated.

First Motif

Rnd 1: Ch 8, join to form a ring, ch 1, [sc, hdc, 3 dc, hdc] 3 times in ring, join in beg sc.

Rnd 2: Ch 1, sc in same st as sl st, [ch 4, sk next 2 sts, sc in next dc, ch 4, sk 2 sts, sc in next sc] 3 times, ending last rep with sk 2 sts, join in beg sc.

Rnd 3: Ch 1, sc in same st as sl st, *[sc, 3 hdc, sc] in ch-4 lp, sc in next sc, rep from * around, ending last rep with [sc, 3 hdc, sc] in ch-4 lp, join in beg sc.

Rnd 4: Ch 1, sc in same st as sl st, *ch 4, sk next 2 sts, sc in next hdc, ch 4, sk next 2 sts, sc in next sc, rep from * around, ending last rep with sk next 2 sts, join in beg sc.

Rnd 5: Ch 1, sc in same st as sl

st, *[sc, 5 hdc, sc] in ch-4 lp, sc in next sc, rep from * around, ending last rep with [sc, 5 hdc, sc] in ch-4 lp, join in beg sc.

Rnd 6: Sl st in next sc and in each of next 2 hdc, sc in next hdc, [ch 5, sk next 7 sts, sc in next hdc] rep around, ending last rep with sk next 7 sts, join in beg sc.

Rnd 7: Ch 1, sc in same st as sl st, *[sc, 7 hdc, sc] in ch-5 lp, sc in next sc, rep from * around, ending last rep with [sc, 7 hdc, sc] in ch-5 lp, join in beg sc.

Rnd 8: Sl st in next sc and in each of next 3 hdc, sc in next hdc, [ch 8, sk next 9 sts, sc in next hdc] rep around, ending last rep with sk next 9 sts, join in beg sc.

Rnd 9: Ch 1, *[sc, ch 3, sc] 5 times in next ch-8 lp, rep from * around, join in beg sc, fasten off.

Second Motif

Rnds 1–8: Rep Rnds 1–8 for First Motif.

Rnd 9: Ch 1, [{sc, ch 3, sc} twice, sc, ch 1, sc in corresponding center ch-3 lp of previous motif, ch 1, sc in working motif, {sc, ch 3, sc} twice] in same ch-8 lp twice, complete as for First Motif.

Continue joining motifs in this manner to form strip of 10 motifs.

To join subsequent strips, join new motif to motif above it, work 1 ch-8 lp in usual manner without joining, join next 2 ch-8 lps to adjoining side motif.

Join 10 strips of 10 motifs each.

Fill-In Motif

Rnd 1: Ch 8, join to form a ring, ch 1, 16 sc in ring, join in beg sc.

Rnd 2: Ch 1, sc in same st as sl st, [ch 8, sc in joining of 2 motifs, ch 8, sc in each of next 2 sc of ring, ch 3, sk next 4 unworked ch-3 lps on snowflake motif, sc in center ch-3 lp, ch 3, sc in each of next 2 sc of ring] 4 times, ending last rep with ch 3, sc in next sc of ring, join in beg sc, fasten off.

Rep Rnds 1 and 2 until all open sps have been filled.

Weave in loose ends. Press with steam iron on cotton setting.

—Designed by Maureen Egan Emlet

My Dahlia Delight

Shown on page 66

Experience Level: Advanced beginner

Size

Tablecloth: 40" in diameter from point to point

Motif: 3½" in diameter

Materials

- Coats & Clark South Maid® crochet cotton size 10 (50 grams per ball): 1 ball each French rose, variegated pink, green and white
- J. & P. Coats Knit-Cro-Sheen crochet cotton size 10: small amounts each light blue, lavender, variegated blue, variegated lavender, variegated green/pink and variegated multicolored
- Size 6 steel crochet hook

Gauge: Work evenly and consistently

Pattern Notes: Join rnds with a sl st unless otherwise stated.

Make flower motifs in any combination of colors, each bordered with green.

Pattern Stitches

2-tr cluster (2-tr cl): Holding back last lp of each tr, make 2 tr in same sp, yo and draw through all 3 lps on hook.

3-tr cluster (3-tr cl): Holding back last lp of each tr, make 3 tr in indicated sts or sp, yo and draw through all 4 lps on hook.

4-tr cluster (4-tr cl): Holding back last lp of each tr, make 4 tr in indicated sts, yo and draw through all 5 lps on hook.

First Motif

Rnd 1: Beg at center with yellow, ch 6, join to form a ring, ch 3 (counts as first dc), 11 dc in ring, join in 3rd ch of beg ch-3, fasten off.

Rnd 2: Attach any color except green or white in any dc, [ch 4 (counts as first tr), 2-tr cl in same st, [ch 3, 3-tr cl in next dc] rep around, ch 3, join in beg cl. (12 cls)

Rnd 3: Sl st to ch-3 sp, ch 4 (counts as first tr), 2-tr cl, ch 5, *3-tr cl in ch-3 sp, ch 5, rep from * around, join in beg cl, fasten off.

Rnd 4: Attach green in any ch-5 sp, ch 4 (counts as first tr), [2-tr cl, ch 3, 3-tr cl, ch 3, 3-tr cl] in ch-5 sp, ch 5, sc in next sp, ch 5, *[3-tr cl, ch 3, 3-tr cl, ch 3, 3-tr cl] in ch-5 sp, ch 5, sc in next sp, ch 5, rep from * around, join in beg cl, fasten off.

Rnd 5: Attach white in first ch-3 sp of group, *ch 3, sc in next ch-3 sp, [ch 5, sc in next sp] 3 times, rep from * around, join in beg sc, fasten off.

Second & Subsequent Motifs

(Make 60)

Rnds 1–4: Rep Rnds 1–4 of First Motif.

Rnd 5: Attach white in first ch-3 sp of tr-cl group, *ch 3, sc in next ch-3 sp, [ch 2, sc in corresponding sp of first motif, ch 2, sc in next sp of 2nd motif] 3 times, rep from * as needed or finish as Rnd 5 of First Motif.

Edging

Rnd 1: Attach white in any sp, ch 5 (counts as first tr, ch 1), [tr, ch 1] twice in same sp, *[tr, ch 1] 3 times in next sp *, rep from * to * around to where motifs are joined tog, sk 2 ch-2 sps, rep from * to * around, join in 4th ch of beg ch-5.

Rnd 2: Sl st to ch-1 sp between tr groups, ch 4 (counts as first tr), 3-tr cl in next 3 ch-1 sps, ch 7, *4-tr cl over same ch-1 sp and next 3 ch-1 sps, ch 7, rep from * around to where motifs are joined, ch 3 between cls (instead of ch 7), continue around, join in beg cl.

Rnd 3: Sl st in each of next 2 chs, ch 5 (counts as first tr, ch 1), [tr, ch 1, tr] in same sp, *ch 2, [tr, ch 1, tr, ch 1, tr] in next ch-7 sp, rep from * around, sk ch-3 sps between motifs, join in 4th ch of beg ch-5.

Rnd 4: Ch 4 (counts as first tr), 3-tr cl over next 2 ch-1 sps and next ch-2 sp, ch 7, *4-tr cl over same sp and next 3 ch-1 sps, ch 7, rep from * around, join in beg cluster.

—Designed by Emma Willey

Flowers Everywhere

Shown on page 67

Experience Level: Intermediate

Size

Table Runner: Approximately 13" x 24"

Large motif: 4¼" in diameter

Filler motif: 1½" in diameter

Materials

- J. & P. Coats Knit-Cro-Sheen 100 percent mercerized crochet cotton (225 yds per skein): 2 skeins new ecru #61A
- Size 7 steel crochet hook
- Aleene's fabric stiffener

Gauge: 9 dc = 1"
To save time, take time to check gauge.

Pattern Note: Join rnds with a sl st unless otherwise stated.

First Motif

Rnd 1: Ch 8, join to form a ring, ch 3 (counts as first dc), 23 dc in ring, join in 3rd ch of beg ch-3.

Rnd 2: Ch 4 (counts as first dc, ch 1), *[dc, ch 1] in next dc, rep from * around, join in 3rd ch of beg ch-4.

Rnd 3: Ch 5 (counts as first dc, ch 2), *[dc, ch 2] in next dc, rep from * around, join in 3rd ch of beg ch-5.

Rnd 4: Sl st in next ch sp, [ch 3 (counts as first dc), dc, ch 3, 2 dc] in same ch sp, *ch 3, sk next ch sp, [2 dc, ch 3, 2 dc] in next ch sp, rep from * around, ending with ch 3, join in 3rd ch of beg ch-3.

Rnd 5: Sl st in next dc, sl st in next ch sp, [ch 3 (counts as first dc), dc, ch 3, 2 dc] in same ch sp, *ch 1, sc in next ch sp, ch 1, [2 dc, ch 3, 2 dc] in next ch sp, rep from * around, ending with ch 1, sc in next ch sp, ch 1, join in 3rd ch of beg ch-3.

Rnds 6 & 7: Sl st in next dc, sl st in next ch sp, [ch 3 (counts as first dc), dc, ch 3, 2 dc] in same ch sp, *ch 3, sc in next sc, ch 3, [2 dc, ch 3, 2 dc] in next ch sp, rep from * around, ending with ch 3, join in 3rd ch of beg ch-3.

Rnd 8: Sl st in next dc, [sl st in next ch] twice, [ch 12, sl st in 3rd ch sp] rep around, ending with ch 12, join in first ch of beg ch-12.

Rnd 9: Ch 1, *[7 sc, ch 3, 7 sc] in next ch sp, rep from * around, join in beg sc, fasten off.

Second & Subsequent Motifs
(Make 14)

Rnds 1–8: Rep Rnds 1–8 of First Motif.

Rnd 9: Ch 1, *[{7 sc, ch 1, sl st in ch sp of previous motif, ch 1, 7 sc} in next ch sp] twice, [7 sc, ch 3, 7 sc] in next ch sp, rep from * as many times as necessary, finish as Rnd 9 of First Motif around rem motif.

Filler Motif *(Make 8)*

Rnd 1: Ch 8, join to form a ring, ch 3 (counts as first dc), 23 dc in ring, join in 3rd ch of beg ch-3.

Rnd 2: Ch 4 (counts as first dc, ch 1), [dc in next dc, ch 1] rep around, join in 3rd ch of beg ch-4.

Rnd 3: *Sl st in next ch sp, ch 5, sl st in ch-3 sp of previous motif, ch 5, sl st in same ch sp, [sl st in next ch sp, ch 3, sl st in same ch sp] 5 times, rep from * around, fasten off.

Finishing

Join motifs in rows of 3 each with filler motifs between each row (see Fig. 1).

Soak runner in fabric stiffener; lay flat to dry. Iron lightly after drying, if necessary.

—Designed by Nazanin S. Fard

FIG. 1
Assembly

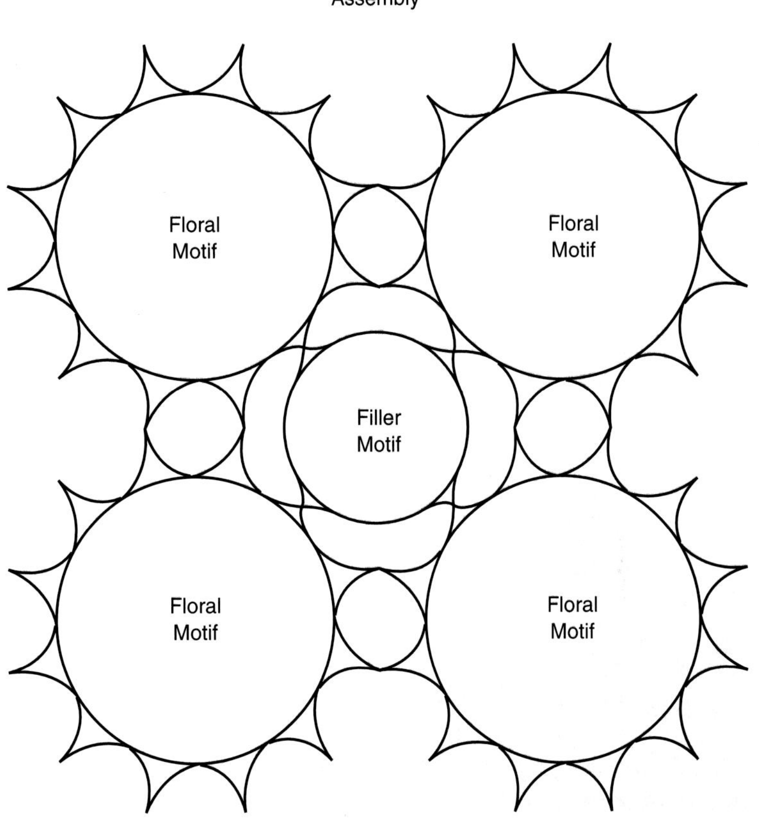

Tips and Hints to Make Crocheting Time Easier and More Enjoyable

Make crocheted edgings from #10 crochet cotton to embellish purchased place mats and napkins for a quick and elegant gift.

To hide yarn ends in projects that are flat, leave about 10" when cutting. Using a tapestry needle, weave the 10" piece through the wrong side of the stitches for about 2"; turn and weave back the opposite way for 2". Tug gently and clip excess yarn.

To mark a stitch on rounds that are not joined, try a bobby pin. It slips easily in and out of stitches and will not harm the yarn or crocheted piece.

For an economical and fragrant filling for stuffed crocheted pieces, save the dryer sheets used when clothes drying.

Store scraps of leftover, non-acrylic yarn in see-through zip-lock bags to use for embroidering features on stuffed toys or for embellishing.

Crocheted flowers of either yarn or thread can be used to embellish plain, purchased fabric pillows.

After completing a larger project such as an afghan or sweater, fluff the item in the clothes dryer on air cycle with a wet bath towel and fragrant dryer sheet for about 10 minutes.

Try using stiff plastic canvas cut to fit instead of cardboard in crocheted items that need a bit of extra sturdiness.

Nursery Delights

Welcome a new life into the world by crocheting a special gift for the little one. Tenderly crocheted coverlets, lacy booties, sweater outfits, a charming teddy bear and an exquisite christening layette are traditional gifts sure to be treasured by the parents today and that precious young one in the years to come.

Whether for decoration or for play, this sweet Beatrice Bear (left) will delight youngsters and adults alike. Instructions for the pretty dress with coordinating bonnet are included for the bear as well as children's sizes ranging from 24 months to toddler's size 2. Instructions begin on page 92.

Crochet this extra-special pair of Victorian Booties (below) for an extra-special occasion—like visiting Grandma for the first time! When Baby outgrows these fancy booties, you'll want to keep them stored safely in a hope chest as a cherished memento of your child's earliest days. Pretty Pink Afghan (right) features a lacy pattern perfect for keeping Baby cozy and warm in the crib. Instructions on pages 97–100.

TREASURY of STORIES
Beatrix Potter

Your child dressed in this lacy Christening Set (left) for his or her baptism will give this treasured event an extra-special touch. The complete layette includes a christening gown, bonnet, booties and baby afghan. For a decorative, yet practical, nursery accent, crochet this clever Baby's Angel (below). Instructions on pages 100–106.

Delicate peach flowers stitched on a solid white background with size 10 crochet cotton form the design on this dainty Embossed Flowers coverlet and pillow set (below). Little Pixie (right), including a sweater, booties, cap and afghan, makes a wonderful gift for the mother-to-be. Whether you make the complete set or just several pieces, this ensemble is appropriate for either boys or girls. *Instructions on pages 106–111.*

Crochet this darling Heart Blanket (left) to delight both mother and child. Each pretty heart motif is crocheted separately and then added to the main body of the afghan for an unusual edge. Silk-embroidered flowers add a caring touch sure to be appreciated and cherished. Love Spoken Here, a delightful filet piece (below), will be a constant reminder of your love for your little one. Instructions on pages 111–113.

Beatrice Bear

Shown on page 82

Experience Level: Intermediate

Size: Bear approximately 20" tall

Materials

- Bernat® Berella 4® worsted weight yarn (3.5 oz/240 yds per ball): 3 balls oak #8796 (MC), 1 ball honey #8795 (CC) and small amount black #8994
- Bernat® Club Classic (1.75 oz/130 yds per ball): 2 balls cream #800 (A) and 5 balls melon tint #803 (B)
- Size G/6 crochet hook
- Size 7 crochet hook or size needed to obtain gauge
- Fiberfill
- Tapestry needle
- 1" lilac ribbon rose with leaves
- ⅛ yd ⅜"-wide cream satin ribbon

  1 yd 1"-wide cream satin ribbon
- 1½ yds ⅝"-wide cream satin ribbon
- Small button

Gauge

Bear: 17 sc and 18 sc rows = 4" with larger hook

Dress and bonnet: 17 sts and 10 rows = 4" with smaller hook

To save time, take time to check gauge.

Pattern Note: Join rnds with a sl st unless otherwise stated.

Pattern Stitches

Sc2tog: [Insert hook in indicated st, yo and draw through lp] twice, yo and draw through all 3 lps on hook.

Puff st: [Yo, insert hook in ch sp, yo, draw up lp] 4 times, yo and draw through all 9 lps on hook, ch 1 to close.

Bear

Body Back *(Make 2)*

Row 1: Beg at bottom with MC and larger hook, ch 4, sc in 2nd ch from hook and in each ch across, ch 1, turn. (3 sc)

Row 2: Sc in first sc, 2 sc in each of last 2 sc, ch 1, turn. (5 sc)

Row 3: 2 sc in first sc, sc in each sc across, ch 1, turn. (6 sc)

Row 4: Sc in each sc across to last sc, 2 sc in last sc, ch 1, turn. (7 sc)

Rows 5–8: Rep Rows 3 and 4. (11 sc)

Row 9: 2 sc in first sc, sc in each sc to last sc, 2 sc in last sc, ch 1, turn. (13 sc)

Row 10: Rep Row 4. (14 sc)

Row 11: Sc in each sc across, ch 1, turn.

Rows 12–14: Rep Row 11.

Row 15: Rep Row 3. (15 sts)

Rows 16 & 17: Rep Row 11.

Row 18: Rep Row 9. (17 sc)

Rows 19–27: Rep Row 11.

Row 28: Sc2tog over first 2 sts, sc in each sc across, ch 1, turn. (16 sc)

Rows 29–31: Rep Row 11.

Row 32: Sc2tog over first 2 sc, sc in each sc to last 2 sc, sc2tog over last 2 sts, ch 1, turn. (14 sc)

Rows 33 & 34: Rep Row 11.

Row 35: Sc in each sc across to last 2 sc, sc2tog over last 2 sc, ch 1, turn. (13 sts)

Row 36: Rep Row 11.

Row 37: Rep Row 32. (11 sts)

Rows 38 & 39: Rep Rows 36 and 37, fasten off. (9 sc at end of Row 39)

With MC and smaller hook, sc evenly sp around outer edge, join in beg sc, fasten off.

Joining body back pieces

Holding both back pieces tog, with MC, sew center back seam from bottom to top.

Body Front *(Make 2)*

Row 1: Beg at bottom, with MC and larger hook, ch 3, sc in 2nd ch from hook, sc in next ch, ch 1, turn. (2 sc)

Row 2: Sc in first sc, 2 sc in last sc, ch 1, turn. (3 sc)

Row 3: Sc in first sc, 2 sc in each of next 2 sc, ch 1, turn. (5 sc)

Row 4: 2 sc in first sc, sc in each sc across to last sc, 2 sc in last sc, ch 1, turn. (7 sc)

Row 5: Sc in each sc across to last sc, 2 sc in last sc, ch 1, turn. (8 sc)

Row 6: 2 sc in first sc, sc in each sc across, ch 1, turn. (9 sc)

Row 7: Rep Row 5. (10 sc)

Row 8: Rep Row 4. (12 sc)

Row 9: Rep Row 5. (13 sc)

Row 10: Sc in each sc across, ch 1, turn.

Rows 11–18: Rep Rows 5 and 10.

Row 19: Rep Row 4. (19 sts)

Rows 20–23: Rep Row 10.

Row 24: Sc in each sc across to last 2 sc, sc2tog over last 2 sc, ch 1, turn. (18 sts)

Row 25: Rep Row 24. (17 sc)

Rows 26–28: Rep Row 10.

Row 29: Sc2tog over first 2 sc, sc in each sc across, ch 1, turn. (16 sts)

Rows 30–32: Rep Row 10.

Row 33: Rep Row 24. (15 sc)

Row 34: Rep Row 10.

Row 35: Sc2tog over first 2 sc, sc in each sc to last 2 sc, sc2tog over last 2 sc, ch 1, turn. (13 sts)

Row 36: Rep Row 10.

Row 37: Rep Row 35. (11 sc)

Row 38: Rep Row 10.

Rows 39 & 40: Rep Rows 37 and 38, fasten off. (9 sts at end of Row 40)

With MC and smaller hook, sc evenly sp around outer edge, join in beg sc, fasten off.

Joining body front pieces
Holding both body front pieces tog, with tapestry ndl and MC, sew center front seam from bottom to top.

Joining Body Front & Body Back Pieces
With WS of body front and body back tog, matching center front and center back seams at bottom and top of body, sew from top of 1 side to top of other side with tapestry ndl and MC.

With fiberfill, stuff evenly through neck opening to desired firmness, set aside.

Side Head *(Make 2)*
Row 1: Beg at bottom with MC and larger hook, ch 19, sc in 2nd ch from hook and in each ch across, ch 1, turn. (18 sc)

Row 2: 2 sc in first sc, sc in each sc to last sc, 2 sc in last sc, ch 1, turn. (20 sc)

Row 3: Sc in each sc across, ch 1, turn.

Row 4: Sc in each sc across to last sc, 2 sc in last sc, ch 1, turn. (21 sc)

Row 5: 2 sc in first sc, sc in each sc across, ch 1, turn. (22 sc)

Row 6: Rep Row 4. (23 sc)

Row 7: Rep Row 3.

Row 8: Rep Row 5. (24 sc)

Rows 9 & 10: Rep Row 3.

Row 11: Sc2tog over first 2 sc, sc in each sc to last 2 sc, sc2tog over last 2 sc, ch 1, turn. (22 sc)

Row 12: Rep Row 11. (20 sc)

Row 13: [Sc2tog over next 2 sc] twice, sc in each sc to last 2 sc, sc2tog over last 2 sc, ch 1, turn. (17 sc)

Row 14: Sc2tog over first 2 sc, sc in each sc to last 4 sc, [sc2tog over next 2 sc] twice, ch 1, turn. (14 sc)

Row 15: Rep Row 13. (11 sc)

Row 16: Rep Row 11, fasten off. (9 sts)

Beg at bottom with MC and smaller hook, sc evenly around outer edge, join in beg sc, fasten off.

Head Inset
Row 1: Beg at bottom with MC and larger hook, ch 8, sc in 2nd ch from hook and in each ch across, ch 1, turn. (7 sc)

Row 2: Sc in each sc across, ch 1, turn.

Rows 3–5: Rep Row 2.

Row 6: 2 sc in first sc, sc in each sc across to last sc, 2 sc in last sc, ch 1, turn. (9 sts)

Rows 7–10: Rep Row 2.

Row 11: Rep Row 6. (11 sc)

Rep Row 2 until piece meas 6½" from beg.

Next Row: Sc2tog over first 2 sc, sc in each sc across, ch 1, turn. (10 sc)

Rep last row 6 times. (4 sts at end of 6th rep)

Next Row: Sc in first sc, sc2tog over next 2 sc, sc in last sc, ch 1, turn. (3 sts)

Next Row: Sc in first sc, sc2tog over last 2 sc, ch 1, turn. (2 sc)

Next Row: Sk first sc, sl st in last sc, fasten off.

Beg at back bottom with MC and smaller hook, sc evenly around outer edge, join in beg sc, fasten off.

Joining Head Pieces
Holding head inset to 1 side head piece, WS tog, matching back edges, sew seam with tapestry ndl and MC from bottom toward nose, easing in fullness.

Sew rem side head piece in same manner.

With tapestry ndl and MC, sew center front seam from nose to bottom of side head pieces.

With fiberfill, stuff evenly to desired firmness through neck opening.

Joining head to body
Position head on body, matching center front seam of head to center front seam of body, and centering center back of head between 2 side head seams. Sew head to body at neck opening with tapestry ndl and MC. Set aside.

Sole *(Make 2)*
Rnd 1: With CC and larger hook, ch 7, sc in 2nd ch from hook, sc in each of next 4 chs, 3 sc in last ch, working on opposite side of beg ch, sc in each of next 4 chs, 2 sc in next ch, join in beg sc. (14 sc)

Rnd 2: Ch 1, 2 sc in same st, sc in each of next 4 sc, 2 sc in each of next 3 sc, sc in each of next 4 sc, 2 sc in each of last 2 sc, join in beg sc. (20 sc)

Rnd 3: Ch 1, 2 sc in same st, sc in each of next 6 sc, 2 sc in each of next 4 sc, sc in each of next 6 sc, 2 sc in each of last 3 sc, join in beg sc. (28 sc)

Rnd 4: Ch 1, sc in same st, sc in each of next 9 sc, 2 sc in each of next 4 sc, sc in each of next 10 sc, 2 sc in each of next 4 sc, join in beg sc, fasten off. (36 sc)

Leg *(Make 4)*

Row 1: Beg at bottom of foot with MC and larger hook, ch 21, sc in 2nd ch from hook and in each ch across, ch 1, turn. (20 sc)

Row 2: Sc in each sc across, ch 1, turn.

Rows 3 & 4: Rep Row 2.

Row 5: Sc in each sc across to last 2 sc, sc2tog over last 2 sc, ch 1, turn. (19 sc)

Row 6: Sc2tog over first 2 sc, sc in each sc across, ch 1, turn. (18 sc)

Rows 7–10: Rep Rows 4 and 5. (14 sc at end of Row 10)

Row 11: Sc in each of first 12 sc, ch 1, turn.

Row 12: 2 sc in first sc, sc in each sc across, ch 1, turn. (13 sts)

Row 13: Rep Row 2.

Rows 14–17: Rep Rows 12 and 13. (15 sc at end of Row 17)

Rows 18–31: Rep Row 2.

Row 32: Sc2tog over first 2 sc, sc in each sc across to last 2 sc, sc2tog over last 2 sc, ch 1, turn. (13 sts)

Rows 33–35: Rep Row 2.

Rows 36 & 37: Rep Row 32. (9 sc at end of Row 37)

Row 38: [Sc2tog over next 2 sc] twice, sc in next sc, [sc2tog over next 2 sc] twice, fasten off. (5 sc)

With MC and smaller hook, sc evenly around outer edge, join in beg sc, fasten off.

Joining Leg Pieces & Sole

Holding 2 leg pieces tog, sew around leg with tapestry ndl and MC from bottom edge to bottom edge, leaving bottom open for sole.

Stuff evenly to desired firmness.

Hold Rnd 4 of sole against bottom edge of foot and sew in position with tapestry ndl and MC.

Arm *(Make 2)*

Row 1: Beg at hand with MC and larger hook, ch 15, sc in 2nd ch from hook and in each ch across, ch 1, turn. (14 sc)

Row 2: 2 sc in first sc, sc in each sc across to last sc, 2 sc in last sc, ch 1, turn. (16 sc)

Row 3: Sc in each of first 8 sc, 2 sc in next sc, sc in each of last 7 sc, ch 1, turn. (17 sc)

Row 4: Sc in each of first 8 sc, 2 sc in each of next 2 sc, sc in each of last 7 sc, ch 1, turn. (19 sc)

Row 5: Sc in first sc, 2 sc in next sc, sc in each of next 7 sc, 2 sc in next sc, sc in each of next 8 st, 2 sc in last sc, ch 1, turn. (22 sc)

Row 6: Sc in each sc across, ch 1, turn.

Rows 7–15: Rep Row 6.

Row 16: Sc in first sc, sc2tog over next 2 sc, sc in each of next 7 sc, 2 sc in each of next 2 sc, sc in each of next 8 sc, sc2tog over last 2 sc, ch 1, turn. (22 sc)

Row 17: Rep Row 16.

Row 18: Rep Row 6.

Rows 19–24: Rep Rows 17 and 18.

Row 25: Rep Row 6.

Row 26: Sc in first sc, sc2tog over next 2 sc, sc in each of next 7 sc, sc2tog over next 2 sc, sc in each of next 8 sc, sc2tog over last 2 sc, ch 1, turn. (19 sc)

Row 27: Sc in first sc, sc2tog over next 2 sc, sc in each of next 6 sc, sc2tog over next 2 sc, sc in each of next 6 sc, sc2tog over last 2 sc, ch 1, turn. (16 sc)

Row 28: Sc in first sc, [sc2tog over next 2 sc] twice, sc in each of next 2 sc, sc2tog over next 2 sc, sc in each of next 3 sc, [sc2tog over next 2 sc] twice, ch 1, turn. (11 sc)

Row 29: Sc in first sc, [sc2tog over next 2 sc] 5 times, fasten off. (6 sc)

With MC and smaller hook, sc evenly around outer edge, join in beg sc, fasten off.

Joining arm pieces

Fold arm in half, with tapestry ndl and MC, sew from bottom of hand to top of arm, leaving an opening for stuffing.

Stuff evenly to desired firmness; sew opening closed.

Outer Ear *(Make 2)*

Row 1: With MC and larger hook, ch 11, sc in 2nd ch from hook and in each ch across, ch 1, turn. (10 sc)

Row 2: Sc in each sc across, ch 1, turn.

Row 3: Rep Row 2.

Row 4: Sc2tog over first 2 sc, sc in each sc across to last 2 sc, sc2tog over last 2 sc, ch 1, turn. (8 sc)

Rows 5 & 6: Rep Row 4, fasten off. (4 sc)

Ear Lining *(Make 2)*

Rows 1–6: With CC, rep Rows 16 of Outer Ear.

Joining Outer Ear & Ear Lining

Rnd 1: Beg at bottom with MC and smaller hook, WS tog, working through both thicknesses, sc evenly around ear, join in beg sc, ch 1, turn.

Rows 2 & 3: Sc evenly along top curved edge of ear, ch 1, turn, fasten off at end of Row 3.

Muzzle

Note: *Do not join rnds; mark end of rnds with CC thread.*

Rnd 1: With MC and larger hook, ch 1, 6 sc in 2nd ch from hook.

Rnd 2: 2 sc in each sc around. (12 sc)

Rnd 3: [Sc in next sc, 2 sc in next sc] rep around. (18 sc)

Rnd 4: [Sc in each of next 2 sc, 2 sc in next sc] rep around. (24 sc)

Rnds 5–7: Sc in each sc around, at end of Rnd 7, join in next sc, fasten off, leaving a 12" length of yarn for sewing.

Stuff muzzle evenly to desired firmness.

Finishing

Joining muzzle & ears to head

With CC, mark line down center front of head from center point of top of head (to be removed later).

Position muzzle on face, matching end of last round of muzzle to center line at Row 2 of head and center of top of muzzle to center line 11 rows from top of head. Sew in position with tapestry ndl and MC.

Position ears on head; sew with tapestry ndl and MC.

Joining arms to body

Match Row 24 of arm to side seam of body; sew along Row 24 to side seam of body with tapestry ndl and MC.

Rep for other arm.

Joining legs to body

Match top of leg to Row 15 of body at side seam; sew with tapestry ndl and MC.

Face

With tapestry ndl and black yarn, embroider nose on muzzle with an overcast st (see photo).

Embroider mouth extending down from center of nose as pictured, using a running st.

Embroider eyes over seams of front of head just above muzzle as pictured, using an overcast st.

Dress

Bodice Front

Row 1: With A and smaller hook, ch 45, dc in 3rd ch from hook and in each ch across, ch 2, turn. (43 dc)

Row 2: Dc in each of first 21 dc, ch 1, sk next dc, dc in each of last 21 dc, ch 2, turn.

Row 3: Dc in each of first 20 dc, ch 1, sk next dc, dc in next ch sp, ch 1, sk next dc, dc in each of last 20 dc, ch 2, turn.

Row 4: Dc in each of first 19 dc, ch 1, sk next dc, dc in next ch sp, dc in next dc, dc in next ch sp, ch 1, sk next dc, dc in each of last 19 dc, ch 2, turn.

Row 5: Dc in each of first 18 dc, ch 1, sk next dc, dc in next ch sp, dc in next dc, ch 1, sk next dc, dc in next dc, dc in next ch sp, ch 1, sk next dc, dc in each of last 18 dc, ch 2, turn.

Row 6: Dc in each of first 17 dc, ch 1, sk next dc, dc in next ch sp, ch 1, sk next dc, dc in next dc, dc in next ch sp, dc in next dc, ch 1, sk next dc, dc in next ch sp, ch 1, sk next dc, dc in each of last 17 dc, ch 2, turn.

Row 7: Dc in each dc and ch sp across, ch 2, turn. (43 dc)

Row 8: Dc in each of first 13 dc, ch 1, turn.

Row 9: Sc in each dc across, fasten off.

Leave next 17 dc free for center front neck, attach A in next dc, ch 2, dc in same st, dc in each of last 12 dc, ch 1, turn.

Row 10: Sc in each dc across, fasten off.

With A, sc evenly sp up 1 side edge and along top of shoulder, fasten off.

Rep along rem side edge and top of shoulder.

Bodice Back

Row 1: With B, ch 46, dc in 3rd ch from hook and in each ch across, ch 2, turn. (44 dc)

Divide for back opening

Row 2: Dc in each of first 22 dc, ch 2, turn.

Rows 3–7: Dc in each dc across, ch 2, turn.

Row 8: Dc in each of first 13 dc, ch 1, turn.

Row 9: Sc in each dc across, fasten off.

Attach B at side edge of Row 1, ch 2, dc in same st, dc in each of rem 21 dc, ch 2, turn. (22 dc)

Rep Rows 3–9.

With B, sc evenly up 1 side edge and along top of shoulder, fasten off.

Rep along rem side edge and top of shoulder.

With tapestry ndl and A, sew bodice front to bodice back at shoulders.

Waistline

Rnd 1: With RS facing, working along underside of beg ch of bodice front and bodice back, attach A with a sl st at center of back, sc in same st, 21 sc evenly across back, 43 sc evenly across front, 21 sc evenly across rem back, join in beg sc. (86 sc)

Rnd 2 (Beading Row): Ch 3, sk next sc, dc in next sc, [ch 1, sk next sc, dc in next sc] rep around, join in 2nd ch of beg ch-3.

Rnd 3: Ch 1, sc in each st and ch sp around, join in beg sc, fasten off. (86 sts)

Skirt

Rnd 1: Attach B where A was fastened off, ch 2 (counts as first dc), 2 dc in same st, [2 dc in next sc, dc in next sc] 14 times, 2 dc in next sc, rep between [] 13 times, 2 dc in next sc, rep between [] 14 times, 2 dc in last sc, join in 2nd ch of beg ch-2. (132 dc)

Rnd 2: Ch 3, sk next dc (counts as first dc, ch 1), dc in each of next 11 dc, [ch 1, sk next dc, dc in each of next 11 dc] rep around, ending last rep with dc in each of next 10 dc, join in 2nd ch of beg ch-3.

Rnd 3: Sl st in ch sp, ch 2, puff st in same ch sp, ch 1, sk next dc, dc in each of next 9 dc, [ch 1, sk next dc, puff st in next ch sp, sk next dc, dc in each of next 9 dc] rep around, ch 1, join in 2nd ch of beg ch-2.

Rnd 4: Sl st in ch-1 sp just made, ch 3, sk first puff st, dc in next ch sp, dc in each of next 9 dc, [dc in next ch sp, ch 1, sk next puff st, dc in next ch sp, dc in each of next 9 dc] rep around, join in 2nd ch of beg ch-3.

Rnd 5: Ch 2, dc in first ch sp, dc in each of next 11 dc, [dc in next ch sp, dc in each of next 11 dc] rep around, ending with dc in each of next 10 dc, join in 2nd ch of beg ch-2.

Rnds 6 & 7: Ch 2, dc in each dc around, join in top of beg ch-2. (132 dc)

Rnd 8: Ch 2 (counts as first dc), dc in each of first 6 dc, [ch 1, sk next dc, dc in each of next 11 dc] rep around to last 5 dc, ch 1, sk next st, dc in each of last 4 dc, join in 2nd ch of beg ch-2.

Rnd 9: Ch 2 (counts as first dc), dc in each of first 5 dc, [ch 1, sk next dc, puff st in next ch sp, sk next dc, dc in each of next 9 dc] rep around, ending with dc in each of last 3 dc, join in 2nd ch of beg ch-2.

Rnd 10: Ch 2 (counts as first dc), dc in each of first 5 dc, [dc in next ch sp, ch 1, sk next puff st, dc in next ch sp, dc in each of next 9 dc] rep around, ending with dc in each of last 3 dc, join in 2nd ch of beg ch-2.

Rnd 11: Ch 2 (counts as first dc), dc in each of first 6 dc, [dc in next ch sp, dc in each of next 11 dc] rep around, ending with dc in each of last 4 dc, join in 2nd ch of beg ch-2.

Rnds 12 & 13: Rep Rnds 6 and 7.

Rnds 14–17: Rep Rnds 2–5, fasten off at end of Rnd 17, attach A.

Rnd 18: Ch 1, sc in same st, sc in each dc around, join in beg sc.

Rnd 19: [Ch 3, sk next sc, sl st in next sc] rep around, join in beg sc.

Rnd 20: Sl st in first ch-3 lp, [ch 3, sl st in next ch-3 sp] rep around, join in beg ch-3 lp, fasten off.

Armhole Edging

Rnd 1: Attach A with sl st at underarm, with RS facing, [ch 3, sk next st, sl st in next st] rep around, join in beg sl st.

Rnd 2: Sl st in first ch-3 lp, [ch 3, sl st in next ch-3 sp] rep around, join in beg ch-3 lp, fasten off.

Rep around rem armhole.

Neck Edges & Back Opening

Row 1: With RS facing, attach A with a sl st at top of left back neck, sc evenly around neck, ending at top of right back neck, turn.

Row 2: [Ch 3, sk next st, sl st in next sc] rep around neck, down left back opening and up right back opening, join in beg ch-3 sp, fasten off.

Finishing

Sew small button to top of right back opening.

Lap left back slightly over right back; use ch-3 sp at top of left back opening for button lp.

Thread ⅜"-wide ribbon through holes at waistband of front, folding raw edges under at sides and tacking in place.

Cut 1 yd of 1"-wide ribbon in half to make 2 pieces for back sash. Fold raw edges under; tack 1 piece to each side of dress. Tie in bow at back.

Attach lavender ribbon rose to center front of bodice in center of heart.

Bonnet

Rnd 1: With B, ch 6, join to form a ring, ch 3 (counts as first dc), 2 dc in ring, ch 1, [3 dc in ring, ch 1] 5 times, join in 3rd ch of beg ch-3. (18 dc)

Rnd 2: Sl st in first dc, ch 3, dc in same st, 2 dc in next dc, 2 dc in next ch sp, ch 1, sk next dc, *[2 dc in next dc] twice, 2 dc in next ch sp, ch 1, sk next st, rep from * around, join in 3rd ch of beg ch-3.

Rnd 3: Sl st in first dc, ch 3 (counts as first dc), dc in same st, dc in each of next 4 dc, 2 dc in next ch sp, ch 1, sk next st, [2 dc in next dc, dc in each of next 4 dc, 2 dc in next ch sp, ch 1, sk next dc] rep around, join in 3rd ch of beg ch-3.

Begin working in rows as follows:

Row 4: Sl st in each of first 2 dc, ch 3 (counts as first dc), dc in same st, dc in each of next 5 dc, dc in next ch sp, ch 1, sk next dc, [dc in each of next 7 dc, dc in next ch sp, ch 1, sk next dc] rep across to last 7 dc, dc in each of last 5 dc, ch 3 (counts as first dc of following row), turn.

Row 5: Dc in each of next 3 dc, [ch 1, sk next dc, dc in next ch sp, dc in each of next 7 dc] rep across, ch 3 (counts as first dc of following row), turn.

Row 6: [Dc in each of next 7 dc, dc in next ch sp, ch 1, sk next dc] rep across to last 3 dc, dc in each of last 3 dc, ch 3 (counts as first dc of following row), turn.

Row 7: Dc in next dc, [ch 1, sk next dc, dc in next ch sp, dc in each of next 8 dc] rep across to last 2 dc, dc in each of last 2 dc, ch 3 (counts as first dc of following row), turn.

Row 8: Dc in each of next 9 dc, ch 14 (for ear opening), sk next [dc, ch 1, 8 dc, ch 1, dc], dc in each of next 7 dc, ch 14 (for ear opening, sk next [ch 1, 8 dc, ch 1, 2 dc], dc in each of next 6 dc, dc in next ch sp, dc in each of last 2 dc, ch 1, turn.

Row 9: Sc in each st and ch sp across, fasten off.

Neck Band

Row 1: With RS facing and A, 27 sc evenly along neck edge, ch 4 (counts as first dc, ch 1 of following row), turn.

Row 2: Sk next sc, dc in next sc, [ch 1, sk next sc, dc in next sc] rep across, ch 1, turn.

Row 3: Sc in each st and ch sp across, fasten off.

Ruffled Edge

Row 1: With RS facing and A, 2 sc in first sc, sc in each sc to last sc, 2 sc in last sc along edge of bonnet, ch 1, turn. (55 sc)

Row 2: Sc in first sc, [ch 3, sk next sc, sc in next sc] rep across, ch 1, turn.

Row 3: [2 sc, 2 hdc, dc] in first ch-3 sp, sc in next ch-3 sp, [11 dc in next ch-3 sp, sc in next ch-3 sp] rep across to last ch-3 sp, [dc, 2 hdc, 2 sc] in last ch-3 sp, ch 1, turn.

Row 4: Sc in first st, ch 1, sk next st, sc in next st, ch 1, sk next st, dc in next st, sc in next st, *dc in next st, [ch 1, sk next st, dc in next st] 5 times, sc in next st, rep from * to last 5 sts, dc in next st, [ch 1, sk next st, sc in next st] twice, fasten off, attach B.

Row 5: Sl st in first st, ch 3, sk first ch sp, sc in next ch sp, *ch 3, sk next st, sl st in next st, [ch 3, sc in next ch sp] 5 times, rep from * 11 times, ch 3, sk next st, sl st in next st, ch 3, sk next st, sc in next ch sp, ch 3, sl st in last st, turn.

Rows 6–8: [Ch 3, sl st in next ch sp] rep across to first st, sl st in last st, turn, fasten off at end of Row 8.

Finishing

Row 1: With B and RS facing, sc evenly along lower edge of bonnet, beg and ending as close to edge of ruffle as possible, ch 1, turn.

Row 2: Sc in each sc across, fasten off.

Cut 2 (26") pieces of ⅝"-wide ribbon; form 3 (1") lps at 1 end of each ribbon, leaving rem lengths of ribbon free. Tack lps tog, forming rosettes.

Attach securely to each lower side of bonnet on A section of frill.

Slip bonnet on bear's head, slipping ears through ear openings; tie ribbons in bow at side of bear's neck, as shown in photo.

— Designed by Women of Design

Victorian Booties

Shown on page 84

Experience Level: Advanced

Size: To fit 3½"-long foot

Materials

- DMC® Cebelia® crochet cotton size 10: 1 ball ecru
- Size 7 steel crochet hook
- 24" ⅜"-wide ribbon
- Tapestry needle
- Needle and matching thread

Gauge: 9 dc = 1"

To save time, take time to check gauge.

Pattern Note: Join rnds with a sl st unless otherwise states

Body

Rnd 1 (RS): Ch 5, join with sl

st to form a ring, ch 1, in ring work [sc, 2 hdc, 2 dc, 2 tr, 2 dtr, 3 trtr, 2 dtr, 2 tr, 2 dc, 2 hdc, sc], join to first sc. (21 sts)

Note: *Loop a short piece of thread around any st to mark last rnd as RS.*

Rnd 2: Ch 1, working in front loops only, sc in next sc, hdc in each of next 2 hdc, 2 dc in each of next 2 dc, 3 dc in next tr, 4 dc in next tr, 5 dc in each of next 7 sts, 4 dc in next tr, 3 dc in next tr, 2 dc in each of next 2 dc, hdc in each of next 2 hdc, sc in last sc, join to first sc. (63 sts)

Rnd 3: Working behind sts of Rnd 2 in free loops of Rnd 1, sl st behind same st, ch 3 (counts as first dc throughout), dc in same st, 2 dc in next free loop and in each free loop around, join to first dc. (42 dc)

Rnd 4: Ch 3, working in back loops only, dc in next 19 dc, 3 dc in each of next 2 dc, dc in last 20 dc, do not join. (46 dc)

Rnd 5: Ch 35, join with sl st to first dc of Rnd 4, being careful not to twist ch, ch 3, 2 dc in same st, working in front loops only, 3 dc in each of next 2 dc, 4 dc in next dc, 5 dc in each of next 38 dc, 4 dc in next dc, 3 dc in each of next 2 dc, 2 dc in last dc, ch 3, sl st in same dc and in first ch.

Rnd 6: Ch 3, dc in next ch and in each ch across; working in free loops of Rnd 4, dc in each dc around, join to first dc, fasten off. (81 dc)

Rnds 7 & 8: Ch 3, dc in both loops of next dc and each dc around, join to first dc, at end of last rnd, fasten off.

Edging

With RS facing and top of body up, join thread with sl st in center front; ch 1, 2 sc in end of next row, sc along opposite side of each ch of ch-35, 2 sc in end of next row; join to first sc, fasten off. (39 sc)

Sole

Rnd 1 (RS): Ch 25 loosely, 3 dc in 4th ch from hook, dc in next 20 chs, 8 dc in last ch (heel), working up opposite side of ch, dc in last 20 chs, join to top of beg ch. (52 sts)

Note: *Mark last rnd as RS.*

Rnd 2: Ch 3, dc in same st, 2 dc in each of next 3 dc, dc in next 20 dc, 2 dc in each of next 8 dc, dc in last 20 dc, join to first dc. (64 dc)

Rnd 3: Ch 3, dc in same st, 2 dc in each of next 7 dc, dc in next 20 dc, [2 dc in next dc, dc in next dc] 3 times, 2 dc in each of next 4 dc, [dc in next dc, 2 dc in next dc] 3 times (toe), dc in last 20 dc, join to first dc, fasten off. (82 dc)

Sew sole to inside loops of body.

Top

Row 1: Ch 22 loosely, dc in 4th ch from hook and in each ch across, ch 3, turn. (20 sts)

Note: *Mark last row as RS.*

Row 2: Working in front loops only, dc in next dc and in each dc across, ch 3, turn.

Row 3: Working in back loops only, dc in next dc and in each dc across, ch 3, turn.

Rows 4–20: [Rep Rows 2 and 3] 8 times, then rep Row 2 once more; at end of last row do not ch, do not fasten off, turn.

Joining Row: With WS to inside and working through both thicknesses of both ends, sl st in each st across, do not fasten off, ch 3, turn.

First ruffle

Working in sts of Joining Row, 4 dc in same st, 5 dc in each of next 19 sts (bottom edge), fasten off. (100 dc)

Bottom edging

With RS facing, join thread with sl st in any row of bottom edge, ch 1, working in end of rows, work 39 sc evenly sp around bottom edge, join to first sc, fasten off. (39 sc)

With WS tog, sew top to body, with first ruffle positioned 1 st to left of 2nd ruffle on body.

Top edging

With RS facing, join thread with sl st in any row of top edge, ch 3, working in end of rows, 4 dc in same row, 5 dc in each row around, join to first dc, fasten off. (100 dc)

Second ruffle

With RS facing, sk 3 rows to right of first ruffle on top, working in free loops, join in first st at base of top, ch 3, 4 dc in same st, 5 dc in each of next 19 sts, fasten off. (100 dc)

Third ruffle

With RS facing, sk 2 rows to right of 2nd ruffle, working in free loops, join in first st at base of top, ch 3, 4 dc in same st, 5 dc in each of next 19 sts, fasten off. (100 dc)

Fourth ruffle

With RS facing, sk 3 rows to right of 3rd ruffle, working in free loops, join in first st at base of top, ch 3, 4 dc in same st, 5 dc in each of next 19 sts, fasten off. (100 dc)

Fifth ruffle

With RS facing, sk 2 rows to right of 4th ruffle, working in free loops, join thread in first st at base of top, ch 3, 4 dc in same st, 5 dc in each of next 19 sts, fasten off. (100 dc)

Sixth ruffle

With RS facing, sk 2 rows to left of 5th ruffle, working in free loops, join in first st at top edge, ch 3, 4 dc in same st, 5 dc in each of next 19 sts, fasten off. (100 dc)

Seventh ruffle

With RS facing, sk 3 rows to left of 6th ruffle, working in free loops, join in first st at top edge, ch 3, 4 dc in same st, 5 dc in each of next 19 sts, fasten off. (100 dc)

Eighth ruffle

With RS facing, sk 2 rows to left of 7th ruffle, working in free loops, join thread with sl st in first st at top edge, ch 3, 4 dc in same st, 5 dc in each of next 19 sts, fasten off. (100 dc)

Rep for 2nd bootie. Cut ribbon into 2 equal lengths, tie each into bow. With sewing needle and thread, sew bow onto front of each bootie as shown.

—Designed by Ann Kirtley courtesy of DMC

Pretty Pink Afghan

Shown on page 85

Experience Level: Advanced beginner

Size: 42" square

Materials

- Coats & Clark Red Heart® Super Sport 3-ply sport weight yarn (5 oz per skein): 3 skeins pink #718
- Size G/6 crochet hook

Gauge: 7 rows = 4"

To save time, take time to check gauge.

Pattern Note: Turning ch-3 counts as first dc of next row throughout.

Pattern Stitch

Cluster (cl): [Yo and draw up lp in indicated st, yo and draw through 2 lps] 3 times, yo and draw through rem 4 lps on hook.

Afghan

Row 1: Ch 143, dc in 4th ch from hook and in each ch across, ch 3, turn. (141 dc)

Row 2: Dc in each of next 2 dc, ch 3, sk 1 dc, sc in next dc, [ch 5, sk 3 dc, sc in next dc] 33 times, ch 3, sk 1 dc, dc in each of last 3 sts, ch 3, turn.

Row 3: Dc in each of next 2 dc, ch 5, sc in ch-5 lp, *11 dc in next lp, sc in next lp, [ch 5, sc in next lp] 4 times, rep from * 4 more times, 11 dc in next lp, sc in next lp, ch 5, dc in each of last 3 sts, ch 3, turn.

Row 4: Dc in each of next 2 dc, ch 3, sc in next lp, *ch 2, cl in next sc, ch 2, sk 3 dc, sc in next dc, ch 5, sk 3 dc, sc in next dc, ch 2, cl in next sc, ch 2, sc in next lp **, [ch 5, sc in next sp] 3 times, rep from * across, ending last rep at **, ch 3, dc in each of last 3 sts, ch 3, turn.

Row 5: Dc in each of next 2 dc, *ch 5, sc in next cl, ch 2, cl in next sc, ch 2, sc in ch-5 lp, ch 2, cl in sc, ch 2, sc in cl **, [ch 5, sc in next lp] 3 times, rep from * across, ending last rep at **, ch 5, dc in each of last 3 sts, ch 3, turn.

Row 6: Dc in each of next 2 dc, ch 3, sc in next lp, *ch 5, sc in cl, ch 2, cl in next sc, ch 2, sc in cl, [ch 5, sc in ch-5 lp] ** 4 times, rep from * across, ending last rep at **, ch 3, dc in each of last 3 sts, ch 3, turn.

Row 7: Dc in each of next 2 dc, *ch 5, sc in ch-5 lp, ch 5, sc in cl, ch 5, sc in ch-5 lp **, ch 5, sc in next lp, 11 dc in next lp, sc in next lp, rep from * across, ending last rep at **, ch 5, dc in each of last 3 sts, ch 3, turn.

Row 8: Dc in each of next 2 dc, ch 3, *sc in next lp, [ch 5, sc in next lp] 3 times **, ch 2, cl in sc, ch 2, sk 3 dc, sc in next dc, ch 5, sk 3 dc, sc in next dc, ch 2, cl in next sc, ch 2, rep from * across, ending last rep at **, ch 3, dc in each of last 3 sts, ch 3, turn.

Row 9: Dc in each of next 2 dc, *[ch 5, sc in ch-5 lp] 3 times **, ch 5, sc in cl, ch 2, cl in next sc, ch 2, sc in next lp, ch 2, cl in next sc, ch 2, sc in next cl, rep from * across, ch 5, dc in each of last 3 sts, ch 3, turn.

Row 10: Dc in each of next 2 dc, ch 3, sc in next lp, [ch 5, sc in next lp] 3 times, *ch 5, sc in cl, ch 2, cl in next sc, ch 2, sc in cl, [ch 5, sc in next lp] 4 times, rep from * across, ch 3, dc in each of last 3 sts, ch 3, turn.

Row 11: Dc in each of next 2 dc, ch 5, sc in ch-5 lp, *11 dc in next lp, sc in next lp **, ch 5, sc in next lp,ch 5, sc in cl, [ch 5, sc in ch-5 lp] twice, rep from * across, ending last rep at **, ch 5, dc in each of last 3 sts, ch 3, turn.

Rows 12–70: Rep Rows 4–11, ending with Row 6.

Row 71: Dc in each of next 2

dc, ch 5, sc in ch-5 lp, *ch 5, sc in cl, [ch 5, sc in next ch-5 lp] ** 5 times, rep from * across, ending last rep at **, ch 5, dc in each of last 3 sts, ch 3, turn.

Row 72: Dc in each of next 2 dc, ch 3, [sc in next lp, ch 5] rep across, sc in last lp, ch 3, dc in each of last 3 sts, ch 3, turn.

Row 73: Dc in each of next 2 dc, dc in ch-3 sp, [tr in sc, 3 dc in ch-5 sp] rep across, tr in last sc, dc in ch-3 sp, dc in each of last 3 sts, do not turn, do not fasten off.

Edging

Rnd 1: Working down side, ch 1, sc over side of dc of first row, ch 5, [sc over side of st of next row, ch 5, sk 1 row] rep to corner, sc over side of st of first row, ch 5, sc in base ch of first dc to form corner lp, [ch 5, sk 3 sts, sc in next st] rep across, ch 5, sc over side of st of first row to form corner lp, [ch 5, sk row, sc over side of st of next row] rep to last row, ch 5, sc over side of st of last row, ch 5, sc in end st to form corner lp, [ch 5, sk 3 sts, sc in next st] rep across, ending with ch 2, dc in beg sc to form last corner lp.

Rnd 2: Sc in dc lp just made, [ch 5, sc in next lp] rep around, ending with ch 2, dc in beg sc to form last lp.

Rnd 3: Sc in dc lp just made, ch 3, sc in same lp, *[ch 5, sc in next lp] twice, ch 5, [sc, ch 3, sc] in next lp, rep from * around, join in beg sc, fasten off.

— Designed by Lucille LaFlamme

Christening Set

Shown on page 86

Experience Level: Intermediate

Size: Newborn

Finished Measurements

Dress: 21½" from front neck edge to lower edge

Booties: 4" sole

Afghan: 43" square

Materials

- Red Heart® 3-ply baby fingering yarn (1¾ oz per skein): 3 skeins white
- Red Heart® 3-ply sport weight yarn (2.5 oz per skein): 7 skeins white
- Size G/6 crochet hook or size needed to obtain gauge
- 3 (½") white buttons
- 4 yds ¼"-wide white satin ribbon
- 11 (½") white ribbon roses
- White sewing thread and needle

Gauge

Dress: First 3 rows = 1¼"

Cap: 10 dc and first 6 rows of back = 2"

Booties: 10 dc = 2"; 3 dc rows = 1¼"

Afghan: 6 dc and 2 dc rows = 1½"

To save time, take time to check gauge.

Pattern Notes: Dress, cap and booties are made with 3-ply baby fingering weight yarn.

Afghan is made with 3-ply sport weight yarn.

Join rnds with a sl st unless otherwise stated.

Beg ch-3 counts as first dc throughout.

Pattern Stitches

Shell: [2 dc, ch 1, 2 d] in indicated st.

3-tr cluster (3-tr cl): Holding back last lp of each tr, make 3 tr in same sp, yo and draw through all 4 lps on hook.

4-tr cluster (4-tr cluster): Holding back last lp of each tr, make 4 tr in same sp, yo and draw through all 5 lps on hook.

Dress

Yoke

Row 1: Beg at neck, ch 61, dc in 4th ch from hook counts as first dc throughout) and in each ch across, turn. (59 dc)

Row 2: Ch 3, dc in each rem dc across, dc in 3rd ch of beg ch-3, turn. (59 dc)

Row 3: Ch 3, dc in each of next 4 dc, 3 dc in next dc, dc in each of next 5 dc, sk 1 dc, shell in next dc, sk 1 dc, dc in each of next 2 dc, [3 dc in next dc, dc in each of next 2 dc] 3 times, sk 1 dc, shell in next dc, sk 1 dc, 2 dc in next dc, 3 dc in next dc, 2 dc in next dc, sk 1 dc, shell in next dc, sk 1 dc, dc in each of next 2 dc, [3 dc in next dc, dc in each of next 2 dc] 3 times, sk 1 dc, shell in next dc, sk 1 dc, dc in each of next 5 dc, 3 dc in next dc, dc in each of last 5 dc, turn.

Row 4: Ch 3, dc in each of next 12 dc, shell in shell sp, sk 2 dc of shell, dc in each of next 3 dc, 3 dc in next dc, [dc in each of next 4 dc, 3 dc in next dc] twice, dc in each of next 3 dc, shell in shell sp, sk 2 dc of shell, dc in each of next 7 dc, shell in shell sp, sk 2 dc of shell, dc in each of next 3 dc, 3 dc in next dc, [dc in each of next 4 dc, 3 dc in next dc] twice, dc in each of next 3

Row 16: Ch 3 (counts as first dc), dc in each of next 5 sc, [dc in each of next 7 dc with ch 1 between (6 ch-1 sps), dc in each of next 6 sc] 3 times, turn.

Row 17: Ch 1, sc in each of next 6 dc, *ch 1, sc in ch-1 sp, [ch 3, sc in next ch-1 sp] 5 times, ch 1, sk dc, sc in each of next 6 dc, rep from * twice, turn.

Row 18: Ch 3 (counts as first dc), dc in each of next 5 sc, [ch 3, sk first ch-3 lp, sc in next lp, ch 5, sk next lp, sc in next lp, ch 3, dc in each of next 6 sc] 3 times, turn.

Row 19: Ch 1, sc in each of next 6 dc, [ch 3, sk ch-3 sp, 7 dc in ch-5 sp, ch 3, sk ch-3 sp, sc in each of next 6 dc] 3 times, turn.

Rows 20–27: [Rep Rows 16–19] twice.

Rows 28 & 29: Rep Rows 16 and 17, fasten off at end of Row 29.

Sew the sides of back section to free sides of Row 12.

Lower edge

Row 1: Attach yarn with a sl st to lower front edge on left side of cap, ch 1, sc over side of each sc, 2 sc over side of each dc along side of cap, sc in each st across edge of back, work opposite side of cap to correspond, turn.

Rows 2 & 3: Ch 1, sc in each st across, turn, fasten off at end of Row 3.

Cut 2 (15") lengths of ribbon; sew end of each ribbon to each side of lower front edge of cap. Sew a ribbon rose over each attached ribbon end.

Booties *(Make 2)*

Instep

Rnd 1: Ch 5, join to form a ring, ch 4, 3-tr cl in ring, [ch 3, 4-tr cl in ring] 6 times, ch 3, sl st in top of beg cl, ch 26, sk next cl, join in top of next 4-tr cl.

Rnd 2: Sl st in same sp, ch 3 (counts as first dc), 2 dc in same ch-3 sp, 3 dc in next ch-3 sp, 5 dc in next ch-3 sp, 3 dc in each of next 2 ch-3 sps, dc in each of next 26 ch, join in 3rd ch of beg ch-3. (43 dc)

Rnd 3: Ch 3, dc in each dc around, join in 3rd ch of beg ch-3.

Rnd 4: Ch 1, sc in same st as sl st, sc in each dc around, join in beg sc.

Sole

Rnd 5: Working in back lps only, ch 1, sc in same sc as sl st, sc in each of next 5 sc, [insert hook in next sc, pull up lp, insert hook in next sc, pull up lp, yo, pull through all 3 lps on hook at once (sc dec made)] 3 times, sc in each of next 17 sc, 2 sc dec, sc in each of next 10 sc, join in beg sc.

Rnd 6: Working in back lps only, ch 1, sc in same sc as sl st, sc in each of next 4 sc, 3 sc dec, sc in each sc around, join in beg sc.

Rnd 7: Ch 1, sc in each sc around, join in beg sc, fasten off.

Sew center seam of sole.

Cuff

Rnd 1: With RS facing, attach yarn with a sl st in unused lp of 16th ch at back of bootie, ch 3, dc in each of next 10 chs, 4 dc in each of next 2 ch-3 lps of Rnd 1, dc in each of next 15 chs, join in 3rd ch of beg ch-3.

Rnd 2: Ch 1, sc in same st as sl st, sc in next dc, [ch 3, sk 2 dc, sc in next dc, ch 5, sk 4 dc, sc in next dc, ch 3, sk 2 dc, sc in each of next 6 dc] twice, join in beg sc.

Rnd 3: Ch 1, sc in same st as sl st, sc in next sc, [ch 3, sk ch-3 sp, 7 dc in ch-5 sp, ch 3, sk ch-3 sp, sc in each of next 6 sc] twice, join in beg sc.

Rnd 4: Ch 3, dc in next sc, [dc in each of next 7 dc with ch 1 between each (6 ch-1 sps), dc in each of next 6 sc] twice, join in 3rd ch of beg ch-3.

Rnd 5: Ch 1, sc in same st as sl st, sc in next dc, *ch 1, sc in ch-1 sp, [ch 3, sc in next ch-1 sp] 5 times, ch 1, sk dc, sc in each of next 6 dc, rep from * once, join in beg sc, fasten off.

Finishing

Weave 18" length of ribbon in Row 1 of Cuff; tie in front. Cut ends to desired length. Sew ribbon rose to center of instep.

Afghan

Row 1: Ch 136, dc in 4th ch from hook and in each ch across, turn. (134 dc counting turning ch)

Row 2: Ch 3 (counts as first dc), dc in each dc across, turn. (134 dc)

Row 3: Ch 1, sc in first dc and in each of next 5 dc, [ch 3, sk 2 dc, sc in next dc, ch 5, sk 4 dc, sc in next dc, ch 3, sk 2 dc, sc in each of next 6 dc] rep across, turn.

Row 4: Ch 1, sc in each of next 6 sc, [ch 3, sk ch-3 sp, 7 dc in ch-5 sp, ch 3, sk ch-3 sp, sc in each of next 6 sc] rep across, turn.

Row 5: Ch 3 (counts as first dc), dc in each of next 5 sc, [dc in each of next 7 dc with ch 1 between (6 ch-1 sps), dc in each of next 6 sc] rep across, turn.

Row 6: Ch 1, sc in each of next 6 dc, *ch 1, sc in ch-1 sp, [ch 3, sc in next sp] 5 times, ch 1, sk dc, sc in each of next 6 dc, rep from * across, turn.

Row 7: Ch 3 (counts as first dc), dc in each of next 5 sc, [ch 3, sk first ch-3 lp, sc in next lp, ch 5, sk next ch-3 lp, sc in next lp, ch 3, dc in each of next 6 sc] rep across, turn.

Row 8: Ch 1, sc in each of next 6 dc, [ch 3, sk ch-3 sp, 7 dc in ch-5 sp, ch 3, sk ch-3 sp, sc in each of next 6 dc] rep across, turn.

Rows 9–91: Rep Rows 5–8, ending with Row 7.

Row 92: Ch 3 (counts as first dc), dc in each of next 5 dc, [2 dc in ch-3 sp, dc in sc, 4 dc over ch-5 sp, dc in sc, 2 dc in ch-3 sp, dc in each of next 6 dc] rep across, turn. (134 dc)

Row 93: Ch 3 (counts as first dc), dc in each dc across, do not turn. (134 dc)

Edging

Rnd 1: Ch 1, sc in top of side of last dc made, ch 4, sc in base of same dc, ch 4, sc in base of next dc, [ch 4, sc over side of next sc] 44 times, ch 4, sk next sc, sc in base of next ch-3 turning ch, ch 4, sc in end st, ch 4, sc in same st. (49 ch-4 lps)

Working along beg ch, [ch 4, sk 2 sts, sc in next st] 43 times, ch 4, sk 3 sts, sc in corner st, ch 4, sc in same st. (45 ch-4 lps)

Rep up side and across top, making [ch 4, sl st] in first sc to form last corner lp.

Rnd 2: Sl st in each of next 2 chs, sc in lp, *[ch 4, sc in next lp] rep across to and including corner lp, ch 4, sc in same st, rep from * around, join in beg sc.

Rnd 3: Sl st in next ch, sl st in lp, ch 3, dc in same lp, ch 3, sl st in 3rd ch from hook (picot), ch 1, 2 dc in same lp, *ch 1, sc in next lp, ch 1, [2 dc, picot, ch 1, 2 dc] in next lp, rep from * around, join in 3rd ch of beg ch-3, fasten off.

Finishing

Cut 4 (12") lengths of ribbon; tie each in a bow in each corner of afghan. Sew ribbon rose to center of each bow.

—Designed by Lucille LaFlamme

Baby's Angel

Shown on page 87

Experience Level: Intermediate

Size: 8" tall

Materials

- 4-ply worsted weight yarn (3 oz per skein): 1 skein pink
  Crochet cotton size 10 (350 yds per ball): 1 ball white
  Size 5 steel crochet hook
- Size G/6 crochet hook or size needed to obtain gauge
- Polyester fiberfill
- Small rubber band
- 4-oz container baby powder
- 1 yd ¼"-wide pink satin ribbon
- 20" ¼"-wide green satin ribbon
- 12 (¼") pink ribbon roses
- Tapestry needle
- Glue (optional)
- Fabric stiffener (optional)

Gauge: 8 sc and 8 sc rnds = 1" with size 10 crochet cotton and size 5 steel crochet hook

4 sc and 4 sc rnds = 1" with 4-ply yarn and size G/6 crochet hook

To save time, take time to check gauge.

Pattern Note: Join rnds with a sl st unless otherwise stated.

Body

Rnd 1: Beg at bottom with pink yarn and G hook, ch 2, 6 sc in 2nd ch from hook, join in beg sc.

Rnd 2: Ch 1, 2 sc in each sc around, join in beg sc.

Rnd 3: Ch 1, sc in first sc, [2 sc in next sc, sc in next sc] rep around, ending with 2 sc in last sc, join in beg sc.

Rnd 4: Ch 1, sc in each of first 2 sc, [2 sc in next sc, sc in each of next 2 sc] rep around, ending with 2 sc in last sc, join in beg sc.

Rnd 5: Working in back lps, ch 1, sc in each sc around, join in beg sc. (24 sc)

Rnds 6–18: Working in both lps, ch 1, sc in each sc around, join in beg sc. (24 sc)

Rnd 19: Rep Rnd 5.

Rnd 20: Working over rubber band, ch 1, sc in each sc around, join in beg sc, fasten off.

Body Lace Covering

Rnd 1: With white cotton and size 5 steel crochet hook, working from top of body toward bottom, join thread with a sc in first free lp at top of body on Rnd 18, [ch 5, sc in next lp] rep around, ending with ch 2, join with dc in beg sc. (24 lps)

Rnd 2: Ch 1, sc in same lp, [ch 5, sc in next ch-5 lp] rep around, ending with ch 2, join with dc in beg sc.

Rnds 3–10: Rep Rnd 2.

Rnd 11: Lay lace covering flat, ch 1, sc in first lp, catching pink free lp of Rnd 4 behind, [ch 1, sc in both ch-5 lp and pink lp] rep around, join in beg sc, fasten off.

Slip work over powder container.

Body Trim

Note: *Trim will be made in straight lace piece; shells will be worked on later.*

Row 1: With white cotton and size 5 hook, ch 7, dc in 4th ch from hook, ch 2, sk 2 chs, 2 dc in last ch, ch 1, turn.

Row 2: [Sk first dc, sc in 2nd dc, sc in each ch, sc in last dc, ch 3, turn.

Row 3: Dc in first sc, ch 2, sk 2 sc, 2 dc in last sc, ch 1, turn.

Rep Rows 2 and 3 until piece measures approximately 14" (28 sps), ending with Row 2, do not ch 3, turn.

Shells

Ch 1, turn to work down side, sc in side of last sc made, [7 dc in end of next sc, sc in end of next sc] rep across side, ending with sc in last ch, fasten off.

Weave ribbon in sps.

Attaching body trim

Place center of body trim at bottom of body over center back of lace covering, attach body trim to lace covering at sc between shells with length of crochet thread, sew around to center front at top of lace covering (Rnd 19), being sure shells are straight and on each side of center (see photo).

Head

Rnd 1: With white cotton and steel hook, ch 3, join to form a ring, 8 sc in ring, join in beg sc.

Rnd 2: Ch 1, 2 sc in each sc around, join in beg sc.

Rnd 3: Ch 1, sc in first sc, [2 sc in next sc, sc in next sc] rep around, ending with 2 sc in last sc, join in beg sc.

Rnd 4: Ch 1, [sc in each of next 2 sc, 2 sc in next sc] rep around, join in beg sc.

Rnd 5: Ch 1, [sc in each of next 3 sc, 2 sc in next sc] rep around, join in beg sc.

Rnd 6: Ch 1, [sc in each of next 4 sc, 2 sc in next sc] rep around, join in beg sc. (48 sc)

Rnds 7–16: Ch 1, sc in each sc around, join in beg sc.

Rnd 17: Ch 1, sc in each of next 4 sc, dec over next 2 sc] rep around, join in beg sc.

Rnd 18: Ch 1, [sc in each of next 3 sc, dec over next 2 sc] rep around, join in beg sc.

Rnd 19: Ch 1, [sc in each of next 2 sc, dec over next 2 sc] rep around, join in beg sc.

Rnd 20: Sc in each sc around, fasten off. (24 sts)

Stuff head with fiberfill to meas approximately 6½" around.

Head Base

Rnd 1: With pink yarn and size G hook, ch 2, 6 sc in 2nd ch from hook, join in beg sc.

Rnd 2: Ch 1, 2 sc in each sc around, join in beg sc.

Rnd 3: Ch 1, sc in first sc, 2 sc in next sc, sc in next sc] rep around, ending with 2 sc in last sc, join in beg sc, fasten off.

Sew head onto base between 2nd and 3rd rnds.

Bodice *(Make 2)*

Row 1 (WS): With pink yarn and size G hook, ch 22, sc in 2nd ch from hook and in each ch across, ch 1, turn. (21 sc)

Rows 28: Sc in each sc across, ch 1, turn, fasten off at end of Row 8.

Bodice Lace Covering

First side

Row 1: With white cotton and size 5 steel crochet hook, with RS facing (Row 2), join thread with a sc in first free lp at beg ch on right side, [ch 5, sc in next lp] rep across, ending with ch 2, dc in last lp, ch 1, turn. (20 ch-5 lps)

Row 2: Sc over dc just made, [ch 5, sc in next lp] rep across, ending with ch 2, dc in last lp, ch 1, turn.

Rows 3–6: Rep Row 2.

Row 7: Sc over dc just made, catching front lp of yarn sc, [ch 5, sc in next lp and in yarn sc below] rep across, sk 6 yarn lps evenly sp, ending with ch 5, sc in last lp, fasten off. (14 lps)

With WS tog (Row 1) and pink yarn length, sew 8 sts on each end of bodice pieces tog, forming neck opening, turn to RS.

Insert head; with yarn, sew head base to neck opening just below head. Open bodice; sew last row of base to inside of bodice.

Second side

Row 1: With size 5 hook, join white cotton with a sl st in base of last sc of first row of lace covering, [ch 5, sl st in base of next thread sc] rep up to head (8 lps), [ch 5, sl st in next st] rep around head in yarn lps (4 lps), [ch 5, sl st in base of next thread sc] 7 times, ch 2, dc in last sc, ch 1, turn. (20 lps)

Rows 2–7: Rep Rows 2–7 of First side.

With yarn length, sew first 4 sts tog at bottom of each end to shape arms.

Bodice Trim

Work as for Body Trim, except work 40 sps. Weave ribbon in spaces.

Attaching bodice trim

With thread, sew trim to bodice with ends at center of face and center back of trim at center back of bodice so that 4 center shells hang just below back of bodice. Bring up over shoulders and down over front.

Hair

Place marker at 12th rnd of head. Place markers to outline face area 2½" around first marker.

Beg at top of head and working around face area, using 2 strands of crochet cotton and tapestry ndl, [bring ndl up through a stitch and back down through same st, forming a lp on right side of work. Bring ndl up on either side of lp and back down on opposite side, locking st, sk 1 st] rep around to last 2 rows of head, fasten off.

Wing

First wing

Row 1: With white cotton and size 5 hook, ch 10, sc in 2nd ch from hook and in each ch across, ch 1, turn.

Row 2: Sc in first sc, [ch 5, sk next sc, sc in next st] 3 times, ch 2, sk next sc, dc in last st, ch 1, turn.

Rows 3–6: Sc in first lp, [ch 5, sc in next lp] 3 times, ch 2, dc in last sc, ch 1, turn.

Row 7: Sc in first lp, [ch 5, sc in next lp] 3 times, ch 5, join in last sc, fasten off.

Second wing

Row 1: Turn first wing, join white cotton in first ch on beg ch, sc across, ch 1, turn. (9 sc)

Rows 27: Rep Rows 27 of First wing.

Shell edging

Join thread with a sl st in end of beg ch, ch 3, 6 dc in same st, sl st in next lp, [7 dc in sc, sl st in next lp] rep around with shell in opposite end of beg ch, fasten off. (20 shells)

Starch, if desired, and allow to dry. With crochet cotton, sew center of wing to center back of bodice between trim and head.

FIG. 1
Ribbon Placement

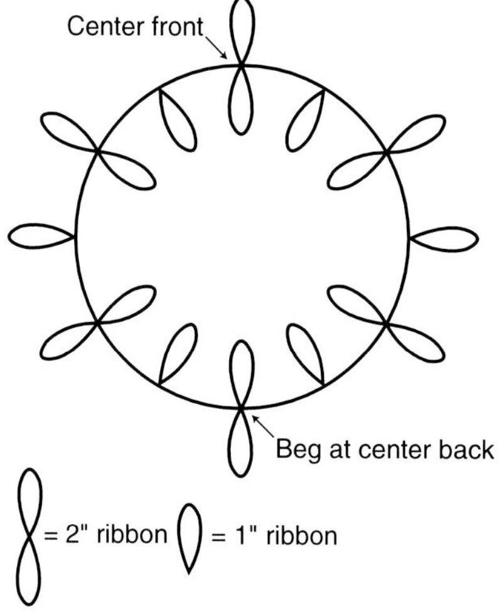

Halo

With white cotton and size 5 hook, ch 54, join to form a ring, ch 1, sc in each ch around, join in beg sc, fasten off.

Cut 6 (2") and 6 (1") pieces of green ribbon; shape into double and single lps as shown in photo. Glue or sew to halo evenly spaced around as in Fig. 1, having double lp at center front of head. Glue or sew 1 ribbon rose over each green ribbon lp.

Place halo over head; fluff hair around and over halo, bringing lps of hair down toward face.

— Designed by Connie Clark

Embossed Flowers

Shown on page 88

Experience Level: Advanced beginner

Size

Pillow Front: 12" square without edge

Coverlet: 24" square without edge

Materials

- DMC® Cebelia® crochet cotton size 10 (50 grams per balls): 7 balls white and 2 balls peach #754
- Size 7 steel crochet hook

Gauge: 12 sts and 4 rows = 1"

To save time, take time to check gauge.

Pattern Note: Join rnds with a sl st unless otherwise stated.

Pattern Stitches: See Instructions for Filet Crochet on page 57.

Embossed flower: With RS facing, work around sides of sp as follows: Attach peach in top left corner, sc in corner, ch 3, 3 dc around post of left dc, [ch 3, sc] in lower left corner, ch 3, dc in each of next 3 dc, [ch 3, sc] in lower right corner, ch 3, 3 dc around post of right dc, [ch 3, sc] in top right corner, ch 3, dc in base of each of next 3 dc, ch 3, join in beg sc. **Note:** *Turn coverlet as flower is*

CHART A
Pillow Front

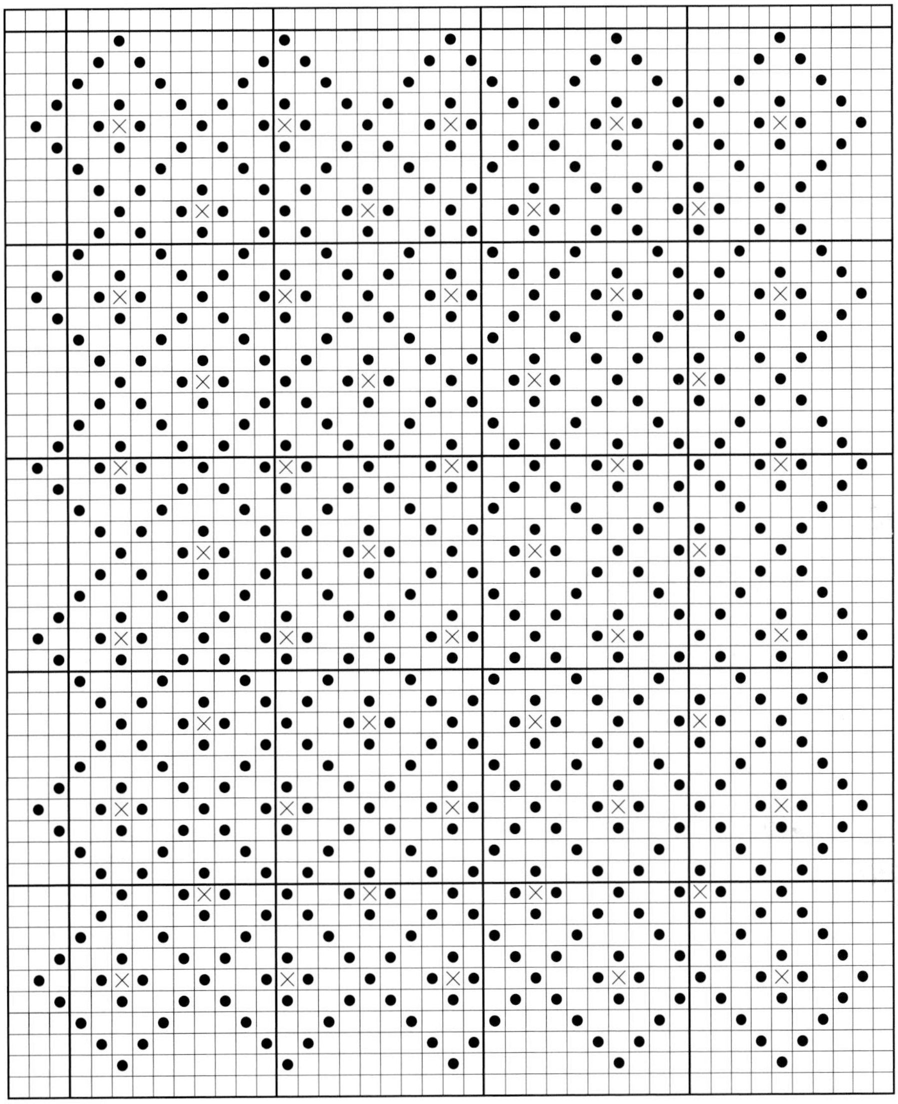

Row 50

Row 40

Row 30

Row 20

Row 10

worked to keep RS facing.

Beg sc cluster (beg sc cl): [Insert hook in next st, draw up a lp] twice, yo and draw through all 3 lps on hook.

Sc cluster (sc cl): [Insert hook in next st, draw up a lp] 3 times, yo and draw through all 4 lps on hook.

Pillow Front

Row 1 (RS): Ch 134, dc in 8th ch from hook, [ch 2, sk 2 chs, dc in next ch] rep across.

Row 2: Beg sp, 4 sps over 4 sps, [bl over bl, 7 sps over 7 sps] 4 times, ending with bl over bl, 5 sps over 5 sps.

Rows 3–51: Continuing with white, follow Chart A, utilizing Pattern Stitches, fasten off.

With peach, work embossed flower as described in Pattern Stitches and indicated on Chart A.

Edge

Rnd 1 (RS): Attach white in corner, ch 3, 3 dc in same sp, [{dc, ch 3, dc} in next dc/row joining, 3 dc in next sp] rep around, working [4 dc, ch 3, 4 dc] in corners, ending with 4 dc, ch 3 in first corner, join in 3rd ch of beg ch-3.

Rnd 2: Sl st in next dc, ch 3, dc in next 2 dc, [{dc, ch 3, dc} in ch-3 sp *, sk 1 dc, dc in each of

STITCH KEY
- ☐ Space (white)
- ⊡ Dc block (white)
- ☒ Embossed flower space (peach #754)

Color number given is for DMC Cebelia.

CHART B
Coverlet

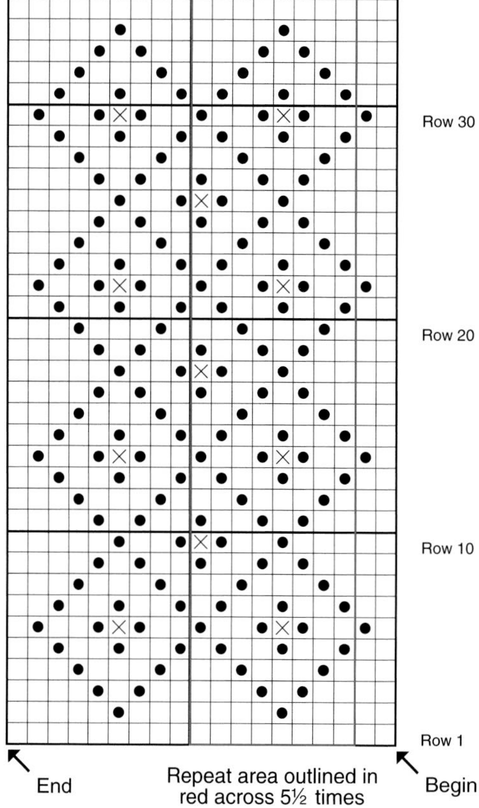

next 3 dc] rep around, ending last rep at *, join in 3rd ch of beg ch-3.

Rnd 3: Sl st in next dc, ch 1, beg sc cl over 2 dc, [ch 3, {dc, ch 3, dc} in ch-3 sp, ch 3 *, sk 1 dc, sc cl over next 3 dc] rep around, ending last rep at *, join in beg sc cl.

Rnd 4: Sl st to ch-3 sp, [sl st, ch 1, sc] in ch-3 sp, [ch 3, {dc, ch 3, dc} in next ch-3 sp, ch 3, sc in each of next 2 ch-3 sps] rep around, ending with ch 3, [dc, ch 3, dc] in next ch-3 sp, ch 3, sc in next ch-3 sp, join in beg sc.

Rnd 5: [4 sc in next ch-3 sp, {2 sc, ch 5, 2 sc} in next ch-3 sp, 4 sc in next ch-3 sp, sc between sc] rep around, join in beg sc, fasten off.

Coverlet

Row 1 (RS): Ch 278, dc in 8th ch from hook, [ch 2, sk 2 chs, dc in next ch] rep across.

Rows 2–25: Follow Chart B, utilizing Pattern Stitches (as established in Pillow Front).

Rep Rows 18–25 for patt, work to desired length to last patt rep.

Work Rows 26–35 to complete coverlet, fasten off.

With peach, work embossed flower as described in Pattern Stitches and indicated on Chart B.

Edge

Rows 1–5: Rep Rows 1–5 of Edge for pillow.

—Designed by Nancy Hearne courtesy of DMC

Little Pixie

Shown on page 89

Experience Level: Intermediate

Size: 3–6 months

Materials

- Red Heart® baby fingering weight yarn (1¾ oz per skein): 9 skeins MC, 2 skeins CC
- Size F/5 crochet hook
- 4 stitch markers

Gauge: 5 dc = 1"

To save time, take time to check gauge.

Pattern Notes: Turning ch-3 counts as first dc throughout.

Join rnds with a sl st unless otherwise indicated.

Pattern Stitch

Shell: 5 dc in indicated st.

Blanket

Row 1: With MC, ch 145, 4 dc in 4th ch from hook, *sk 2 chs, sc in next ch **, sk next 2 chs, 5 dc in next ch, rep from * across, ending last rep at **, ch 3, turn. (24 shells)

Row 2: 4 dc in first sc, *sc in 3rd dc of next shell **, 5 dc in next sc, rep from * across, ending last rep at **, ch 3, turn.

Rows 3–12: Rep Row 2, ending with ch 1, turn at end of Row 12.

Row 13: Sc in each st across, ch 3, turn.

Row 14: Dc in each sc across, ch 1, turn.

Row 15: Sc in each dc across, ch 3, turn.

Row 16: 4 dc in first sc, *sk next 2 sc, sc in next sc, sk next 2 sc, 5 dc in next sc, rep from * across, ending with sc, ch 2, turn.

[Rep Rows 2–16] 3 times, rep Rows 3–12 once, do not turn.

Trim

Rnd 1: Sc evenly around blanket, working 4 sc in each corner st, 2 sc in each dc row and 1 sc in each sc row, sc in each st across top and in each ch of foundation ch, join in beg sc, ch 3, turn.

Rnd 2: 4 dc in first sc, *sk next 2 sc, sc in next sc, sk next 2 sc, 5 dc in next sc, rep from * around blanket, join in 3rd ch of turning ch-3, fasten off MC, attach CC, ch 1, turn.

Rnd 3: Sc in each st around blanket, working 4 sc in each corner st, join in beg sc, ch 3, turn.

Rnd 4: Dc in each sc around, working 3 dc in each corner, join in 3rd ch of turning ch-3, ch 1, turn.

Rnd 5: Sc in each dc around blanket, working 3 sc in each corner, join in beg sc, fasten off CC, attach MC, ch 3, turn.

Rnd 6: 4 dc in first sc, *sk next 2 sc **, sc in next sc, sk next 2 sc, 5 dc in next sc, rep from * around, ending last rep at **, join in 3rd ch of turning ch-3, fasten off MC, attach CC, ch 1, turn.

Rnd 7: Sc in each st, working 3 sc in 3rd dc in each shell around blanket, join in beg sc, fasten off.

Weave in loose ends. Apply fringe if desired.

Sweater

Row 1: Beg at yoke with MC, ch 13, place marker (in last ch made), ch 13, place marker, ch 29, place marker, ch 13, place marker, ch 15, sc in 2nd ch from hook and in each ch to first marker, 4 sc in marked ch st, *sc in each ch to next marker, 4 sc in marked ch st, rep from * across, move markers to 2nd sc of each 4-sc group, fasten off MC, attach CC, ch 1, turn. (94 sc)

Row 2: Sc in each st to first marker, *4 sc in marked st, sc in each sc to next marker, rep from * across, move markers to 2nd sc of each 4-sc group, ch 3, turn. (106 sc)

Row 3: Dc in each sc to first marker, *4 dc in marked st, dc in each sc to next marker, rep from * across, ch 1, move markers to 2nd dc of each 4-sc group. (118 dc)

Row 4: Sc in each dc to first marker, *4 sc in marked st, sc in each dc to next marker, rep from * across, fasten off CC, attach MC, ch 3, turn. (130 sc)

Row 5: 3 dc in first sc, *sk next 2 sc, sc in next sc **, sk next 2 sc, 5 dc in next sc, rep from * across, ending last rep at **, ending with sc, ch 2, turn. (21½ shells)

Row 6: 3 dc in first sc, *sc in 3rd dc in first shell **, 5 dc in sc, rep from * across, ending last rep at **, fasten off MC, attach CC, move markers to middle dc of shells directly above previously marked sts, ch 1, turn.

Rows 7–11: Rep Rows 2–6.

Rows 12 & 13: Rep Rows 2 and 3.

Row 14: Sc in each dc to first marker, sc in 2nd marked st for left underarm, sc in each dc to 3rd marked st, sc in 4th marked st for right underarm, sc in each dc to end of row, fasten off CC, attach MC, ch 3, turn.

Begin Sweater Body

Row 15: 3 dc in first sc, *sk next 2 sc, sc in next sc, sk next 2 sc, 5 dc in next sc, rep from * across, ending with sc, ch 3, turn.

Row 16: 3 dc in first sc, *sc in 3rd dc of next shell, 5 dc in next sc, rep from * across.

[Rep Row 16] 13 times, fasten off.

Weave in loose ends.

Neck Trim

Row 1: With WS facing, attach MC in first ch of foundation ch (right corner of neck), ch 1, sc in same ch, sc in each ch to left corner, ch 1, turn.

Row 2: Sc in each sc to right corner, fasten off MC, attach CC, ch 1, turn.

Rnd 3: Sc evenly around sweater, working 3 sc in each corner st, 1 sc in each sc row and 2 sc in each dc row, join in beg sc, turn.

Rnd 4: Ch 3, 2 dc in first sc, dc in each sc around sweater, working 3 dc in 2nd sc of each 3-sc corner group, join in 3rd ch of beg ch-3, ch 1, turn.

Rnd 5: Sc in each of first 3 dc, *dec 1, sc in each of next 3 dc, rep from * to left corner, sc in each dc around sweater, join in beg sc, fasten off CC, attach MC, ch 3, turn.

Rnd 6: 4 dc in first sc, *sk next 2 sc, sc in next sc, sk next 2 sc, 5 dc in next sc, rep from * around sweater, fasten off.

Work in loose ends.

With 1 strand each color, ch 100. Weave ch through Rnd 3 of neck trim around sweater neck; gather to fit and tie bow. Make 2

(1") pompons with a strand of each color of yarn; attach pompon to each end of chain.

Sleeve

Rnd 1: Attach CC in underarm st, sc in each dc around sleeve (count sc to get same number on each sleeve), join in beg sc, fasten off CC, attach MC, ch 3, turn. (42 sc)

Rnd 2: 4 dc in beg sc, *sk 2 sc, sc in next sc, sk next 2 sc, 5 dc in next sc, rep from * across, ending with sc, join in 3rd ch of turning ch-3, ch 3, turn.

Rnds 3–13: 4 dc in first sc, *sc in 3rd dc of next shell, 5 dc in next sc, rep from * across, join in 3rd ch of turning ch-3, ch 3, turn, fasten off MC at end of Rnd 13, attach CC, ch 1, turn.

Rnd 14: Sc in each st around sleeve, join in beg sc, ch 3, turn.

Rnd 15: Dc in each sc around sleeve, join in 3rd ch of turning ch-3, ch 1, turn.

Rnd 16: Sc in each of first 2 dc, *dec 1, dc in each of next 2 sc, rep from * around sleeve, fasten off CC, attach MC, ch 3, turn.

Rnd 17: 4 dc in first sc, *sk next sc, sc in next sc, sk next sc, 5 dc in next sc, rep from * around sleeve, join in 3rd ch of turning ch-3, ch 1, turn.

Rnd 18: Sc in first st, dec 1, *sc in next st, dec 1, rep from * around sleeve, join in beg sc, fasten off.

Work in loose ends.

With CC, ch 50. Weave through dc rnd of trim; gather to fit and tie in a bow. Make 4 (¾") pompons with a strand of each color of yarn; attach 1 pompon to each end of ch.

Booties (*Make 2*)

Row 1: With MC, ch 29, sc in 2nd ch from hook and in each rem ch across, ch 3, turn. (28 sc)

Row 2: 4 dc in first sc, *sk next 2 sc, sc in next sc **, sk next 2 sc, 5 dc in next sc, rep from * across (5 shells), ending last rep at **, ch 3, turn.

Rows 3–16: 4 dc in sc, *sc in 3rd dc of next shell **, 5 dc in next sc, rep from * across, ending last rep at **, ch 3, turn, at end of Row 16, sc down left side, fasten off.

Work in loose ends. Fold square into triangle with right sides tog.

Beg at right corner, sc 2 sides tog, 3 sc in left corner (bootie sole), sc in each of next 11 sts, sl st in next st (forms bootie back), fasten off.

Work in loose ends. Turn bootie right side out.

Trim

Row 1: Attach CC in top of back seam, sc around pointed edge to beg sc, join in beg sc, ch 3, turn.

Row 2: Dc in each sc around top of bootie, working 3 dc in corner st, join in 3rd ch of turning ch-3, ch 1, turn.

Row 3: Sc in each dc around trim, join in beg sc, fasten off.

Work in loose ends. Fold point down to form bootie front.

With CC, ch 60. Weave through dc row of trim; gather to fit and tie in bow. Make 4 (1") pompons with a strand of each color of yarn; attach pompon to each end of ch.

Cap

Rnd 1: With MC, ch 64, join in beg ch, ch 1, turn.

Rnd 2: Sc in each ch around, join in beg sc, ch 1, turn.

Rnds 3–6: Rep Rnd 2, at the end of Rnd 6, ch 3, turn.

Rnd 7: 4 dc in first sc, *sk next sc, sc in next sc **, sk next sc, 5 dc in next sc, rep from * around, ending last rep at **, join in 3rd ch of turning ch-3, ch 3, turn.

Rnd 8: 4 dc in first sc, *sc in 3rd dc of next shell **, 5 dc in next sc, rep from * around, ending last rep at **, join in 3rd ch of turning ch-3, ch 3, turn.

Rnds 9 & 10: Rep Rnd 8, at end of Rnd 10, ch 1, turn.

Rnd 11: Sc in each st around cap, join in beg sc, ch 3, turn. (96 sc)

Rnd 12: Dc in each sc around, join in 3rd ch of beg ch-3, ch 1, turn.

Rnd 13: Sc in each dc around, join in beg sc, ch 1, turn.

Rnd 14: Sc in first sc, *dec 1, sc in next sc, rep from * around, join in beg sc, ch 1, turn. (64 sts)

Rnd 15: Rep Rnd 14, ending with sc in last sc, ch 1, turn. (43 sc)

Rnd 16: Sc in first sc, *sc in each of next 2 sc **, dec 1, rep from * around, ending last rep at **, join in beg sc, ch 1, turn. (33 sc)

Rnd 17: Sc in each sc around, join in beg sc, ch 1, turn.

Rnd 18: Rep Row 14. (22 sts)

Rnd 19: Sc in first sc, *dec 1, rep from * around, join in beg sc, ch 1, turn. (11 sts)

Rnd 20: Rep Rnd 19, ending with sc in last sc, join in beg sc, do not ch 1, turn, fasten off, leaving 6" length.

Gather rem 6 sts; anchor yarn.

Weave in loose ends.

Trim

Rnd 1: Attach CC in first sc in cap front, sc in each ch st across, join in beg sc, ch 1, turn.

Rnd 2: Sc in front lp only of each sc around cap front, join in beg sc, ch 3, turn.

Rnd 3: 4 dc in first sc, *sk next sc, sc in next sc, sk next sc, 5 dc in next sc, rep from * around cap, ending with sc, join in 3rd ch of turning ch-3, ch 3, turn.

Rnd 4: 4 dc in sc, *sc in 3rd dc in next shell, 5 dc in next sc, rep from * across, join in 3rd ch of turning ch-3, ch 3, turn.

Rnd 5: Rep Rnd 4, fasten off CC, attach MC, ch 1, turn.

Rnd 6: Sc in each st around cap, fasten off.

Weave in loose ends. Fold cap in half, place marker in 12th st on each side of cap center.

Earflap *(Make 2)*

Row 1: Attach MC in 12th sc, sc in first sc, sc in each of next 7 sc, ch 1, turn.

Row 2: Sc in each sc across, ch 1, turn.

Rows 3–5: Rep Row 2.

Row 6: Sc in first sc, dec 1 sc, sc in each of next 2 sc, dec 1 sc, sc in last sc, ch 1, turn.

Row 7: Sc in each sc across, ch 1, turn.

Row 8: [Sc, dec 1 sc] twice, ch 1, turn.

Row 9: Sc in first sc, dec 1, sc in last sc, fasten off.

Weave in loose ends.

With RS facing, attach CC at right side of earflap, sc evenly around earflap, fasten off.

Weave in loose ends. Working with 1 strand each MC and CC, attach yarn at end of earflap, ch 40, fasten off.

Make 2 (1") pompons with a strand of each color of yarn; attach 1 pompon to each end of ch.

Make a 2" pompon with a strand of each color of yarn; attach to top of cap.

—Designed by Alice Hyche

Heart Blanket

Shown on page 90

Experience Level: Intermediate

Size: Approximately 37" x 46"

Materials

- Bernat® Club Classic® DK cotton/acrylic blend yarn (50 grams/130 yds per ball): 9 balls cream #800 (MC) and 4 balls melon tint #803 (CC)
- Size G/6 crochet hook
- Size 7 steel crochet hook or size needed to obtain gauge
- 4 yds ½"-wide cream satin ribbon
- 16 (1") lilac ribbon roses with leaves
- 16 (1") cream ribbon roses with leaves
- Tapestry needle

Gauge: 16 sts and 9 rows = 4" with larger hook

To save time, take time to check gauge.

Pattern Note: Join rnds with a sl st unless otherwise stated.

Pattern Stitches

Sc3tog: [Insert hook in next st, yo and draw up lp] 3 times, yo and draw through all 4 lps on hook.

Puff st: [Yo, insert hook in ch sp, yo and draw up lp] 4 times, yo and draw through all 9 lps on hook, ch 1 to close st.

Afghan

Row 1: With larger hook and MC, ch 119, dc in 3rd ch from hook, dc in each ch across, ch 2, turn. (117 sts)

Row 2: Dc in each dc across, ch 2, turn.

Rows 3 & 4: Rep Row 2.

Row 5: Dc in each of first 10 dc, [ch 1, sk next st, dc in each of next 11 sts] rep across to last 11 dc, ch 1, sk next dc, dc in each of last 10 dc, ch 2, turn.

Row 6: Dc in each of first 8 dc, [ch 1, sk next dc, dc in next dc, puff st in next ch sp, dc in next dc, ch 1, sk next dc, dc in each of next 7 dc] rep across to last dc, dc in last dc, ch 2, turn.

Row 7: Dc in each of first 8 dc, [dc in next ch sp, dc in next dc, ch 1, sk next puff st, dc in next dc, dc in next ch sp, dc in each of next 7 dc] rep across to last dc, dc in last dc, ch 2, turn.

Row 8: Dc in each of first 10 dc, [dc in next ch sp, dc in each of next 11 dc] rep across to last 11 sts, dc in next ch sp, dc in each of last 10 dc, ch 2, turn.

Rows 9 & 10: Rep Row 2.

Row 11: Dc in each of first 4 dc, [ch 1, sk next st, dc in each of next 11 dc] rep across to last 5 dc, ch 1, sk next dc, dc in each of last 4 dc, ch 2, turn.

Row 12: Dc in each of first 2 dc, [ch 1, sk next dc, dc in next dc, puff st in next ch sp, dc in next dc, ch 1, sk next dc, dc in each of next 7 dc] rep across to last 7 sts, ch 1, sk next dc, dc in next dc, puff st in next ch sp, dc in next dc, ch 1, sk next dc, dc in each of last 2 dc, ch 2, turn.

Row 13: Dc in each of first 2 dc, [dc in next ch sp, dc in next dc, ch 1, sk next puff st, dc in next dc, dc in next ch sp, dc in each of next 7 dc] rep across to last 7 sts, dc in next ch sp, dc in next dc, ch 1, sk next puff st, dc in next dc, dc in next ch sp, dc in each of last 2 dc, ch 2, turn.

Row 14: Dc in each of first 4 dc, [dc in next ch sp, dc in each of next 11 dc] rep across to last 5 sts, dc in next ch sp, dc in each of last 4 dc, ch 2, turn.

Rows 15–74: Rep Rows 3–14.

Rows 75–82: Rep Rows 3–10.

Rows 83 & 84: Rep Row 2, fasten off at end of Row 84.

Edging

Rnd 1: With MC and smaller hook, RS facing, sc evenly around outer edge, working 2 dc in side of each dc row and 3 sc in each corner, join in beg sc.

Rnd 2: Ch 2, sk next sc, dc in next sc, [ch 1, sk next sc, dc in next sc] rep around, working [dc, ch 1, dc] in each corner st, join in 2nd ch of beg ch-2.

Rnd 3: Ch 1, sc in each st and ch sp around, working 3 sc in each corner ch-1 sp, fasten off.

Hearts *(Make 32)*

Rnd 1: With smaller hook and CC, ch 15, dc in 3rd ch from hook, 2 dc in same st, dc in each of next 4 chs, insert hook in next ch, yo and draw up lp, sk next ch, insert hook in next ch, yo and draw up lp, yo and draw through all 3 lps on hook, dc in each of next 4 chs, 3 dc in last ch, working on opposite side of beg ch, dc in each of next 5 chs, 3 dc in next ch, dc in each of next 5 chs, sk last ch, join in top of beg dc.

Rnd 2: Ch 2, dc in next st, 3 dc in next dc, dc in each of next 4 dc, sc3tog over next 3 sts, dc in each of next 4 dc, 3 dc in next dc, dc in each of next 7 dc, 3 dc in next dc, dc in each of next 6 dc, join in 2nd ch of beg ch-2.

Rnd 3: Ch 2, 3 dc in next dc, dc in next dc, 3 dc in next dc, dc in each of next 4 dc, sc3tog over next 3 sts, dc in each of next 4 dc, 3 dc in next dc, dc in next dc, 3 dc in next dc, dc in each of next 7 dc, 3 dc in next dc, dc in each of next 7 dc, join in beg dc.

Rnd 4: Ch 1, sc in same st, sc in next st, 2 sc in each of next 5 dc, sc in each of next 4 dc, sl st in each of next 3 sts, sc in each of next 4 dc, 2 sc in each of next 5 dc, sc in each of next 9 dc, [sc, ch 1, sc] in next dc, sc in each of next 8 dc, join in beg sc, fasten off.

Joining hearts

(Make 2 strips of 7 hearts & 2 strips of 9 hearts each)

With CC and tapestry ndl, join hearts tog in strips by sewing edge-to-edge in 10th, 11th, 12th and 13th sts (counted down from center of heart along side).

Tack strip of 7 hearts to each end of afghan, and strip of 9 hearts to each side of afghan at each rounded hump.

Join hearts at corners by easing tog and sewing in place.

Finishing

Weave ribbon through filet holes around outer edge of blanket; sew ends tog on WS.

Sew 1 ribbon rose in center of each heart, alternating lavender and cream colors.

— Designed by Women of Design

Love Spoken Here

Shown on page 91

Experience Level: Intermediate

Size: 24" wide x 17" high without tassels and rod loops

Materials

- DMC® Cebelia® crochet cotton size 10 (50 grams per ball): 2 balls white
- Size 7 steel hook
- 3½" piece of cardboard

Gauge: 10 dc and 3 rows = 1"

To save time, take time to check gauge.

Pattern Notes: For chart, work Row 1 and all odd-numbered rows from right to left. Work even-numbered rows from left to right.

To inc at beg of row: Ch 5, dc in 4th ch from hook and in each of next ch.

To inc at end of row: After last dc of row, [yo, draw up a lp at base of last st, yo and draw through 1 lp on hook, {yo and draw through 2 lps on hook} twice] 2 times.

To dec at beg of row: Sl st in each of first 4 sts, ch 3 (counts as first dc).

To dec at end of row: Leave last 3 sts unworked.

Work 2 dc in ch-2 sp to fill in sp.

Pattern Stitch

2-tr cluster (2-tr cl): Keeping last lp of each tr on hook, 2 tr in same st, yo and draw through all 3 lps on hook.

Wall Hanging

Row 1: Ch 147, dc in 4th ch from hook and in each ch

across, ch 5, turn.

Row 2: Sk first 3 dc, dc in next dc, [ch 2, sk 2 dc, dc in next dc] rep across, inc at end of row, ch 5, turn.

Row 3: Dc in 4th ch from hook and in each of next 2 chs, dc in next dc, [ch 2, dc in next dc] rep across, ch 5, turn.

Follow chart, inc and dec as indicated, do not fasten off after last row.

Lower Scalloped Edge

With RS facing, attach in lower right-hand corner, *[ch 5, 2-tr cl in 5th ch from hook, sc in corner st of next row] 7 times, ch 5, sc in next corner st (the ch-5 will be over the 2 even rows on lower end of scallop), [ch 5, 2-tr cl in 5th ch from hook, sc in center st of next 2 even rows] 7 times, rep from * across, fasten off.

Rod Loops

Attach cotton with sc in top right-hand corner st, ch 15, 2 sc over side of dc, 3 sc in each of next 3 sps, ch 15, [3 sc in each of next 4 sps, ch 15] rep across, 2 sc over end dc, ch 15, sl st in corner st, fasten off.

Tassels *(Make 5)*

Wrap thread 25 times around cardboard. Cut 1 end; tie over free ch-5 at lower end of each scallop.

—Designed by Lucille LaFlamme

Thread Tip

When making a thread motif design that is difficult to follow or crochet, try making it out of worsted weight yarn first. That will enable you to see the stitches better and practice the motif before using the more difficult thread.

STITCH KEY

☐ Space
◙ Dc block

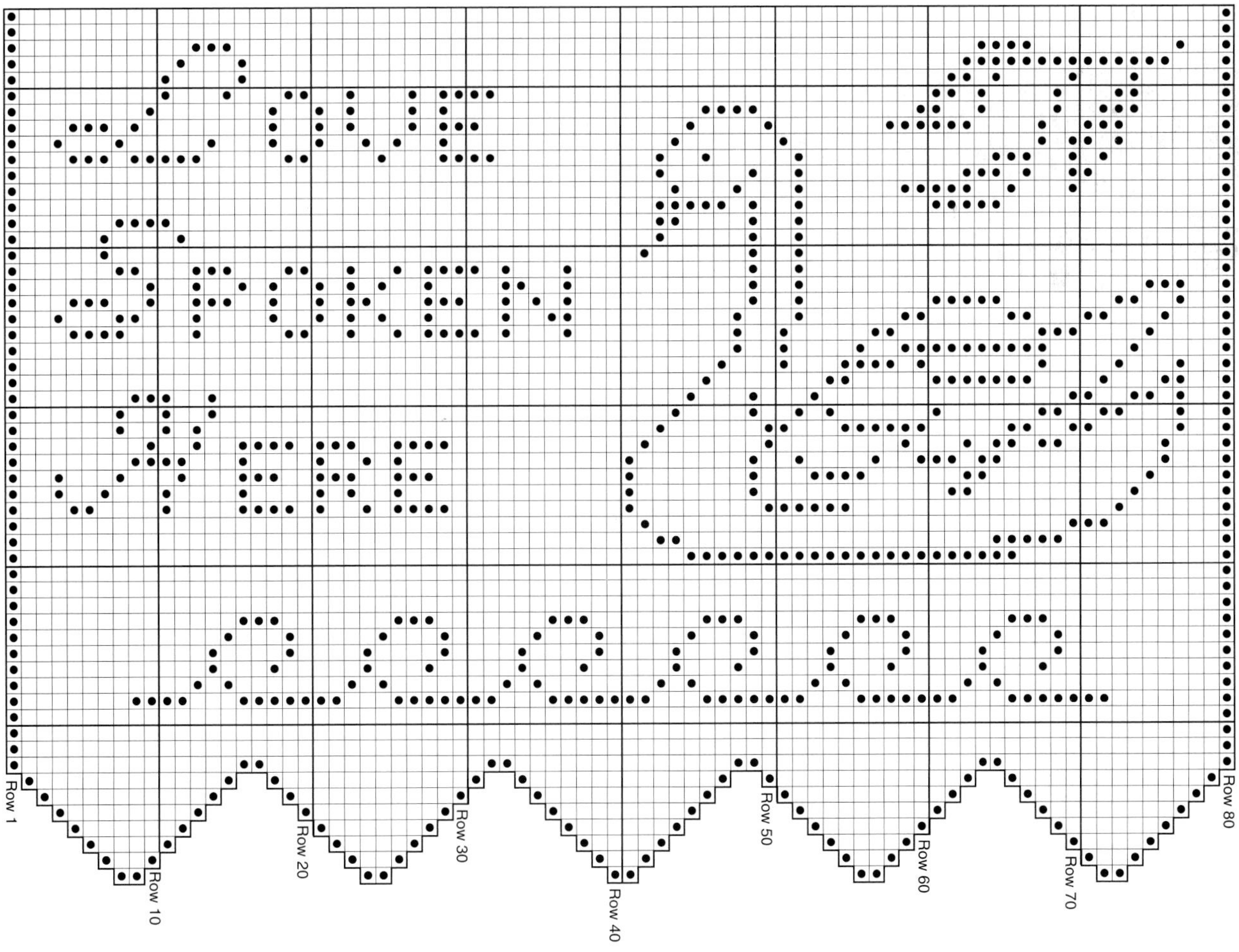

Row 1 · Row 10 · Row 20 · Row 30 · Row 40 · Row 50 · Row 60 · Row 70 · Row 80

Christmas Traditions

Every family has cherished traditions that help to make the holidays special. A tree trimmed with delicate ornaments, pretty stockings hung from the mantel, handsome tree skirts circling the tree and other crocheted accents will bring classic elegance to your holiday decor.

Give your holiday decor an elegant Victorian feel with this lovely Victorian Set of matching stocking and tree skirt. Instructions begin on page 124.

Little Angel (below) makes an exquisite treetop angel or mantel decoration. Give your holiday entertaining a cheerful touch with a complete set of red-and-green place mats and napkin rings included in this Festive Table Set (right). Instructions on pages 125–127.

Drape this gorgeous Snowdrops tablecloth (left) over a table for serving a fanciful spread. Stitched with bright crochet cotton and metallic thread, two easy-to-crochet Floral Ornaments (right and below) make special gifts. Instructions on pages 127–130.

Three lacy ornaments including a fan, suncatcher and bow comprise this classic set of Dainty Ornaments (below). Angels give your home a blessing on this heirloom-quality filet piece, Angels' Blessing (right). Instructions on pages 130–134.

For a more relaxed, country decorating theme, Country Hearts tree skirt (right) is the perfect addition to your holiday decorating. A ruffled edging gives it just a touch of frill. *Instructions begin on page 135.*

Victorian Set

Shown on page 114

Experience Level: Intermediate

Size

Tree skirt panel: Approximately 5¼" at top; 17" from top to bottom

Tree skirt circumference: 156"

Stocking: 6" across x 16" long

Materials

- Lion Brand Jiffy® yarn (3 oz/ 135 yds per skein): 14 skeins forest green #131 (MC)
- Lion Brand Jamie® yarn (1.75 oz/196 yds per skein): 6 skeins white #200 (CC)
- Size K/10½ afghan hook
- Size H/8 crochet hook or size needed to obtain gauge
- 7 pairs hooks-and-eyes
- 5¾ yds ⅜"-wide red ribbon with metallic edging
- 8½ yds ⅛"-wide red ribbon with metallic edging
- 4¾ yds gold-red-and-green Christmas cord
- ⅜ yd metallic plaid fabric for rosettes
- 24 (10mm) gold jingle bells
- 3 (15mm) gold jingle bells
- Sewing needle and thread
- 9 safety pins

Gauge: 17 sts and 21 rows = 5" with size K10½ afghan hook over afghan knit st

To save time, take time to check gauge.

Tree Skirt

Panel *(Make 8)*

With afghan hook and MC, ch 18, draw up a lp in 2nd ch from hook and in each ch across, keeping all lps on hook, yo and draw through 1 lp, [yo and draw through 2 lps] rep across (last lp counts as first st of next row).

Row 1 (afghan knit st): Draw up a lp in center of each lp across, keeping all lps on hook, yo and draw through 1 lp, [yo and draw through 2 lps] rep across (last lp counts as first st of next row).

Row 2: Work afghan knit st over 18 sts.

Row 3: Continuing in afghan knit st, inc 1 st at each end.

Rows 4 & 5: Work afghan knit st evenly across.

Rows 6–72: Rep Rows 3–5 until piece meas 17", ending with Row 3. (66 sts in Row 72)

Note: *Do not sl st or sc into last row.*

Joining

Sew pieces tog to form a circle, leaving 1 seam unsewn.

Lower Edging

Bottom

Row 1: With crochet hook and CC, beg at unsewn seam edge at right-hand side of work with RS facing, sc in each st across bottom edge, ch 3, turn.

Row 2 (WS): Ch 3 (counts as first dc), dc in front lp (of WS) of first sc, [2 dc in front lp of next sc] rep across, turn.

Row 3 (RS): Sl st to sp between first and 2nd dc, ch 3, dc in same sp, [sk 2 dc, 2 dc in next sp between dc] rep across, turn.

Picot edging

Row 4 (WS): [Ch 2, sl st in 2nd ch from hook, sl st in each of next 2 dc] rep across, ending with sl st in last dc, fasten off.

Top

Row 1: Attach CC at edge of sc row with RS facing, dc across sc row on rem front lp of each sc, with skirt away from you and bottom lower edge toward you, ch 3, turn.

Rows 2–4: Rep Rows 2–4 of Bottom Lower Edging.

Upper Edging

Bottom

Row 1: With crochet hook and CC, beg at unsewn seam, sc across top edge of skirt, ch 3, turn.

Rows 2–4: Rep Rows 2–4 of Bottom Lower Edging.

Top

Row 1: Attach CC at edge of sc row with RS facing, dc across sc row on rem front lp of each sc, ch 3, turn.

Rows 2–4: Rep Rows 2–4 of top lower edging.

Unsewn Seam Edging

With crochet hook and MC, sc evenly across unsewn seam edge, fasten off.

Rep for rem unsewn seam.

Finishing

Sew hooks-and-eyes evenly sp on underside of unsewn seam edges.

Weave 4½ yds of ⅜"-wide ribbon through dc row of lower edging, working over 2 and under 1 dc. Sew ends down at unsewn edge. Sew inner edge of dc row to skirt edge to hold down.

Weave 2½ yds of ⅛"-wide ribbon through dc sts of upper edging; pull to gather; tie.

Rosettes

Cut plaid fabric into 8 (3" x 13½") pieces. Sew seam at short edge to form a tube. Fold tube lengthwise with WS inside; gather raw inside edge tightly to form rosette. Fasten securely.

Rosette Trim

Cut red-green-and gold cord into 8 (15¾") pieces. Knot ends of cord; for a 2-lp bow shape and sew at rosette center (Fig. 1).

FIG. 1
Two Loop
Bow Shape

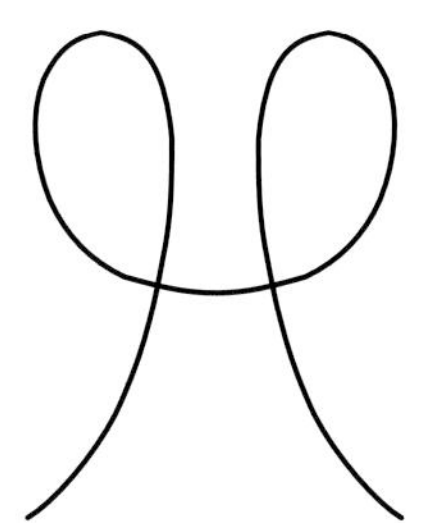

Cut 8 (27") pieces ⅛"-wide ribbon; form each into a 4-lp bow shape and sew over cord. Sew 3 (10mm) bells in center.

Pin rosettes on lower edging with safety pins at each seam. Remove before laundering tree skirt.

Stocking

Beg at top with afghan hook and MC, ch 40, draw up a lp in 2nd ch from hook and in each ch across, keeping all lps on hook, yo and draw through 1 lp, [yo and draw through 2 lps] rep across (last lp counts as first st of next row.

Work evenly in afghan knit st (see Row 1 of Tree Skirt) until piece measures 9".

Heel Shaping

Draw up a lp in each of next 4 sts (last lp from previous row counts as first st), insert hook first in next st, then in next st, draw up 1 lp through both sts (1-st dec), draw up a lp in next st.

Work 2nd part of Row 1 over rem 7 sts.

Continue to dec over first half of heel until 2 sts rem, fasten off.

Work heel shaping over last 8 sts of stocking, mirroring shaping.

Foot

Work over first 2 sts, draw up a total of 6 lps over side of first half of heel, draw up a lp over center 24 sts, draw up a total of 6 lps over side of 2nd half of heel, work over rem 2 sts. (40 sts)

*Work over first 8 sts, work 2 tog, work across to within last 10 sts, work 2 tog, work across rem 8 sts.

Work 1 row even *. Work from * to * once.

Work even over rem 36 sts until foot meas 4½" from heel.

Toe Shaping

Divide sts in half with 18 sts for each side of foot. Work 1-st dec over first 2 sts, draw up a lp in next 14 sts, work 1-st dec over next 2 sts (do not work over rem 18 sts).

Dec 1 st at each end of each row until 6 sts rem, fasten off.

Attach MC in 19th st of last long row, work as for other side, when 6 sts rem, with WS facing, sl st this side to other side to join end of toe.

Edging

Work as for Tree Skirt Upper Edging.

Finishing

Sew back seam and front toe seam. Sew edging back seam.

Weave ⅜"-wide ribbon through dc row of edging, as for Tree Skirt. Cut length to fit.

Rosette

Make rosette from 3½" x 15" piece of plaid fabric in same manner as for Tree Skirt.

Rosette trim

Make a 4-lp bow shape from 1¼ yds red-gold-and-green cord

FIG. 2
Four Loop
Bow Shape

(Fig. 2); sew in center of rosette.

Make a 4-lp bow shape with rem ⅜"-wide ribbon; sew over cord.

Sew 3 (15 mm) jingle bells to center of rosette. Pin rosette to edge of stocking with safety pin.

Hanger

With crochet hook, attach MC at top edge of back seam below edging, ch 12, sl st to attaching sp, fasten off.

—Designed by Michele Maks Thompson courtesy of Designs for America

Little Angel

Shown on page 116

Experience Level: Advanced beginner

Size: Approximately 5½" tall x 4¼" in diameter

Materials

- J. & P. Coats South Maid® crochet cotton size 10 (350 yds per ball): 1 ball cream #430
- Cotton ball
- Funnel
- Plastic wrap
- Size 5 steel crochet hook
- Fabric stiffener
- Hot-glue gun

- Curly doll hair
- 16" ½"-wide mauve feather-edged ribbon
- 5" gold cord
- 6 (¾"-diameter) mauve silk flowers with leaves
- 12" length gold metallic thread

Gauge: Work evenly and consistently

Pattern Note: Join rnds with a sl st unless otherwise stated.

Angel

Rnd 1: Beg at head, ch 3, 19 hdc in first ch, join in 2nd ch of beg ch-3. (20 hdc)

Rnds 2–7: Ch 2 (counts as first hdc), hdc in each st around, join in 2nd ch of beg ch-2.

Rnd 8: Ch 1, sc in same sp, [sk 1 st, sc in next st] rep around, join in beg sc. (10 sc)

Rnd 9: Ch 4 (counts as first dc, ch 1), dc, ch 1 in same sp, [dc, ch 1] twice in each st around, join in 3rd ch of beg ch-4. (40 sts)

Rnd 10: Ch 3 (counts as first dc), dc in each of next 4 sts, [sk 1 st, dc in next st, ch 8, sl st in dc just made, dc in next st, dc in next st, ch 10, sl st in dc just made, dc in next st, dc in next st, ch 12, sl st in dc just made, dc in next st, dc in next st, ch 10, sl st in dc just made, dc in next st, dc in next st, ch 8, sl st in dc just made, dc in next st, sk 1 st], dc in each of next 8 sts, rep between [] once, dc in each of last 3 sts, join in 3rd ch of beg ch-3.

Rnd 11: Ch 1, sc in same sp, sc in each of next 4 sts, [{hdc, ch 2} in each of next 7 chs of ch-8 lp, hdc in last ch, sl st in center dc between lps, {hdc, ch 2} in each of next 9 chs of ch-10 lp, hdc in last ch, sl st in center dc between lps, {hdc, ch 2} in each of next 11 chs of ch-12 lp, hdc in last ch, sl st in center dc between lps, {hdc, ch 2} in each of next 9 chs of ch-10 lp, hdc in last ch, sl st in center dc between lps, {hdc, ch 2} in each of next 7 chs of ch-8 lp, hdc in last ch, sk next dc], sc in each of next 8 dc, rep between [] once, sc in each of last 4 dc, join in beg sc.

Rnd 12: Ch 1, sc in same sp, sc in each of next 3 sts, sk all lps, sc in front lp of each of next 8 sc, sk lps, sc in each of last 4 sc, join in beg sc.

Rnd 13: Ch 3 (counts as first dc), dc in each st around, join in 3rd ch of beg ch-3. (16 dc)

Rnd 14: Ch 5 (counts as first dc, ch 2), [dc, ch 2] in each st around, join in 3rd ch of beg ch-5.

Rnd 15: Ch 2 (counts as first hdc), hdc in each st around, join in 2nd ch of beg ch-2. (48 hdc)

Rnd 16: Ch 3 (counts as first dc), dc in next st, [ch 2, sk 1 st, dc in each of next 2 sts] rep around, ch 2, join in 3rd ch of beg ch-3.

Rnd 17: Sl st to first ch of next ch-2 sp, ch 3 (counts as first dc), dc in next ch, [ch 2, sk 2 dc, dc in each of next 2 chs] rep around, ch 2, join in 3rd ch of beg ch-3.

Rnd 18: Sl st to first ch of next ch-2 sp, ch 3 (counts as first dc), dc in next ch, [ch 4, sk 2 dc, dc in each of next 2 chs] rep around, ch 4, join in 3rd ch of beg ch-3.

Rnd 19: Sl st to 2nd ch of next ch-4 sp, ch 3 (counts as first dc), dc in next ch, [ch 12, sl st in 11th ch from hook, ch 2, dc in 2nd and 3rd chs of next ch-4 sp] rep around, ending last rep with sl st in 11th ch from hook, join in 3rd ch of beg ch-3.

Rnd 20: Ch 1, sc in same sp, sc in next dc, [{hdc, ch 2} in each of first 9 chs of ch-10 lp}, hdc in last ch, sc in each of next 2 dc] rep around, join in beg sc, fasten off.

Finishing

Insert cotton ball into head; cinch neck.

Cover funnel with plastic wrap. Stiffen angel; place over funnel to dry, shaping wings and ruffle.

Apply doll hair according to manufacturer's instructions. Shape gold cord into ring; glue ends. Glue on top of head over hair, as shown in photo. Glue 1 silk flower over cord.

Weave length of mauve ribbon through Rnd 18; trim ends and secure with glue on underside of skirt.

Glue silk flowers evenly sp around skirt above ribbon.

Wrap rem ribbon around waist; trim ends and secure with glue at back.

Thread gold metallic thread through body opening under wings. Knot ends to form hanging lp.

—Designed by Jo Ann Maxwell

Festive Table Set

Shown on page 117

Experience Level: Beginner

Size

Place Mat: Approximately 11" x 16¼"

Napkin Ring: Approximately 2" in diameter x 2½" tall

Materials

- Red Heart® Classic™ 4-ply

acrylic worsted weight yarn (3½ oz per skein): 3 skeins each cherry red #912 and paddy green #686

- Size G/6 crochet hook or size needed to obtain gauge
- Yarn needle

Gauge: 5 sts = 1"; 5 rows = 2"

To save time, take time to check gauge.

Pattern Note: Join rnds with a sl st unless otherwise stated.

Place Mat

Row 1: With cherry red yarn, ch 62, sc in 2nd ch from hook and in each rem ch across, ch 1, turn. (61 sc)

Row 2: Sc in each sc across, ch 3, turn.

Row 3: Sk first sc, dc in each of next 3 sc, dc in sk sc, [sk next sc, dc in next 3 sc, dc in sk sc] 14 times, ch 1, turn.

Row 4: Sc in each st across, fasten off.

Rows 5–28: Attach paddy green yarn, [rep Rows 2–4] 8 times, alternating colors, ending with red stripe. (5 cherry red stripes; 4 paddy green stripes)

Border

Rnd 1: Attach paddy green yarn in any st, sc in each st around, working 4 sc in each corner st, join in beg sc, ch 1, turn.

Rnd 2: Sc in each sc around, working 4 sc in each corner st, join in beg sc, ch 3, turn.

Rnd 3: Sk first sc, *dc in each of next 3 sc, dc in sk sc, sk next sc, rep from * around, join in 3rd ch of beg ch-3, ch 1, turn.

Rnd 4: Sc in each st around, working 4 sc in each corner st, join in beg sc, ch 1, turn.

Rnd 5: Rep Row 4, ending with ch 3, turn.

Rnd 6: 2 dc in first sc, sk next sc, *3 dc in next sc, sk next sc, rep from * around, join in 3rd ch of turning ch-3, fasten off.

Weave in loose ends.

Napkin Ring

Row 1: With cherry red yarn, ch 26, sc in 2nd ch from hook, sc in each rem ch across, ch 1, turn.

Row 2: Sc in each sc across, ch 3, turn.

Row 3: Sk first sc, dc in each of next 3 sc, dc in sk sc, [sk next sc, dc in next 3 sc, dc in sk sc] 5 times, ch 1, turn. (6 cross-st groups)

Row 4: Sc in each sc across, ch 1, turn.

Row 5: Rep Row 4.

Border

Row 1: Attach paddy green yarn in bottom left corner, ch 1, sc in each st around sides and ends, working 2 sc in each corner st, ch 3, turn.

Row 2: 2 dc in first sc, sk next sc, *3 dc in next sc, sk next sc, rep from * across side, fasten off.

Attach paddy green yarn in upper right corner, rep Row 2 from * across side, fasten off.

Weave in loose ends.

With yarn ndl and paddy green yarn, st ends tog.

Bow

With paddy green yarn, ch 35, fasten off.

Weave through cross-st sps at seam; tie in bow.

— Designed by Alice Hyche

Snowdrops

Shown on page 118

Experience Level: Intermediate

Size: 32" excluding fringe

Materials

- DMC® Cebelia® crochet cotton size 10 (50 grams per ball): 3 balls white
- Size 7 steel crochet hook
- 5" piece cardboard

Gauge: Rnds 1–3 of snowflake motif = 2½"

Pattern Note: Join rnds with a sl st unless otherwise stated.

Pattern Stitches

2-dc cluster (2-dc cl): Keeping last lp of each dc on hook, 2 dc in ring, yo, draw through all 3 lps on hook.

3-dc cluster (3-dc cl): Keeping last lp of each dc on hook, 3 dc in ring, yo, draw through all 4 lps on hook.

Trtr: Yo 4 times, insert hook in st, yo, draw lp through, [yo, draw through 2 lps on hook] 5 times.

First Snowflake Motif

Rnd 1: Ch 6, join to form a ring, ch 3, 2-dc cl in ring, [ch 3, 3-dc cl in ring] 5 times, dc in top of first cl.

Rnd 2: Sl st in sp over dc just made, ch 10, [dc in next sp, ch 7] 5 times, join in 3rd ch of beg ch-10.

Rnd 3: Ch 1, *[sc, hdc, dc, 5 tr, dc, hdc, sc] in sp, ch 3, rep from * around, join in beg sc.

Rnd 4: Sl st to 3rd tr, ch 1, sc in same tr, *ch 5, [dc, ch 3, dc] in ch-3 sp, ch 5, sc in 3rd tr of next tr group, rep from * around, ending with ch 2, dc in beg sc.

Rnd 5: Sc in sp over dc just made, [ch 7, sc in next ch-5 sp, ch 5, sc in ch-3 sp, ch 4, sl st in sc (picot), ch 5, sc in next ch-5 sp] rep around, join in beg sc.

Rnd 6: Sl st in each of next 4 chs, ch 7, tr in same ch as last sl st, ch 4, sl st in tr (picot), ch 3, tr in same ch, *ch 7, sc in next picot, ch 7, [tr, ch 3, tr, picot, ch 3, tr] in 4th ch of ch-7 sp, rep from * around, ending with ch 7, sc in next picot, ch 7, join in 4th ch of beg ch-7, fasten off.

Second & Subsequent Snowflake Motifs

Rnds 1–5: Rep Rnds 1–5 for First Snowflake Motif.

Rnd 6 (Joining Rnd): Sl st in each of next 4 chs, ch 7, tr in same ch as sl st, ch 2, sl st in picot on previous motif, ch 2, sl st in tr just made on new motif to close joining picot, ch 3, tr in same ch, ch 7, sc in next picot, ch 7, [tr, ch 3, tr, joining picot in next free picot on previous motif, ch 3, tr] in 4th ch of ch-7 sp, *ch 7, sc in next picot, ch 7, [tr, ch 3, tr, picot, ch 3, tr] in 4th ch of ch-7 sp, rep from * around, ending with ch 7, sc in next picot, ch 7, join in 4th ch of beg ch-7, fasten off.

Join subsequent motifs in first free picot to right of previous joining, join in joined picot of 2 previous motifs, join in next free picot on just completed motif. Complete new motif as before.

Join 5 motifs around center motif.

Join 6th motif first to free picot on first motif, then in 2 joining picots on center motif, and last to the free picot on previous motif. Complete new motif as before.

Surrounding Border

Rnd 1: Attach cotton with sc in first free picot on any motif, *ch 9, [tr, ch 3, tr] in sc, ch 9, sc in next picot, ch 9, [trtr, ch 3, trtr] in next sc, ch 7, trtr in next tr, sk motif joining, trtr in next tr, ch 7, [trtr, ch 3, trtr] in next sc, ch 9, sc in next picot, rep from * around, join in beg sc.

Rnd 2: Ch 3, dc in each of next 45 sts, [sk 2 trtr sts, dc in each of next 67 sts] rep around, ending with sk 2 trtr sts, dc in each of last 21 sts, join in 3rd ch of beg ch-3. (67 dc in each scallop)

Rnd 3: Ch 1, sc in same st as sl st, [ch 9, sk 7 dc, sc in next dc] 5 times, *ch 11, sk 10 dc, sc in next dc, [ch 9, sk 7 dc, sc in next dc] 7 times, rep from * around, ending with ch 9, sk 7 dc, sc in next dc, ch 9, sk 7 dc, join in beg sc.

Rnd 4: Sl st in each of next 5 chs, ch 6, dc in same ch as sl st, [ch 5, {dc, ch 3, dc} in 5th ch of next ch-9 sp] 4 times, *ch 5, [dc, ch 3, dc] in 6th ch of ch-11 sp, [ch 5, {dc, ch 3, dc} in 5th ch of ch-9 sp] 7 times, rep from * around, ending with [ch 5, {dc, ch 3, dc} in 5th ch of ch-9 sp] twice, ch 5, join in 3rd ch of beg ch-6.

Rnd 5: Ch 6, dc in next dc, [ch 7, dc in next dc, ch 3, dc in next dc] rep around, ending with ch 7, join in 3rd ch of beg ch-6.

Rnd 6: Ch 3, dc in next dc, *ch 3, [dc, ch 3, dc] in 4th ch of ch-7, ch 3, [dc in next dc] twice, rep from * around, ending with ch 3, join in 3rd ch of beg ch-3.

Rnd 7: Sl st in dc, sl st in each of next 3 chs and in next dc, ch 6, dc in next dc, [ch 7, sk 2 dc, dc in next dc, ch 3, dc in next dc] rep around, ending with ch 7, join in 3rd ch of beg ch-6.

Rnd 8: Rep Rnd 6.

Rnd 9: Sl st in dc, sl st in each of next 3 chs and in next dc, ch 6, dc in next dc, [ch 9, sk 2 dc, dc in next dc, ch 3, dc in next dc] rep around, ending with ch 9, join in 3rd ch of beg ch-6.

Rnd 10: Ch 3, dc in next dc, *ch 4, [dc, ch 3, dc] in 5th ch of ch-9 sp, ch 4, [dc in next dc] twice, rep from * around, ending with ch 4, join in 3rd ch of beg ch-3.

Rnd 11: Sl st in dc, sl st in each of next 4 chs and in next dc, ch 6, dc in next dc, [ch 9, sk 2 dc, dc in next dc, ch 3, dc in next dc] rep around, ending with ch 9, join in 3rd ch of beg ch-6.

Rnd 12: Rep Rnd 10.

Rnd 13: Sl st in dc, sl st in each of next 4 chs and in next dc, ch 6, dc in next dc, [ch 11, sk 2 dc, dc in next dc, ch 3, dc in next dc] rep around, ending with ch 11, join in 3rd ch of beg ch-6.

Rnd 14: Ch 3, dc in next dc, *ch 5, [dc, ch 3, dc] in 6th ch of ch-11, ch 5, [dc in next dc] twice, rep from * around, ending with ch 5, join in 3rd ch of beg ch-3.

Rnd 15: Sl st in dc, sl st in each of next 5 chs and in next dc, ch 6, dc in next dc, [ch 13, sk 2 dc, dc in next dc, ch 3, dc in next dc] rep around, ending with ch 6, join in 3rd ch of beg ch-6.

Rnd 16: Ch 3, dc in next dc, *ch 6, [dc, ch 3, dc] in 7th ch of ch-13 sp, ch 6, dc in dc, dc in next dc, rep from * around, join in 3rd ch of beg ch-3.

Rnd 17: Sl st in dc, sl st in each of next 6 chs and in next dc, sl st in next sp, ch 3, 4 dc in same sp, [ch 13, 5 dc in next ch-3 sp] rep around, join in 3rd ch of beg ch-3.

Rnd 18: Sl st in each of next 2 dc, ch 3, [2 dc, ch 2, 3 dc] in same dc as last sl st, *ch 5, sc over next ch-13 sp, ch 5, sk 2 dc, [3 dc, ch 2, 3 dc] in next dc, rep from * around, ending with ch 5, sc over next ch-13 sp, ch 5, join in 3rd ch of beg ch-3.

Rnd 19: Sl st in each of next 2 dc and in next ch-2 sp, ch 3, [2 dc, ch 2, 3 dc] in same sp, *ch 6, sc in next sc, ch 6, [3 dc, ch 2, 3 dc] in next ch-2 sp, rep from * around, ending with ch 6, sc in next sc, join in 3rd ch of beg ch-3.

Rnd 20: Sl st in each of next 2 dc and in next ch-2 sp, ch 3, [2 dc, ch 2, 3 dc] in same sp, *ch 7, sc in next sc, ch 7, [3 dc, ch 2, 3 dc] in next ch-2 sp, rep from * around, ending with ch 7, sc in next sc, join in 3rd ch of beg ch-3.

Rnd 21: Sl st in each of next 2 dc and in next ch-2 sp, ch 3, [2 dc, ch 2, 3 dc] in same sp, *ch 9, sc in next sc, ch 9, [3 dc, ch 2, 3 dc] in next ch-2 sp, rep from * around, ending with ch 9, sc in next sc, ch 9, join in 3rd ch of beg ch-3.

Rnd 22: Sl st in each of next 2 dc and in next ch-2 sp, ch 3, [2 dc, ch 2, 3 dc] in same sp, *ch 10, sc in next sc, ch 10, [3 dc, ch 2, 3 dc] in next ch-2 sp, rep from * around, ending with ch 10, sc in next sc, ch 10, join in 3rd ch of beg ch-3.

Rnd 23: Ch 3, [2 dc, ch 2, 3 dc] in same st as sl st, *[3 dc, ch 3, 3 dc] in next ch-2 sp, sk 2 dc, [3 dc, ch 2, 3 dc] in next dc, ch 7, sc in next sc, ch 7**, [3 dc, ch 2, 3 dc] in first dc of next dc group, rep from * around, ending last rep at **, join in 3rd ch of beg ch-3.

Rnd 24: Sl st in each of next 2 dc and in next ch-2 sp, ch 10, *[tr, ch 3, tr] in same sp, ch 3, [dc, ch 5, dc] in next sp, ch 3, [tr, ch 3, tr, ch 3, dtr] in next sp **, sk ch-7 sps, dtr in next ch-2 sp, ch 3, rep from * around, ending last rep at **, join in 3rd ch of beg ch-3, fasten off.

Tassels *(Make 48)*

Wrap cotton around cardboard 15 times. Cut lps at 1 end; insert rem lp end through ch-5 sp on outer edge. Bring ends through lp; knot. Trim ends evenly.

Rep for each ch-5 sp around.

—Designed by Lucille LaFlamme

Floral Ornaments

Shown on page 119

Experience Level: Intermediate

Size

Bell: Approximately 4¼" tall x 4½" wide at base

French horn: Approximately 3¾" tall x 6" long

Materials

- Anchor® pearl cotton (5 grams per ball): 1 ball blue #0130
- DMC® Brilliant knitting/crochet cotton: small amounts each red #666 and green #910
- Kreinik Japan thread #7: gold
- Kreinik very fine (#4) braid (12 yds per skein): 1 skein each red #110 and silver #001
- Kreinik blending filament (55 yds per skein): 1 skein green #009 HL
- Size 4 steel crochet hook or size needed to obtain gauge
- Size 8 steel crochet hook or size needed to obtain gauge
- 2 (5" x 12") pieces muslin
- Pres-On® self-adhesive bell picture frame #FSB-12
- Pres-On® self-adhesive French horn picture frame #FSF-12
- 4 (5"-square) pieces Pellon® batting
- 2 photographs
- 1½ yds ecru 2mm string pearls
- Low-temp glue gun
- Fabric glue stick

Gauge

Bell: 12 dc = 1"

French horn: 7 dc = 1"

To save time, take time to check gauge.

Pattern Note: Join rnds with a sl st unless otherwise stated.

Pattern Stitch

Sl ring: Instead of beg ch, place yarn over hook as if to make a ch, do not pull tight, work sts in ring.

Bell With Roses

Roses *(Make 2)*

Rnd 1: With size 8 hook, holding pearl cotton and silver braid tog, make sl ring (see Pattern Stitch), ch 3, 11 dc in ring, join in 3rd ch of beg ch-3.

Pull ends of thread to close slip ring.

Rnd 2: *Ch 4, sk 1 dc, sl st in next dc, rep from * around, join in same dc as beg sl st. (6 ch sps)

Rnd 3: *[Sc, hdc, 4 dc, hdc, sc] in next ch sp, rep from * around, join in beg sc. (6 petals)

Rnd 4: Holding petals forward,

sl st in next unworked dc on Rnd 1, [ch 5, sl st in next unworked dc] rep around, join in first ch of beg ch-5. (6 ch sps)

Rnd 5: *[Sc, hdc, 6 dc, hdc, sc] in next ch sp, rep from * around, join in beg sc, fasten off.

Finishing

Assemble frame according to manufacturer's instructions.

Glue string pearls around oval opening. Glue 1 end of string pearls at top of frame; glue again in same sp 3½" from beg end. Continue to glue string pearls around outer seam; trim.

Glue roses to frame as shown.

French Horn With Poinsettia

Poinsettia

Rnd 1: With gold Japan thread and size 4 hook, ch 5, join to form a ring, [ch 5, sl st in next ch] rep around, join in 5th ch of beg ch-5, fasten off. (5 ch sps)

Rnd 2: Working in beg-ch ring, attach red braid and red cotton held tog in any ch, [ch 1, sl st in next ch] 4 times, join in beg ch.

Rnd 3: Sl st in next ch sp, [ch 10, sc in 2nd ch from hook, hdc in next ch, dc in each of next 2 chs, tr in next ch, dc in each of next 2 chs, hdc in next ch, sc in last ch, sl st in base ch sp, ch 2, sl st in next ch sp] 4 times, sl st in next ch-2 lp, rep between [] 4 times, fasten off. (8 petals)

Leaf

Row 1: With size 4 hook, holding green cotton and green blending filament tog, ch 16, sc in 2nd ch from hook, sc in each of next 13 chs, 3 sc in next ch, working on opposite side of beg ch, sc in each of next 14 chs, ch 1, turn.

Row 2: Working in back lps only from this point on, sc in each of next 11 sts, ch 1, turn.

Row 3: Sk first st, sc in each of next 11 sts, 3 sc in next st, sc in each of next 12 sts, ch 1, turn.

Row 4: Sk first st, sc in each of next 12 sts, 3 sc in next st, sc in each of next 10 sts, ch 1, turn.

Row 5: Sk first st, sc in each of next 10 sts, 3 sc in next st, sc in each of next 10 sts, ch 1, turn.

Row 6: Sk first st, sc in each of next 10 sts, 3 sc in next st, sc in each of next 8 sts, ch 1, turn.

Row 7: Sk first st, sc in each of next 8 sts, 3 sc in next st, sc in each of next 8 sts, ch 1, turn.

Row 8: Sk first st, sc in each of next 8 sts, 3 sc in next st, sc in each of next 6 sts, fasten off.

Finishing

Assemble frame following manufacturer's instructions.

Glue string pearls around round opening and around outer seam as for bell frame.

Glue poinsettia and leaf in place as shown in photo.

—Designed by Nazanin S. Fard

Dainty Ornaments

Shown on page 120

Experience Level: Advanced beginner

Size

Bow: Approximately 5" across x 6" long

Suncatcher: Approximately 6" in diameter x 8½" long (without tassel)

Fan: Approximately 7" across x 6" long

Materials

- J. & P. Coats South Maid® crochet cotton size 10 (350 yds per ball): 1 ball each cream #430 and new ecru #429
- Size 5 steel crochet hook or size needed to obtain gauge
- Hot-glue gun
- Fabric stiffener

Gauge

Bow: 8 hdc = 1"

Suncatcher: First 2 rnds = 1¾"

Fan: 2 shells = 1"

To save time, take time to check gauge

Pattern Note: Join rnds with a sl st unless otherwise stated.

Pattern Stitches

Lover's knot (Lk): Draw up a long lp on hook (indicated length), yo, draw lp through, sc in back strand of long lp.

Picot: Ch 3, sl st in sc just made.

Bow

Additional Materials

- 3 (¾"-long) silk holly leaves
- Scrap of glittered pink tulle
- ¾"-diameter mauve silk poinsettia
- 1¼"-diameter mauve silk poinsettia
- 4 small sprigs glittered gold baby's breath
- 6" length gold cord

Bow

Rnd 1: With cream South Maid crochet cotton, ch 5, join to form a ring, ch 1, sc in ring, ch 31, sl st in first sc, 6 sc in ring, ch 31, sl st in 6th sc, 5 sc in ring, join in beg sc.

Rnd 2: [Beg in first ch of ch-31, sc in next ch, hdc in next ch, {2 hdc in next ch, hdc in next ch} 4 times, 2 hdc in each of next 11 chs, {hdc in next ch, 2 hdc in next ch} 4 times, hdc in next ch, sc in last ch], sl st in beg sc again, sc in each of next 5 sc, sl st in next sc, rep between [], sl st in sc of ch-31 lp, sc in each of next 2 sc, *ch 34, hdc in 3rd ch from hook and in each rem ch *, sc in each of next 2 sc, rep from * to *, sc in next sc, sl st in beg sc.

Rnd 3: Working in back lps only, sc in first sc of ch-31 lp, [ch 4, sk 1 st, sc in next st, {ch 4, sk 2 sts, sc in next st} 15 times, ch 4, sk 1 st, sc in next st], sl st to first sc of next ch-31 lp, sc in first sc, rep between [], sl st in next sc, *sc in first ch of ch-34, **[ch 4, sk 2 sts, sc] 10 times **, [ch 4, sc, ch 4, sc, ch 4] in ch-2 sp at end of ch-34, sk hdc, sc in next hdc, rep from ** to **, sl st in next sc, rep from * around, fasten off.

Finishing

Stiffen bow; lay flat to dry.

Glue holly leaves to bow, using photo as a guide.

Cut tulle into 4"-diameter circle. Make gathering st on outer edge of circle; draw to center and flatten. Glue to center of bow over leaves with gathered side down.

Glue ¾"-diameter poinsettia in center of tulle. Glue 1¼"-diameter poinsettia onto bow above first poinsettia, using photo as a guide.

Glue 1 sprig of baby's breath under tulle over each leaf and under edge of large poinsettia.

Fold gold cord in half, forming hanging lp; glue ends to back of bow just above center sp.

Suncatcher

Additional Materials

- 3" rose-colored tassel
- 14" ¼"-wide feather-edged double-faced burgundy ribbon
- 45" ⅛"-wide dark teal green ribbon
- 8 (⅜"-diameter) rose-colored ribbon roses
- 4 (⅜"-diameter) burgundy ribbon roses
- 13 small sprigs gold glittered baby's breath

Suncatcher

Rnd 1: With South Maid ecru, ch 5, join to form a ring, ch 7 (counts as first tr, ch 3), [tr, ch 3] 9 times in ring, join in 4th ch of beg ch-7.

Rnd 2: Ch 3 (counts as first dc), [dc, ch 2, 2 dc] in same sp, **ch 3, *sc, picot in next tr, sc in each of next 3 chs, rep from * twice, sc, picot in next tr, ch 3 **, [2 dc, ch 2, 2 dc] (shell) in next tr, rep from ** to **, join in 3rd ch of beg ch-3.

Rnd 3: Ch 6 (counts as first tr, ch 2), *[tr, ch 2] in next dc, [tr, ch 3, tr] in ch-2 sp, ch 2, [tr, ch 2] in next dc, tr in next dc, ch 5, sk next picot, tr in back lp of center sc between picots, [ch 7, sk next picot, tr in back lp of center sc] twice, ch 5 *, tr in next dc of shell, ch 2, rep from * to *, join in 4th ch of beg ch-6.

Rnd 4: Ch 1, sc in same sp, **picot, sc in each of next 2 chs, [sc, picot] in next tr, ch 2, dc in next tr, ch 2, [dc, ch 3, dc] in next ch-3 sp, ch 2, dc in next tr, ch 2, [sc, picot] in next tr, sc in each of next 2 chs, [sc, picot] in next tr, *[sc in next ch, 2 sc in next ch] twice, sc in next ch *, sc in next tr, [sc in each of next 2 chs, 2 sc in next ch, sc in next ch, 2 sc in next ch, sc in each of next 2 chs, sc in next tr] twice **, rep from * to *, sc in next tr, rep from ** to **, join in beg sc.

Rnd 5: Sl st to next ch-3 sp, ch 3 (counts as first dc), {dc, ch 3, 2 dc} in same sp, **ch 9, sk 2 picots, dc in back lp of 3rd sc, ch 3, sk 1 sc, dc in back lp of next sc, *ch 7, sk 6 sts, [{dc, ch 3} in back lp of next st, sk 1 st, dc in next st] *, ch 7, sk 7 sts, rep between [] once, rep from * to * once, ch 9 **, shell in next ch-3 sp, rep from ** to **, join in 3rd ch of beg ch-3.

Rnd 6: Ch 5 (counts as first dc, ch 2), *tr in next dc, ch 2, [tr, ch 3, tr] in next ch-3 sp, [ch 2, tr in next dc] twice, **[ch 3, sc, ch 3] in next ch-9 sp **, [dc in next dc, ch 2, {dc, ch 2} in each of next 4 sts, sc in next ch-7 sp, ch 2] 3 times, dc in next dc, ch 2, {dc, ch 2} in each of next 4 sts, rep from ** to ** once *, dc in next dc, ch 2, rep from * to * once, join in 3rd ch of beg ch-5.

Rnd 7: *[{Sc, hdc} in next ch, {hdc, sc} in next ch, sl st in next tr] twice *, [sc, hdc] in next ch, 2 hdc in next ch, [hdc, sc] in next ch, sl st in next tr, rep from * to * once, ch 3, {sc, picot} in next sc, ch 3, **[sl st in next dc, {sc, hdc} in next ch, {hdc, sc} in next ch, sl st in next dc] 4 times, ch 2, {sc, picot} in next sc, ch 2, rep from ** 3 times, at the end of 3rd rep instead of ch 2, sc, picot, ch 2, work ch 3, {sc, picot} in next sc, ch 3, sl st in next dc, rep from * once, join in beg sc, fasten off.

Finishing

Stiffen suncatcher; lay flat to dry.

Glue tassel to 1 end. Cut 2 (4") lengths of burgundy ribbon; tie into bows. Glue 1 bow over spot where tassel is glued. Glue other bow at opposite tip of suncatcher, using photo as a guide.

Cut dark teal green ribbon into 16 pieces, varying in length from ¾"–1½". Fold each piece into a lp. Glue 1 lp each to backs of 2 rose-colored ribbon rose; glue 2 lps each to backs of 2 rose-colored ribbon roses; glue 2 lps each to backs of 2 burgundy ribbon roses; glue 3 lps each to backs of 2 burgundy ribbon roses.

Using photo as a guide, glue 3 rose-colored ribbon roses over each burgundy bow, having rose with 1 lp on 1 end, rose with 2 lps on opposite end, and rose without lp in center of each cluster. Glue small sprigs of baby's breath around ribbons and roses.

Again using photo as guide, glue 2 ribbon rose clusters around center of suncatcher, with each cluster made up of 2 burgundy ribbon roses (1 with 2 lps and 1 with 3 lps) with 1 rose-colored ribbon rose (without lps) in middle.

Glue rem sprigs of baby's breath around each cluster.

Trim rem burgundy ribbon to desired length for hanging lp; fold in half and glue ends to back of suncatcher at top.

Fan

Additional Materials

- 8 x 16mm teardrop pearl
- 4 (1") purple roses with leaves
- 20 (6mm) pearl beads
- Beading needle
- Heavy-duty thread
- 4 (8mm) light purple round faceted beads
- 20" ⅜"-wide feather-edged lavender ribbon
- Nylon thread

Fan

Rnd 1: Beg at handle with South Maid cream crochet cotton, ch 15, join to form a ring, ch 1, 2 sc in each ch around, join in back lp of beg sc.

Rnd 2: Working in back lps only, sc in same sc and in each of next 3 sc, ch 3, sk 3 sc, sc in next sc, *ch 3, sk 2 sc, sc in next sc *, [ch 3, sk 2 sc, {sc, picot} in next sc], ch 3, sk 2 sc, dc in next sc, ch 5, sl st in 5th ch from hook, ch 1, dc in next sc, rep between [] once, rep from * to * twice, ch 3, sk 3 sc, join in beg sc.

Row 3: Ch 3 (counts as first dc), 2 dc in same sc, 2 dc in each of next 2 sc, 3 dc in last sc, turn.

Row 4: Ch 5 (counts as first tr, ch 1), [tr, ch 2] in each of next 7 dc, tr in next dc, ch 1, tr in 3rd ch of ch-3, turn.

Row 5: Ch 4 (counts as first dc, ch 1), [2 dc, ch 3] in each of next 7 tr, 2 dc in next tr, ch 1, sk 1 ch, dc in next ch (4th ch of turning ch-5), turn.

Row 6: Ch 4 (counts as first dc, ch 1), [2 dc, ch 2, 2 dc (shell)] in 2nd ch of ch-3 sp, shell in 2nd ch of each of next 6 ch-3 sps, ch 1, dc in 3rd ch of turning ch-4, turn.

Row 7: Ch 4 (counts as first dc, ch 1), [shell, ch 1] in each shell across, dc in 3rd ch of turning ch-4, turn.

Row 8: Ch 5 (counts as first dc, ch 1), [shell, ch 2] in each ch across, dc in 3rd ch of turning ch-4, turn.

Row 9: Ch 3 (counts as first dc), *[dc, {ch 2, tr} 4 times, ch 2, dc] in next shell sp, sc in next ch-2 sp between shells, rep from * 6 times, omitting last sc on last rep, sk 1 ch, dc in 3rd ch of turning ch-5, turn.

Row 10: Ch 1, sc in same st, sc in next dc, [{ch 3, sc} in next tr] 4 times, ch 3, sc in next dc, sk next sc, sc in next dc] 7 times, sc in 3rd ch of turning ch-3, turn.

Row 11: Sl st in first sc, *[sc in next ch, 3 sc in next ch, sc in next ch, sl st in next sc] 5 times, sl st in next sc between scallops, rep from * 6 times, sl st in last sc, fasten off.

Finishing

Stiffen fan. Pin to blocking board, shaping ruffled edges and handle. Let dry.

With beading ndl, thread pearls onto heavy-duty thread; knot ends of thread to form 4 circles of 5 pearls each. Glue 3 circles of pearls on fan as shown in photo; glue light purple round faceted bead in center of each circle.

Glue purple ribbon roses on fan as shown in photo.

Cut ribbon in half; tie into double bow. Glue to fan above handle as shown in photo. Glue rem circle of pearls and faceted bead over knot in bow.

Thread pearl drop onto nylon thread; glue ends of thread to fan so that pearl drop hangs freely in handle opening.

—Designed by Jo Ann Maxwell

Angels' Blessing

Shown on page 121

Experience Level: Intermediate

Size: 21" wide x 27" long including rod loops and fringe loops, excluding tassel

Materials

- DMC® Cebelia® crochet cotton size 10 (50 grams per ball): 3 balls white
- Size 8 steel crochet hook
- 4½" piece cardboard
- Sewing needle and white sewing thread
- 10" ⅛"-wide gold ribbon

Gauge: 7 sps and 7 rows = 2"

To save time, take time to check gauge.

Pattern Note: Work odd-numbered rows left to right, and even-numbered rows right to left on graph.

Pattern Stitches

See Instructions for Filet Crochet on page 57.

Long decorative picot (ldp): Ch 5, sc in center of next sp, ch 4, sl st in sc (picot), ch 5, dc in next indicated st as shown on chart. Long ch over this picot in next row is ch-8.

Short decorative picot (sdp): Ch 3, sc and picot in indicated st as shown on chart, ch 3, dc in next indicted st as shown on chart. Long ch over this picot in next row is ch-5.

Wall Hanging

Row 1: Ch 212, dc in 8th ch from hook, [ch 2, sk 2 chs, dc in next ch] rep across, ch 5, turn. (69 sps)

Row 2: [Dc in next dc, ch 2] rep across, ending with dc in 3rd ch of end sp.

Continue to follow chart, making sps or solid blocks as indicated, ending last row with ch 1, turn.

Rod loops

Next Row: 2 sc in sp, sc in dc, *ch 20, [2 sc in next sp, sc in dc] 6 times, rep from * 9 times, ch 20, [2 sc in next sp, sc in dc] 7 times, ch 20, 2 sc in last sp.

Side edging

Ch 3, *2 dc in sp, ch 5, sl st in 4th ch from hook, ch 1, 3 dc in same sp, ch 3, sk 1 sp, sc in next sp, ch 4, sl st in sc (picot), ch 3, sk 1 sp, dc in next sp, ch 7, sl st in last dc of previous 3-dc group, [4 sc, picot, 4 sc] over ch-7, sl st in dc, rep from * 18 times, 2 dc in same sp, ch 5, sl st in 4th ch from hook, ch 1, 2 dc in same sp, ch 3, sc in same sp.

Lower edge fringe

2 sc in sp, ch 15, sc in same sp, ch 15, sc in dc, *ch 17, sc in next sp, ch 17, sc in dc, ch 19, sc in next sp, ch 19, sc in dc, ch 21, sc in next sp, ch 21, sc in dc, ch 23, sc in next sp, ch 23, sc in dc, ch 25, sc in next sp, ch 25, sc in dc, ch 27, sc in next sp, ch 27, sc in dc, ch 29, sc in next sp, ch 29, sc in dc, ch 31, sc in next sp, ch 31, sc in dc, ch 33, sc in next sp, ch 33, sc in dc, ch 35, sc in next sp, ch 35, sc in dc, ch 37, continue in this patt inc 2 chs in each sp until ch-47 has been completed for 2 sps, continue in this patt, dec 2 chs in each sp until ch-15 has been completed for 2 lps, 2 sc in 35th sp, ch 15, sc in next sp, ch 15, sc in dc, rep from * to last sp on lower edge, [{ch 15, sc} in last sp] twice, 2 sc in same sp.

Side edging

Work same as for previous side edging, ending with 2 dc, ch 3, sl st in first sc on rod lp row, fasten off.

Skirt Edging

Top *(Make 2)*

Row 1: Ch 116, dc in 8th ch from hook, [ch 2, sk 2 chs, dc in next ch] rep across, turn. (37 sps)

Row 2: Rep as for side edging, fasten off.

Middle *(Make 2)*

Row 1: Ch 152, dc in 8th ch from hook, [ch 2, sk 2 chs, dc in next ch] rep across, turn. (49 sps)

Row 2: Rep as for side edging, fasten off.

Lower *(Make 2)*

Row 1: Ch 104, dc in 8th ch from hook, [ch 2, sk 2 chs, dc in next ch] rep across, turn. (33 sps)

Row 2: Rep as for side edging, fasten off.

Finishing

With sewing needle and white thread, stitch each skirt edging in place as indicated on chart, easing in fullness.

Tack end of gold ribbon in place in top of large heart just above first ldp. Weave through sps to angels' hands; tie rem length in bow to secure.

Tassel

Wrap cotton around cardboard 50 times. Cut 1 lp end. Insert 1 cut end through sp indicated on chart. Fold strands in half; knot with length of cotton ¾" from top. Trim ends evenly.

— Designed by Lucille LaFlamme

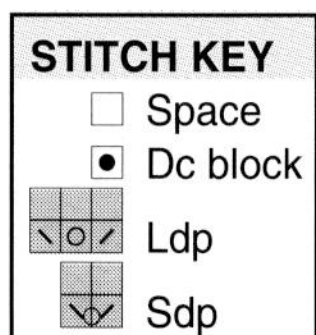

Row 70
Row 60
Tie ribbon between han
Row 50
Edging Row 1
Edging Row 2
Row 40
Edging Row 3
Row 30
Row 20
Row 10
Row 1

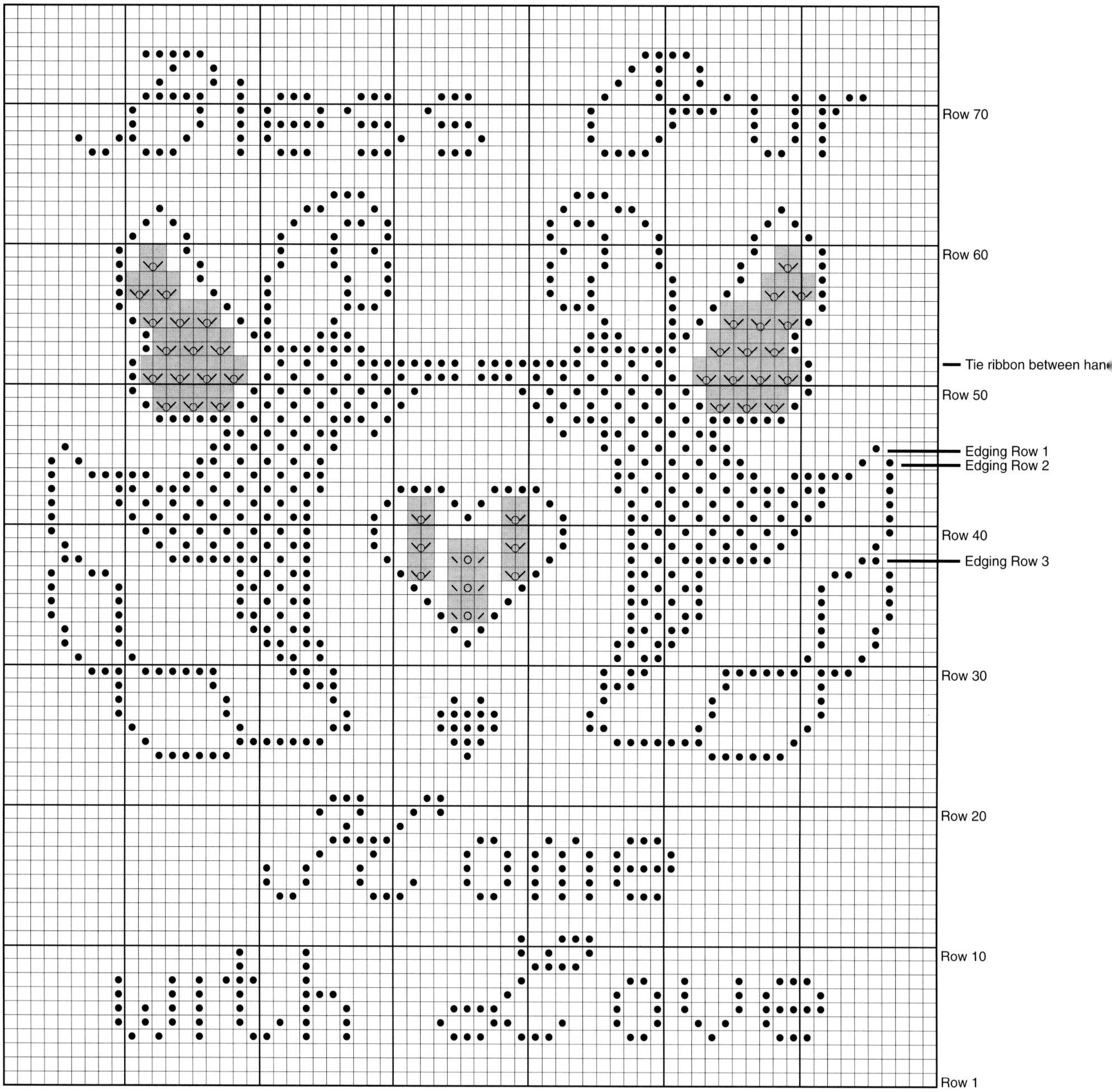

Country Hearts

Shown on page 122

Experience Level: Intermediate

Size: 27" in diameter

Materials

- 4-ply worsted weight acrylic yarn: 32 oz off-white and 6 oz each hunter green and burgundy
- Size H/8 crochet hook
- Tapestry needle

Gauge: 3 dc = 1"; 7 dc rows = 4"

To save time, take time to check gauge.

Pattern Note: When changing colors on the panel to form the wreath, hold the dark green yarn on the wrong side of the panel, crocheting over the yarn every once in a while to keep it flat.

Panel *(Make 6)*

Row 1: Beg at top of panel with off-white yarn, ch 7, sc in 2nd ch from hook and in each ch across, ch 3, turn. (6 sc)

Row 2: Dc in same sc as ch-3, dc in each sc across until last sc, 2 dc in last sc of row, ch 3, turn. (8 dc)

Rows 3–18: Dc in same dc as ch-3, dc in each dc across until last dc, 2 dc in last dc of row, ch 3, turn. (40 dc at end of Row 18)

Row 19: Dc in same dc as ch-3, dc in each of next 14 dc, change to hunter green, fpdc around posts of next 10 dc, change to off-white, dc in each of next 14 dc, 2 dc in last dc of row, ch 3, turn. (42 sts)

Row 20: Dc in same dc as ch-3, dc in each of next 13 dc, change to hunter green, bpdc around post of next dc, change to off-white, dc in each of next 12 sts, change to hunter green, bpdc around post of next dc, change to off-white, dc in each of next 13 dc, 2 dc in last dc of row, ch 3, turn. (44 sts)

Row 21: Dc in same dc as ch-3, dc in each of next 12 dc, change to hunter green, fpdc around post of next dc, change to off-white, dc in each of next 16 dc, change to hunter green, fpdc around post of next dc, change to off-white, dc in each of next 12 dc, 2 dc in last dc of row, ch 3, turn. (46 sts)

Row 22: Dc in same dc as ch-3, dc in each of next 11 dc, change to hunter green, bpdc around post of next dc, change to off-white, dc in each of next 20 sts, change to hunter green, bpdc around post of next dc, change to off-white, dc in each of next 11 dc, 2 dc in last dc of row, ch 3, turn. (48 sts)

Row 23: Dc in same dc as ch-3, dc in each of next 10 dc, change to hunter green, fpdc around post of next dc, change to off-white, dc in each of next 24 dc, change to hunter green, fpdc around post of next dc, change to off-white, dc in each of next 10 dc, 2 dc in last dc of row, ch 3, turn. (50 sts)

Row 24: Dc in same dc as ch-3, dc in each of next 9 dc, change to hunter green, bpdc around post of next dc, change to off-white, dc in each of next 28 sts, change to hunter green, bpdc around post of next dc, change to off-white, dc in each of next 9 dc, 2 dc in last dc of row, ch 3, turn. (52 sts)

Row 25: Dc in same dc as ch-3, dc in each of next 10 dc, change to hunter green, fpdc around post of next dc, change to off-white, dc in next 28 dc, change to hunter green, fpdc around post of next dc, change to off-white, dc in each of next 10 dc, 2 dc in last row of ch-3, turn. (54 sts)

Row 26: Dc in same dc as ch-3, dc in each of next 11 dc, change to hunter green, bpdc around post of next dc, change to off-white, dc in next 28 sts, change to hunter green, bpdc around post of next dc, change to off-white, dc in each of next 11 dc, 2 dc in last dc of row, ch 3, turn. (56 sts)

Row 27: Dc in same dc as ch-3, dc in each of next 12 dc, change to hunter green, fpdc around post of next dc, change to off-white, dc in each of next 28 dc, change to hunter green, fpdc around post of next dc, change to off-white, dc in next 12 dc, 2 dc in last dc of row, ch 3, turn. (58 sts)

Row 28: Dc in same dc as ch-3, dc in each of next 13 dc, change to hunter green, bpdc around post of next dc, change to off-white, dc in each of next 28 sts, change to hunter green, bpdc around post of next dc, change to off-white, dc in each of next 13 dc, 2 dc in last dc of row, ch 3, turn. (60 sts)

Row 29: Dc in same dc as ch-3, dc in each of next 14 dc, change to hunter green, fpdc around post of next dc, change to off-white, dc in each of next 28 dc, change to hunter green, fpdc around post of next dc, change to off-white, dc in each of next 14 dc, 2 dc in last dc of row, ch 3, turn. (62 sts)

Row 30: Dc in same dc as ch-3, dc in each of next 17 dc, change to hunter green, bpdc around post of next dc, change to off-white, dc in next 24 sts, change to hunter green, bpdc around post of next dc, change to off-white, dc in each of next 17 dc, 2 dc in last dc of row, ch 3, turn. (64 sts)

Row 31: Dc in same dc as ch-3, dc in each of next 20 dc, change to hunter green, fpdc around post of next dc, change to off-white, dc in each of next 20 dc, change to hunter green, fpdc around post of next dc, change to off-white, dc in each of next 20 dc, 2 dc in last dc of row, ch 3, turn. (66 sts)

Row 32: Dc in same dc as ch-3, dc in each of next 23 dc, change to hunter green, bpdc around post of next dc, change to off-white, dc in each of next 16 sts, change to hunter green, bpdc around post of next dc, change to off-white, dc in each of next 23 dc, 2 dc in last dc of row, ch 3, turn. (68 sts)

Row 33: Dc in same dc as ch-3, dc in each of next 26 dc, change to hunter green, fpdc around post of next dc, change to off-white, dc in each of next 12 dc, change to hunter green, fpdc around post of next dc, change to off-white, dc in each of next 26 dc, 2 dc in last dc of row, ch 3, turn. (70 sts)

Row 34: Dc in same dc as ch-3, dc in each of next 29 dc, change to hunter green, bpdc around post of next 10 dc, change to off-white, dc in each of next 29 dc, 2 dc in last dc of row, ch 3, turn. (72 sts)

Row 35: Dc in same dc as ch-3, dc in each st across row until last dc of row, 2 dc in last dc of row, ch 3, turn. (74 dc)

Rows 36–37: Dc in same dc as ch-3, dc in each dc across row until last dc of row, 2 dc in last dc of row, ch 3, turn, at end of Row 37, ch 1, turn. (78 dc at end of Row 37)

Row 38: 2 sc in first dc, sc in each of next 8 dc, hdc in each of next 10 dc, dc in each of next 10 dc, tr in each of next 20 dc, dc in each of next 10 dc, hdc in each of next 10 dc, sc in each of next 8 dc, 2 sc in 3rd ch of beg ch-3, ch 1, turn. (80 sts)

Row 39: Sc in each of next 10 sc, hdc in each of next 10 hdc, dc in each of next 10 dc, tr in each of next 20 tr, dc in each of next 10 dc, hdc in each of next 10 hdc, sc in each of last 10 sc, ch 1, turn. (80 sts)

Row 40: 2 sc in first sc, sc in each of next 9 sc, hdc in each of next 10 hdc, dc in each of next 10 dc, tr in each of next 20 tr, dc in each of next 10 dc, hdc in each of next 10 hdc, sc in each of next 9 sc, 2 sc in last sc of row, fasten off. (82 sts)

Wreath

Rnd 1: With hunter green, work over the posts made in each panel. With bottom of panel facing you, begin at Row 29 on RS of panel, sl st around post, sc around same post, sc around each of next 4 posts, [ch 2, sc around next post] 5 times, sc around each of next 9 posts, rep between [] 5 times, sc around each of next 4 posts, rep between [] 5 times, sc around each of next 9 posts, rep between [] 4 times, ch 2, join with a sl st in beg sc.

Rnd 2: Ch 1, sc in beg sc, ch 2, sc in 2nd ch from hook, sc in same st as beg sc, *sc, ch 2, sc in 2nd ch from hook, sc in same st, sc in next st, rep from * around in each sc and ch-2 sp, join with a sl st in beg sc, fasten off.

Thread tapestry ndl with a 36" length of burgundy yarn. Sew wreath to panel by taking ¼" running sts around wreath between Rnds 1 and 2 of wreath. Tie ends of yarn in a bow. Do not pull yarn; wreath should lie flat. Cut excess yarn.

Heart Appliqué

Row 1 (RS): Beg at bottom of heart with burgundy, ch 2, 3 sc in 2nd ch from hook, ch 1, turn.

Row 2: 2 sc in first sc, sc in next sc, 2 sc in last sc, ch 1, turn. (5 sc)

Row 3: Sc in each sc across, ch 1, turn.

Row 4: 2 sc in first sc, sc in each sc to last sc, 2 sc in last sc, ch 1, turn. (7 sc)

Row 5: Rep Row 3.

Row 6: Rep Row 4. (9 sc)

Row 7: Rep Row 3.

Row 8: Rep Row 4. (11 sc)

Right side of heart

Row 9: Sc in each of next 6 sc, ch 1, turn.

Row 10: Sc first 2 sc tog, sc in each of next 2 sc, sc last 2 sc tog. (4 sc)

Row 11: Sc in first sc, sc next 2 sc tog, sc in last sc, fasten off. (3 sc)

Left side of heart

Row 9: Sl st in same st as 6th sc of right side, sc in same st, sc in each of next 5 sc, ch 1, turn. (6 sc)

Rows 10 & 11: Rep Rows 10 and 11 of right side.

Edging

Rnd 1: With burgundy and RS facing, sl st in opposite side of beg ch, 2 sc, ch 1, 2 sc in same st, working around edge of heart, sc in end of each row and in each st around with a sl st in 6th st of Row 8. ***Note:*** *Same st as divide of heart, this st already has 2 sc in it. Join with a sl st in beg sc, fasten off burgundy.*

Rnd 2: Working in back lps, with off-white, sl st in beg sc of left heart divide, sc in same st, ch 2, *sc in next st, ch 2 *, rep from * to * to ch-1 sp, sc, ch 2, sc in ch-1 sp at bottom of heart, rep from * to * around, join with a sl st in beg sc, fasten off.

Thread tapestry ndl with burgundy. Using photo as a guide, sew heart appliqué in center of wreath.

Joining

Thread tapestry ndl with off-white. Sew panels tog, matching rows with RS facing. Make a complete circle, leaving first and last panels separated.

Ruffle

Row 1: With WS facing and off-white, sl st in first st, sc in each st across all 6 panels, ch 3, turn. ***Note:*** *Do not sc in seams.* (492 sc)

Row 2: Working in back lps only, 2 dc in next sc, *dc in next sc, 2 dc in next sc, rep from * across, ch 3, turn. (738 dc)

Row 3: Working in both lps, rep Row 2, ch 1, turn. (1,107 dc)

Row 4: Working in front lps, [*sc in next dc, {dc, ch 2, dc} in next dc, sc in next dc] (patt set), rep from * across, fasten off. (369 patt sets)

Row 5: Working in both lps, sl st in first sc with hunter green, sc in same st, sc in next dc, sc, ch 2, sc in next ch-2 sp, sc in next sc, *sc in next sc, sc in next dc, {sc, ch 2, sc} in next ch-2 sp, sc in next sc, rep from * across, fasten off.

Ruffle Edging

With burgundy in unworked lps of Row 1 of ruffle, sl st in first st, sc in same st, ch 2, *sc in next st, ch 2, rep from * across, sc in last st, fasten off.

Working in unworked lps of Row 3 of ruffle, sl st in first st, ch 2, *sl st in next st, ch 2, rep from * across, sl st in last st, fasten off.

Panel Edging

With RS facing and off-white yarn, sl st in end of Row 40 of left panel, sc in end of next 2 rows, 2 sc in end of each dc row to top corner, working on opposite side of beg ch, work 3 sc in first st, sc in each st across top until last st, 3 sc in last st, working down right panel, 2 dc in end of each row until last 3 rows, sc in end of next 2 rows, sl st in end of Row 40.

Ties

Sl st in top left back corner of skirt, ch 25, fasten off.

Rep on right back corner.

— Designed by Adele Mogavero

Tips & Techniques for Crocheters

When working into the ends of rows of a tightly crocheted piece, it is sometimes difficult to push the hook into the stitches. Use a hook one or two sizes smaller than the hook you are working with to help push through the end of row and draw a loop through; then complete stitch with larger hook.

When you complete a crochet project that will be given away, take a picture of the item to put in a scrapbook. You will savor the satisfaction of having completed the project, and also start a nice portfolio of your work.

To utilize the sales at your local craft store, keep a notebook in your purse of projects you plan on making, along with a list of all the necessary supplies needed for that project.

When making crocheted hot pads or pot holders that will be functional, place two thicknesses of heat-resistant material between the front and back pieces to prevent burnt fingers.

Doily Accents

Crochet a collection of lovely doilies to accent your home with their subtle beauty. Perfect for adding a decorative touch to the living room, dining room, study and bedroom, these doilies will bring back memories of visits to Grandmother's house.

This exquisite filet masterpiece, Victorian Rose, is striking enough to stand alone. You will want to give this beautiful piece a prominent position in your home, whether with a collection of framed family photos or framed and hung on the wall. Instructions on page 148.

GREENLEAF
Aromatic Bath
Crystals
Foxgloves
GREENLEAF
Aromatic Bath
Crystals
Water
Lilies

Placed on a bedside table, Tulip Whispers (below) is the perfect accent for a crystal vase filled with flowers to make a special houseguest feel at home. Daydream Doily (left) is thus named for its enchanting curves and lacy, open feel. *Instructions on pages 150–151.*

A traditional favorite, the pineapple pattern never loses its appeal to both crocheter and admirer. Pineapple Wheel (below) is no exception! The hours of work you put into crocheting this enchanting Forever Yours (right), stitch by stitch, will surely demonstrate your affection for a loved one. Instructions on pages 151–154.

The Rose Garden
Talcum Powder
Toilet Soap

Doilies with an unusual shape provide a welcome change of pace to a home decorated with crocheted pieces. Oval Beauty will bring an elegant look to a bureau or buffet.
Instructions on page 154.

Square Treasure (below) provides a small end table with a unique accent, and Victorian Floral (right) will bring the beauty of flowers into your home all year-round. *Instructions on page 155–156.*

Victorian Rose

Shown on page 138

Experience Level: Intermediate

Size

Approximately 21" x 22" before blocking

Materials

- DMC® Cebelia® crochet cotton size 30 (50 grams per ball): 2 balls ecru naturel
- Size 12 steel crochet hook or size needed to obtain gauge

Gauge: 16 sts and 6 rows = 1"

Pattern Stitches

See Instructions For Filet Crochet on page 57.

Bl and sp over a bar: Dc in each of next 3 chs, ch 2, sk 2 chs, dc in next dc.

2 bls over a bar: Dc in each of next 5 chs, dc in next dc.

Sp and bl over a bar: Ch 2, sk 2 chs, dc in each of next 3 chs, dc in next dc.

2 sps over a bar: Ch 2, sk 2 chs, dc in next ch, ch 2, sk 2 chs, dc in next dc.

Lacet: Ch 3, sk 2 sts, sc in next st, ch 3, sk 2 sts, dc in next st.

Bar: Ch 5, sk 5 sts, dc in next st/dc.

Doily

Row 1 (RS): Ch 372, dc in 4th ch from hook and in each ch across, ch 3, turn.

Row 2: Dc in each of next 3 dc, [ch 2, sk 2 dc, dc in next dc] rep across, ending with dc in each of last 3 dc, dc in 3rd ch of turning ch-3.

Row 3: Beg bl, 22 sps over 22 sps, 6 bls over 6 sps, 10 sps over 10 sps, bl over a sp, 44 sps over 44 sps, bl over a sp, 10 sps over 10 sps, 6 bls over 6 sps, 21 sps over 21 sps, bl over a bl, turn.

Rows 4–123: Follow Chart A, utilizing Pattern Stitches, fasten off.

— Designed by Nancy Hearne, courtesy of DMC

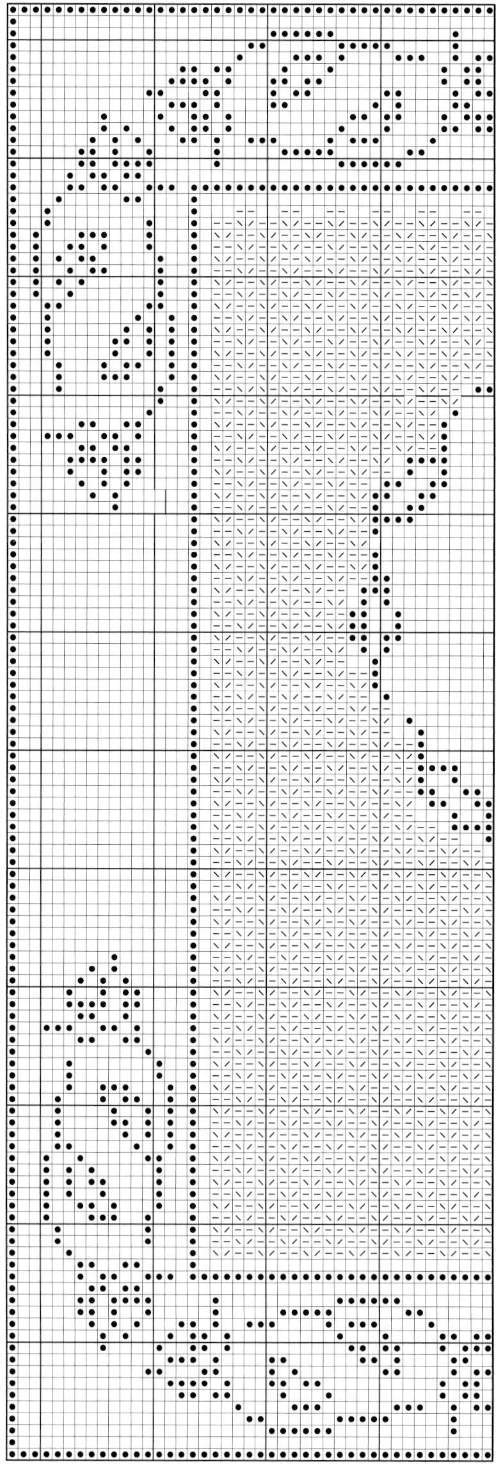

STITCH KEY
- ☐ Space
- ⦿ Block
- ⧄ Lacet
- ⊟ Bar

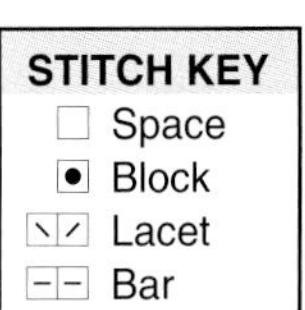

CHART A

Note: Work both graphs simultaneously.

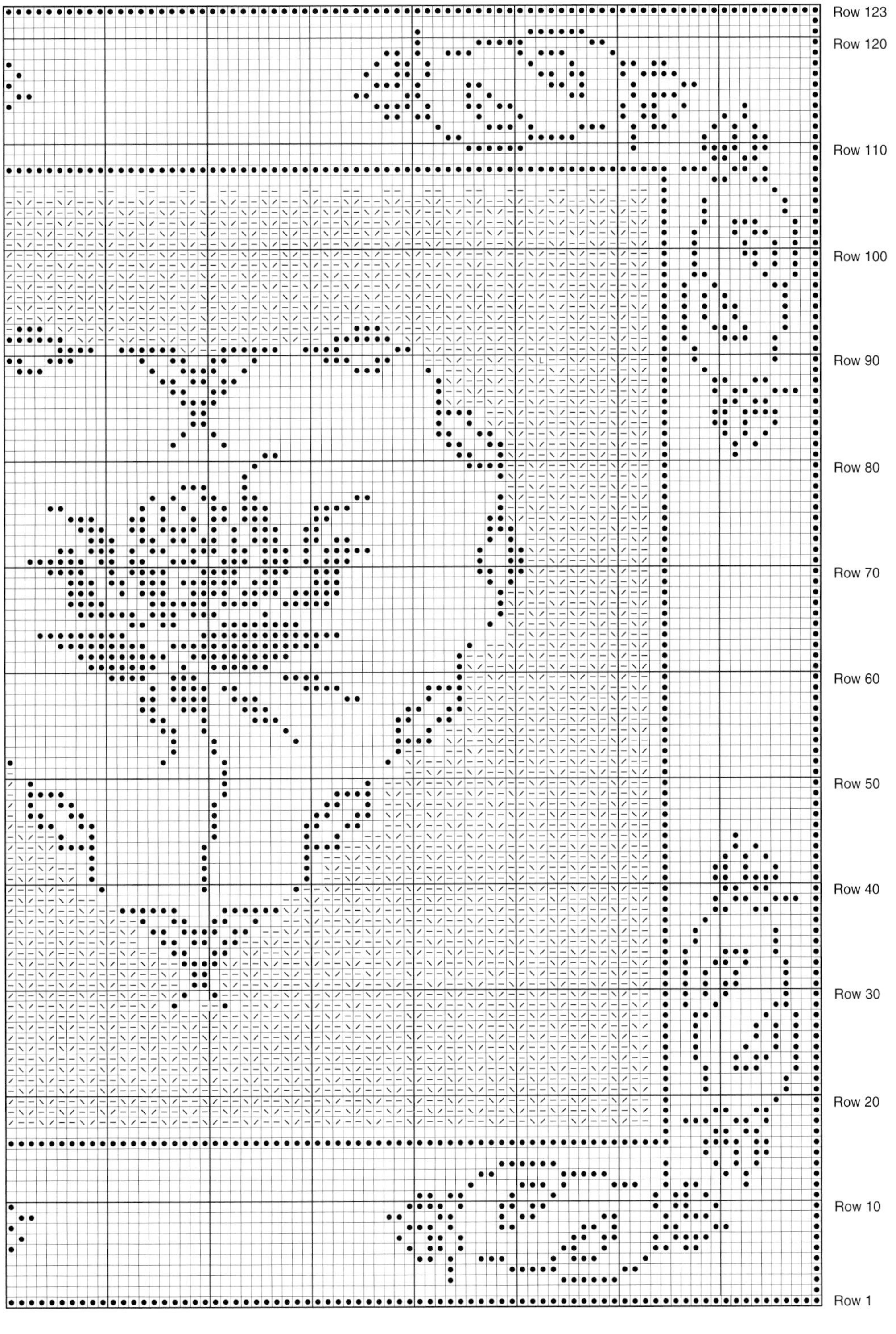

Row 123
Row 120
Row 110
Row 100
Row 90
Row 80
Row 70
Row 60
Row 50
Row 40
Row 30
Row 20
Row 10
Row 1

Daydream Doily

Shown on page 140

Experience Level: Intermediate

Size: 16" in diameter

Materials

- DMC® Cebelia® crochet cotton size 10 (282 yds per ball): 1 ball light tan #619
- Size 6 steel crochet hook or size needed to obtain gauge

Gauge: 6 dc = ½"

To save time, take time to check gauge.

Pattern Note: Join rnds with a sl st unless otherwise stated.

Doily

Rnd 1: Ch 8, join to form a ring, ch 2, dc in ring, ch 2, *[work dc in ring, keeping last lp on hook] twice, yo, draw through rem lps on hook (dc cl made), ch 2, rep from * 10 times, join in top of beg dc.

Rnd 2: Ch 1, sc in next ch-2 sp, *ch 13, sc in same sp, [ch 3, sc in next sp] twice, rep from * around, ending with ch 3, sc in next sp, ch 3, join in beg sc.

Rnd 3: Sl st in ch-13 lp, ch 3, 10 dc in lp, ch 2, 11 dc in same lp, sc in ch-3 lp, ch 15, sc in next lp, *11 dc in next lp, ch 2, 11 dc in same lp, sc in next lp, ch 15, sc in next lp, rep from * around, join in 3rd ch of beg ch-3.

Rnd 4: Sl st to sp at tip of petal, ch 1, *sc in ch-2 sp, ch 7, 3 dc in ch-15 lp, ch 7, rep from * around, join in beg sc.

Rnd 5: Ch 3, 2 dc in same st, ch 7, dc cl in next dc, ch 3, sk next dc, dc cl in next dc, ch 7, *3 dc in next sc, ch 7, dc cl in next dc, ch 3, sk next dc, dc cl in next dc, ch 7, rep from * around, join in 3rd ch of beg ch-3.

Rnd 6: Ch 2, dc in same st, ch 3, sk next dc, dc cl in next dc, ch 3, [sk next 2 sts, 2-dc cl in next st, ch 3] twice, [sk next 3 sts, dc cl in next st, ch 3] twice, sk next 2 sts, dc cl in next st, ch 3, sk next 2 sts, *dc cl in next dc, ch 3, sk next dc, dc cl in next dc, ch 3, [sk next 2 sts, dc cl in next st, ch 3] twice, [sk next 3 sts, dc cl in next st, ch 3] twice, sk next 2 sts, dc cl in next st, ch 3, sk next 2 sts, rep from * around, join in beg dc. (42 dc cls)

Rnd 7: Sl st in each of next 2 sts, ch 2, dc in same st, [ch 3, sk next 3 sts, dc cl in next st] twice, ch 3, *dc cl in next st, ch 3, sk next 2 sts, dc cl in next st, [ch 3, sk next 3 sts, dc cl in next st] twice, ch 3, dc cl in next st, ch 3, sk next 2 sts, dc cl in next st, [ch 3, sk next 3 sts, dc cl in next st] 3 times, ch 3, rep from * around, dc cl in next st, ch 3, sk next 2 sts, dc cl in next st, [ch 3, sk next 3 sts, dc cl in next st] twice, ch 3, dc cl in next st, ch 3, sk next 2 sts, dc cl in next st, ch 3, join in beg dc. (54 dc cls)

Rnds 8 & 9: Sl st in each of next 2 sts, ch 2, dc in same st, *ch 3, sk next 3 sts, dc cl in next st, rep from * around, ch 3, join in beg dc.

Rnd 10: Sl st in each of next 2 sts, ch 3, 2 dc in same st, *ch 5, 3 dc in center st of next ch-3 lp, rep from * around, ch 5, join in 3rd ch of beg ch-3.

Rnd 11: Sl st in each of next 5 sts, ch 3, 2 dc in same st, *ch 6, 3 dc in center st of next ch-5 lp, rep from * around, ch 6, join in 3rd ch of beg ch-3.

Rnd 12: Sl st in each of next 5 sts, ch 3, 2 dc in same st, *ch 7, 3 dc in 3rd ch of next ch-6 lp, rep from * around, ch 7, join in 3rd ch of beg ch-3.

Rnds 13 & 14: Sl st in each of next 6 sts, ch 3, 2 dc in same st, *ch 8, 3 dc in 4th ch of next lp, rep from * around, ch 8, join in 3rd ch of beg ch-3.

Rnd 15: Sl st in each of next 6 sts, ch 3, 2 dc in same st, *ch 9, 3 dc in 4th ch of next lp, rep from * around, ch 9, join in 3rd ch of beg ch-3.

Rnd 16: Sl st in each of next 7 sts, ch 3, 2 dc in same st, *ch 10, 3 dc in 5th ch of next lp, rep from * around, ch 10, join in 3rd ch of beg ch-3.

Rnd 17: Sl st in each of next 7 sts, ch 3, 2 dc in same st, *ch 11, 3 dc in 5th ch of next lp, rep from * around, ch 11, join in 3rd ch of beg ch-3.

Rnd 18: Sl st in each of next 8 sts, ch 3, 2 dc in same st, *ch 11, 3 dc in 6th ch of next lp, rep from * around, ch 11, join in 3rd ch of beg ch-3.

Rnd 19: Ch 2, dc in same st, ch 3, sk next st, dc cl in next st, *[ch 3, sk next 2 sts, dc cl in next st] 4 times, ch 3, sk next st, dc cl in next st, rep from * around, [ch 3, sk next 2 sts, dc cl in next st] 3 times, ending with ch 1, dc in top of beg dc to set up hook in center of last ch lp.

Rnd 20: Ch 1, sc in same lp, *ch 6, sl st in 3rd ch from hook, ch 3, sk next sp, sc in center st of next sp, ch 5, sk next cl, sc in next cl, ch 3, sc in same st, ch 5, sk next sp, sc in center st of next sp, rep from * around, join in beg sc, fasten off.

— Designed by Zelda Workman

Tulip Whispers

Shown on page 141

Experience Level: Intermediate

Size: Approximately 7" in diameter

Materials

- Crochet cotton size 10 (225 yds per ball): ½ ball white
- Size 7 steel crochet hook
- Fabric stiffener

Gauge: 9 sc = 1"
To save time, take time to check gauge

Pattern Note: Join rnds with a sl st unless otherwise stated.

Doily

Rnd 1: Ch 16, join to form a ring, ch 3 (counts as first dc), 31 dc in ring, join in 3rd ch of beg ch-3.

Rnd 2: Ch 11, [sk 3 dc, tr in next dc, ch 7] rep around, ending with tr, ch 4, tr in 4th ch of beg ch-11. (8 ch-4 sps)

Rnd 3: Ch 27, sl st in 3rd ch of ch-27 (counts as first dc, ch-24 lp), 5 dc in same ch sp, [5 dc in next ch sp, ch 24, sl st in first ch, 5 dc in same ch sp] rep around, ending with 4 dc in last ch sp, join in 3rd ch of beg ch-27. (8 petals)

First petal

Row 4: [Ch 3, sk 1 ch, dc] 5 times, ch 3, sk 1 ch, {dc, ch 3, dc in} next ch, [ch 3, sk 1 ch, dc] 5 times, ending with ch 3, sk 1 ch, sl st in next ch, turn.

Row 5: Ch 2, 2 dc in next ch sp, [3 dc in next ch sp] twice, *[dc, ch 5, dc] in next ch sp, dc in next dc, rep from * 5 times, [dc, ch 5, dc] in next ch sp, [3 dc in next ch sp] twice, 2 dc in next ch sp, ch 2, sl st in last ch, fasten off.

Second–seventh petals
*With finished petal to the right, attach cotton in 5th dc before next ch-24 lp, rep Row 4 of first petal.

Row 5: Ch 2, 2 dc in next ch sp, [3 dc in next ch sp] twice, *[dc, ch 5, dc] in next ch sp, dc in next dc, rep from * 5 times, in next ch sp work dc, ch 2, sl st in first ch-5 sp of previous petal directly adjacent, ch 2, dc in same ch sp, [3 dc in next ch sp] twice, 2 dc in next ch sp, ch 2, sl st in last ch, fasten off.

Rep from * 5 more times.

Eighth petal
With finished petal to the right, attach cotton in 5th dc before last ch-24 lp, rep Row 4 of first petal.

Row 5: Ch 2, 2 dc in next ch sp, [3 dc in next ch sp] twice, in next ch sp work dc, ch 2, sl st in 7th ch-5 sp of first petal, ch 2, dc in same ch sp, dc in next dc, *[dc, ch 5, dc] in next ch sp, dc in next dc, rep from * 4 times, in next ch sp work dc, ch 2, sl st in first ch-5 sp of previous petal directly adjacent, ch 2, dc in same ch sp, [3 dc in next ch sp] twice, 2 dc in next ch sp, ch 2, sl st in last ch, fasten off.

Joining petals

Rnd 6: Attach thread to the top ch-5 sp of any petal, [ch 5, sl st in next ch-5 sp] twice, *ch 5, sl st in ch-5 sp on next petal, [ch 5, sl st in next ch-5 sp] 4 times, rep from * around, ending with ch 5, sl st in next ch-5 sp. Ch 5, join in first ch of beg ch-5.

Rnd 7: Ch 1, *[3 sc, ch 3, sl st in first ch (picot), 3 sc] in next ch sp, rep from * around, ending with sl st in first ch, fasten off.

Stiffen doily and block to size.

—Designed by Nazanin S. Fard

Pineapple Wheel

Shown on page 142

Experience Level: Advanced

Size: Approximately 15"

Materials

- J. & P. Coats South Maid® crochet cotton size 10 (350 yds per ball): 1 ball ecru
- Size 7 steel crochet hook

Gauge: First 3 rnds = 3"

Pattern Notes: Ch-3 at beg of shell row counts as dc throughout.

Join rnds with a sl st in 3rd ch of beg ch-3 unless otherwise stated.

Pattern Stitches

Beg shell: [Ch 3, 2 dc, ch 3, 2 dc] in same sp.

Shell: [3 dc, ch 3, 3 dc] in same sp.

Shell inc: [3 dc, ch 3, 3 dc, ch 3, 3 dc] in same sp.

Doily

Rnd 1: Ch 8, join to form a ring, ch 4 (counts as first tr), 23 tr in ring, join in 4th ch of beg ch-4. (24 tr)

Rnd 2: Ch 7, [tr in tr, ch 3] rep around, join in 4th ch of beg ch-7. (24 ch-3 sps)

Rnd 3: Sl st in ch-3 sp, ch 3

(counts as first dc), 2 dc in same sp, 3 dc in each ch-3 sp around, join in 3rd ch of beg ch-3. (24 ch-3 groups)

Rnd 4: Ch 7, sk 2 dc, tr in next dc, [ch 3, sk 2 dc, tr in next dc] rep around, ch 3, join in 4th ch of beg ch-7. (24 sps)

Rnd 5: Sl st in first sp, [sc, ch 3, sc] in each sp around, join in beg sc. (24 ch-3 sps)

Rnd 6: Sl st in ch-3 lp, beg shell in same lp, shell in each lp around, join in 3rd ch of beg shell ch-3.

Rnd 7: Sl st to ch-3 sp, beg shell in same sp, shell in each shell around, join in 3rd ch of beg shell ch-3.

Rnd 8: Rep Rnd 7, working ch 1 between shells.

Rnd 9: Sl st to ch-3 sp of shell, beg shell in same sp, ch 2, [9 tr in next shell, ch 2, shell in shell, ch 2 *, shell in shell, ch 2] rep around, ending last rep at *, join in 3rd ch of beg shell ch-3. (8 pineapples)

Rnd 10: Sl st to ch-3 sp of shell, beg shell in same sp, ch 2, *dc in next tr, [ch 1, dc in next tr] 8 times, ch 2, shell in next shell, ch 2] twice, rep from * around, ending with shell in next shell, ch 2 once, join in 3rd ch of beg shell ch-3.

Rnd 11: Sl st to ch-3 sp of shell, beg shell in same sp, *ch 2, dc in ch-1 sp in pineapple, [ch 1, dc in ch-1 sp of pineapple] 7 times, ch 2, shell in shell, ch 3 **, shell in shell, rep from * around, ending last rep at **, join in 3rd ch of beg shell ch-3.

Rnd 12: Sl st to ch-3 sp of shell, beg shell in same sp, *ch 2, dc in ch-1 sp of pineapple, [dc in ch-1 sp of pineapple] 6 times, ch 2, shell in shell, ch 5 **, shell in shell, rep from * around, ending last rep at **, join in 3rd ch of beg shell ch-3.

Rnd 13: Sl st to ch-3 sp of shell, [ch 3, 2 dc, ch 3, 3 dc, ch 3, 3 dc] in same sp (beg shell inc), *ch 2, dc in ch-1 sp, [ch 1, dc in ch-1 sp] 5 times, ch 2, shell inc in next shell **, ch 5, shell inc in next shell, rep from * around, ending last rep at **, join in 3rd ch of beg ch-3.

Rnd 14: Sl st to ch-3 sp of shell, beg shell, ch 1, shell in next ch-3 sp, *ch 2, dc in ch-1 sp, [ch 1, dc in next sp] 4 times, ch 2, shell in next ch-3 sp, ch 1, shell in next ch-3 sp, ch 5 **, shell in next ch-3 sp, ch 1, shell in next ch-3 sp, rep from * around, ending last rep at **, join in 3rd ch of beg ch-3.

Rnd 15: Sl st to ch-3 sp of shell, beg shell in same sp, ch 3, *shell in shell, ch 2, dc in next ch-1 sp, [ch 1, dc in next ch-1 sp] 3 times, ch 2, shell in shell, ch 3, shell in shell, ch 5 **, shell in shell, ch 3, rep from * around, ending last rep at **, join in 3rd ch of beg ch-3.

Rnd 16: Sl st to ch-3 sp of shell, beg shell in same sp, ch 5, shell in shell, *ch 2, dc in next ch-1 sp, [ch 1, dc in next ch-1 sp] twice, ch 2, shell in shell, ch 5, shell in shell, ch 7 **, shell in shell, ch 5, shell in shell, rep from * around, ending last rep at **, join in 3rd ch of beg ch-3.

Rnd 17: Sl st to ch-3 sp of shell, beg shell in same sp, ch 7, shell in next shell, *ch 2, dc in next ch-1 sp, ch 1, dc in next ch-1 sp, ch 2, shell in next shell, ch 7, shell in next shell, ch 9 **, shell in next shell, ch 7, shell in next shell, rep from * around, ending last rep at **, join in 3rd ch of beg ch-3.

Rnd 18: Sl st to ch-3 sp of shell, beg shell in shell, ch 7, *shell in next 2 shells, ch 7, shell in shell, ch 9 **, shell in shell, ch 7, rep from * around, ending last rep at **, fasten off.

— Designed by Evelyn Sturtz

Forever Yours

Shown on page 143

Experience Level: Intermediate

Size: 14" in diameter

Materials

- DMC® Cebelia® crochet cotton size 10 (50 grams per ball): 1 ball ecru naturel
- Size 8 steel hook

Gauge: Rnds 13 = 2"

Pattern Note: Join rnds with a sl st unless otherwise stated.

Pattern Stitches

2-dc cluster (2-dc cl): Keeping last lp of each dc on hook, 2 dc in indicated st or sts, yo and draw through all 3 lps on hook.

3-dc cluster (3-dc cl): Keeping last lp of each dc on hook, 3 dc in indicated st or sts, yo and draw through all 4 lps on hook.

Doily

Rnd 1: Ch 9, join to form a ring, ch 3, 23 dc in ring, join in 3rd ch of beg ch-3.

Rnd 2: Ch 3, dc in each of next 2 dc, [ch 3, dc in each of next 3 dc] 7 times, ch 3, join in 3rd ch of beg ch-3.

Rnd 3: Ch 3, dc in each of next

2 dc, [ch 4, sc in next sp, ch 4, dc in each of next 3 dc] rep around, ending with ch 4, sc in next sp, ch 4, join in 3rd ch of beg ch-3.

Rnd 4: Ch 3, 2-dc cl over next 2 dc, *[ch 3, sc in next sp] twice, ch 3, 3-dc cl over next 3 dc, rep from * around, ending with [ch 3, sc in next sp] twice, ch 3, join in top of first cl.

Rnd 5: Ch 3, *[3 dc in next sp, dc in next sc] twice, 3 dc in next sp, [dc, ch 3, dc] in cl, rep from * around, ending with [3 dc in next sp, dc in next sc] twice, 3 dc in next sp, dc in same cl as beg ch-3, ch 3, join in 3rd ch of beg ch-3.

Rnd 6: Sl st in each of next 2 dc, ch 3, dc in each of next 8 dc, ch 3, sc in next sp, [ch 3, sk 2 dc, dc in each of next 9 dc, ch 3, sc in next sp] rep around, ch 3, join in 3rd ch of beg ch-3.

Rnd 7: Sl st in each of next 2 dc, ch 3, dc in each of next 4 dc, [ch 4, sc in next sp] twice, *ch 4, sk 2 dc, dc in each of next 5 dc, [ch 4, sc in next sp] twice, rep from * around, ch 4, join in 3rd ch of beg ch-3.

Rnd 8: Sl st in each of next 2 dc, ch 3, dc in same dc as last sl st, [ch 4, sc in next sp] 3 times, *ch 4, sk 2 dc, 2 dc in next dc, [ch 4, sc in next sp] 3 times, rep from * around, ch 4, join in 3rd ch of beg ch-3.

Rnd 9: Sl st in dc and in each of next 2 chs, ch 1, sc in same sp, [ch 5, sc in next sp] rep around to within last sp, ch 2, join with dc in beg sc.

Rnds 10 & 11: Sc in dc sp just made, [ch 6, sc in next sp] rep around to within last sp, ch 3, join with dc in beg sc.

Rnd 12: Sc in dc sp just made, [ch 7, sc in next sp] rep around to within last sp, ch 3, join with tr in beg sc.

Rnd 13: Ch 3, 4 dc in tr sp just made, ch 2, sc in next sp, ch 4, sl st in sc just made (picot), [ch 2, 9 dc in next sp, ch 2, sc and picot in next sp] rep around, ch 2, 4 dc in first half of beg sp, join in 3rd ch of beg ch-3.

Rnd 14: Ch 3, dc in each of next 3 dc, ch 2, 3-dc cl in next dc, ch 4, sl st in top of cl for picot, [ch 3, 3-dc cl and picot in next dc, ch 2, dc in each of next 7 dc, ch 2, 3-dc cl and picot in next dc] rep around, ch 3, 3-dc cl and picot in next dc, ch 2, dc in each of next 3 dc, join in 3rd ch of beg ch-3.

Rnd 15: Ch 3, dc in each of next 2 dc, ch 2, 3-dc cl and picot in next dc, [ch 7, sk both cls, 3-dc cl and picot in next dc, ch 2, dc in each of next 5 dc, ch 2, 3-dc cl and picot in next dc] rep around, ch 7, sk both cls, 3-dc cl and picot in next dc, ch 2, dc in each of next 2 dc, join in 3rd ch of beg ch-3.

Rnd 16: Ch 3, dc in next dc, ch 2, 3-dc cl and picot in next dc, [ch 5, sc in next sp, ch 5, 3-dc cl and picot in next dc, ch 2, dc in each of next 3 dc, ch 2, 3-dc cl and picot in next dc] rep around, ch 5, sc in next sp, ch 5, 3-dc cl and picot in next dc, ch 2, dc in next dc, join in 3rd ch of beg ch-3.

Rnd 17: Ch 5, 3-dc cl and picot in dc, [ch 5, dc in next sp] twice, *ch 5, 3-dc cl and picot in next dc, ch 2, dc in next dc, ch 2, 3-dc cl and picot in next dc, [ch 5, dc in next sp] twice, rep from * around, ch 5, 3-dc cl and picot in next dc, ch 2, join in 3rd ch of beg ch-5.

Rnd 18: Ch 3, 2-dc cl and picot in same st as sl st, *[ch 5, dc in next sp] 3 times, ch 5, 3-dc cl and picot in next dc, rep from * around, [ch 5, dc in next sp] 3 times, ch 2, join with dc in 3rd ch of beg ch-3.

Rnd 19: Ch 11, tr in next sp, [ch 5, tr in next sp] 3 times, *ch 7, tr in next sp, [ch 5, tr in next sp] 3 times, rep from * around, ending with ch 5, join in 4th ch of beg ch-11.

Rnd 20: Sl st in each of next 4 chs, ch 3, [2 dc, ch 3, 3 dc] in same ch as last sl st, *[ch 2, {dc, ch 2, dc} in 3rd ch of next ch-5 sp] 3 times, ch 2, [3 dc, ch 3, 3 dc] in 4th ch of ch-7 sp, rep from * around, [ch 2, {dc, ch 2, dc} in 3rd ch of next ch-5 sp] 3 times, ch 2, join in 3rd ch of beg ch-3.

Rnd 21: Ch 3, dc in each of next 2 dc, *ch 3, sc in next sp, ch 3, dc in each of next 3 dc, dc in next sp, [ch 2, sk next sp, {dc, ch 2, dc} in next sp] twice, ch 2, sk next sp, dc in next sp, dc in each of next 3 dc, rep from * around, ending with dc in next sp, join in 3rd ch of beg ch-3.

Rnd 22: Ch 7, sk 2 dc, sc in next sp, *ch 4, sc in next sp, ch 4, sk 2 dc, dc in each of next 2 dc, 2 dc in next sp, ch 1, sk next sp, [dc, ch 2, dc] in next sp, ch 1, sk next sp, 2 dc in next sp, dc in each of next 2 dc, ch 4, sc in next sp, rep from * around, ending with 2 dc in next sp, dc in next dc, join in 3rd ch of beg ch-7.

Rnd 23: Sl st in next ch, sc in next sp, *ch 4, sc in next sp, ch 4, sl st in sc just made (picot), ch 4, sc in next sp, ch 4, sk 2 dc, dc in each of next 2 dc, dc in next sp, dc in next dc, dc in next sp, ch 4, sl st in dc just made (picot), dc in same sp, dc in next dc, dc in next sp, dc in each of next 2 dc, sk 2 dc, ch 4, sc in next sp, rep from * around, join in beg sc, fasten off.

— Designed by Lucille LaFlamme

Oval Beauty

Shown on page 145

Experience Level: Advanced

Size: 10" x 15½"

Materials

- DMC® Cebelia® crochet cotton size 10 (50 grams per ball): 1 ball ecru naturel
- Size 8 steel crochet hook

Gauge: Center strip and Rnd 1 = ¾" x 6"

Pattern Note: Join rnds with a sl st unless otherwise stated.

Pattern Stitches

2-dc cluster (2-dc cl): Keeping last lp of each dc on hook, dc in each of next 2 dc, yo and draw through all 3 lps on hook.

3-dc cluster (3-dc cl): Keeping last lp of each dc on hook, dc in each of next 3 dc, yo and draw through all 4 lps on hook.

Doily

Center Strip: Ch 10, join to form a ring, [ch 5, tr in 5th ch from hook] 8 times, ch 10, join in 10th ch from hook.

Rnd 1: Sl st in next sp over side of tr, ch 3, 4 dc in sp, [5 dc in next sp over side of tr] 7 times, 17 dc in end lp, [5 dc in next sp] 8 times, 17 dc in end lp, join in 3rd ch of beg ch-3.

Rnd 2: Sl st in each of next 2 dc, ch 7, dc in 4th ch from hook, dc in same dc as last sl st, [ch 2, sk 4 dc, {dc, ch 4, dc in 4th ch from hook, dc} in same dc] 8 times, [ch 2, sk 2 dc, {dc, ch 4, dc in 4th ch from hook, dc} in same dc] 4 times, [ch 2, sk 4 dc, {dc, ch 4, dc in 4th ch from hook, dc} in same dc] 9 times, [ch 2, sk 2 dc, {dc, ch 4, dc in 4th ch from hook, dc} in same dc] 4 times, join with hdc in 3rd ch of beg ch-7.

Rnd 3: Ch 11, tr in next ch-2 sp, [ch 7, tr in next ch-2 sp] 8 times, ch 7, [tr, ch 7, tr] in next ch-2 sp, ch 7, [tr, ch 7, tr] in next ch-2 sp, [ch 7, tr in next ch-2 sp] 11 times, ch 7, [tr, ch 7, tr] in next ch-2 sp, ch 7, [tr, ch 7, tr] in next ch-2 sp, ch 7, tr in next ch-2 sp, ch 3, join with tr in 4th ch of beg ch-11.

Rnd 4: Ch 11, [tr in next sp, ch 7] 11 times, [tr, ch 7, tr] in next sp, [ch 7, tr in next sp] 14 times, ch 7, [tr, ch 7, tr] in next sp, [ch 7, tr in next sp] twice, ch 3, tr in 4th ch of ch-11.

Rnd 5: Ch 11, [tr in next sp, ch 7] 12 times, [tr, ch 7, tr] in next sp, [ch 7, tr in next sp] 15 times, ch 7, [tr, ch 7, tr] in next sp, [ch 7, tr in next sp] twice, ch 7, join in 4th ch of beg ch-11.

Rnd 6: Sl st in next sp, ch 3, 6 dc in same sp, 7 dc in each sp around, join in 3rd ch of beg ch-3.

Rnd 7: Sl st in each of next 3 dc, ch 7, dc in 4th ch from hook, dc in same dc as last sl st, [ch 3, sk 6 dc, {dc, ch 4, dc in 4th ch from hook, dc} in same dc] 12 times, ch 5, sk 6 dc, [dc, ch 4, dc in 4th ch from hook, dc] in same dc, ch 5 [sk 6 dc, {dc, ch 4, dc in 4th ch from hook, dc} in same dc, ch 3] 15 times, sk 6 dc, [dc, ch 4, dc in 4th ch from hook, dc] in same dc, ch 5, sk 6 dc, [dc, ch 4, dc in 4th ch from hook, dc] in same dc, ch 5, [sk 6 dc, {dc, ch 4, dc in 4th ch from hook} in same dc, ch 3] twice, sk 6 dc, [dc, ch 4, dc in 4th ch from hook, dc] in same dc, join with ch 1, dc in 3rd ch of beg ch-7.

Rnd 8: Sl st in dc sp just made, ch 7, tr in same sp, *[ch 5, {tr, ch 3, tr} in center ch of next ch-3] 10 times *, [ch 7, {tr, ch 3, tr} in center ch of next sp] 7 times, rep from * to * once, [ch 7, { tr, ch 3, tr} in center ch of next sp] 6 times, ch 7, join in 4th ch of beg ch-7.

Rnd 9: Sl st in next ch, ch 1, sc in next sp, [ch 2, 7 dc in next sp, ch 2, sc in next sp] rep around, ch 2, join in beg sc.

Rnd 10: Sl st in each of next 2 chs and next 2 dc, ch 3, dc in each of next 4 dc, [ch 5, sc in next sc, ch 5, sk 1 dc, dc in each of next 5 dc] rep around, ch 5, sc in next sc, ch 5, join in 3rd ch of beg ch-3.

Rnd 11: Sl st in next dc, ch 3, 2 dc over next 2 dc, *[ch 4, dc in each of next 2 sps, ch 4, sk 1 dc, 3-dc cl over next 3 dc] 9 times *, [ch 4, dc in next sp, ch 3, dc in next sp, ch 4, sk 1 dc, 3-dc cl over next 3 dc] 8 times, rep from * to * once, [ch 4, dc in next sp, ch 3, dc in next sp, ch 4, sk 1 dc, 3-dc cl over next 3 dc] 7 times, ending with ch 4, dc in next sp, ch 3, dc in next sp, ch

4, join in top of beg cl.

Rnd 12: Ch 6, *[dc in next sp, ch 3, dc in next sp, ch 3, dc in cl, ch 3] 9 times *, [{dc in next sp, ch 3} 3 times, dc in cl, ch 3] 8 times, rep from * to * once, [{dc in next sp, ch 3} 3 times, dc in cl, ch 3] 7 times, [dc in next sp, ch 3] 3 times, join in 3rd ch of beg ch-6.

Rnd 13: Ch 7, dc in 4th ch from hook, tr in same ch, dc in same st as beg ch-7, *ch 1, sc in next dc, ch 1, [dc, ch 4, dc in 4th ch from hook, tr in same ch, dc] in same dc, rep from * around, ch 1, sc in next dc, ch 1, join in 3rd ch of beg ch-7, fasten off.

— Designed by Lucille LaFlamme

Square Treasure

Shown on page 146

Experience Level: Intermediate

Size: 15" square

Materials

- Crochet cotton size 10: 400 yds ecru
- Size 7 steel crochet hook

Gauge: First rnd = 1"

To save time, take time to check gauge.

Pattern Notes: Beg ch-3 counts as first dc throughout.

Join rnds with a sl st in 3rd ch of beg ch-3 unless otherwise stated.

Pattern Stitches

Picot: Ch 3, sl st in same st.

Shell: [2 dc, ch 3 2 dc] in same sp.

V-st: [Dc, ch 3, dc] in same place.

Inc: 2 sts in same st.

Dec: Dc 2 sts tog.

First Motif

Rnd 1: Ch 6, join to form a ring, ch 3, 23 dc in ring, join. (24 dc)

Rnd 2: Ch 3, dc in next 2 dc, ch 2, [dc in each of next 3 sts, ch 2] 7 times, join. (8 petals)

Rnd 3: Ch 3, [inc in first st, dc in next dc, inc in last dc, ch 2] 8 times, join.

Rnd 4: Ch 3, [inc in first st, dc in each of next 3 dc, inc in last dc, ch 2] 8 times, join.

Rnd 5: Ch 3, [inc in first st, dc in each of next 5 dc, inc in last dc, ch 2] 8 times, join.

Rnd 6: Ch 3, [inc in first st, dc in each of next 7 dc, inc in last dc, ch 2] 8 times, join.

Rnd 7: Ch 3, [dc in each dc, ch 5] 8 times, join.

Note: *At beg of Rnds 8–11, ch 2, dc in next dc for beg dec that is within brackets.*

Rnd 8: Ch 2, *[dec, dc in each of next 7 dc, dec], ch 5, sc in next ch-5 sp, ch 5, rep between [] once, ch 2, V-st in next V-st, rep from * 3 times, join.

Rnd 9: Ch 2, *[dec, dc in each of next 5 dc, dec], {ch 5, sc in next ch-5 sp} twice, ch 5, rep between [] once, ch 2, {2 dc, ch 3, 2 dc, ch 3, 2 dc} in corner ch-5 sp, ch 2, rep from * 3 times, join.

Rnd 10: Ch 2, *[dec, dc in each of next 3 dc], {ch 5, sc in next ch-5 sp} 3 times, ch 5, rep between [] once, ch 2, shell in next shell, ch 5, shell in next shell, ch 2, rep from *3 times, join.

Rnd 11: Ch 2, *[dec, dc in next dc, dec], {ch 5, sc in next ch-5 sp} 4 times, ch 5, rep between [] once, ch 2, shell in next shell, ch 2, V-st in next ch-5 corner sp, ch 2, shell in next shell, ch 2, rep from * 3 times, join.

Rnd 12: Ch 2, *[dec over 3 dc], {ch 5, sc in next ch-5 sp} 5 times, ch 5, rep between [] once, ch 2, shell in shell, ch 2, [shell, picot, dc, ch 3, 2 dc] in corner V-st, ch 2, shell in shell, ch 2, rep from * 3 times, fasten off.

Second–Fourth Motifs

Rnds 1–11: Rep Rnds 1–11 of First Motif.

Joining

Rnd 12: With RS facing, join motifs as follows: Replace center st of 2 ch-3 lps on each end and 6 ch-5 lps in middle with a sc worked in corresponding ch lp of 2nd motif on 1 side of motif.

Join 2nd motif to first motif, finish rem 3 sides as in rem 3 sides of Rnd 12 of first motif.

Join 3rd motif to 2nd motif in same manner.

Join 4th motif to first motif, then join to 3rd motif as in first joining to form a square (Fig. 1).

FIG. 1
Joining Diagram

Motif 2	Motif 1
Motif 3	Motif 4

Border

Rnd 1: Attach thread in first shell sp on any corner, *shell in shell, ch 2, shell in next shell, ch 2, [dc in next ch-2 sp, ch 5, dc in next sp] 7 times, ch 2, shell in shell, ch 2, shell in next shell, ch 5, sk motif joining, shell in next shell, ch 2, shell in next shell, ch 2, rep between [] once, ch 2, shell in shell, ch 2, shell in next shell, ch 5 for corner, rep from * 4 times, ending last rep with ch 2, dc in 3rd ch of beg ch-3.

Rnd 2: Ch 3, dc in same st, *[ch 2, shell in next shell, ch 2, shell in next shell, ch 2, V-st in next ch-5 sp, ch 2, dc in next ch-5 sp] 3 times, ch 2, V-st in next ch-5 sp, ch 2, shell in next shell, ch 2, shell in next shell, ch 2, sc in next ch-5 sp, ch 3, sc in same ch-5 sp, rep between [] once, ch 2, V-st in next ch-5 sp, ch 2, shell in next shell, ch 2, shell in next shell, ch 2, shell in next corner sp, rep from * 4 times, ending last rep with 2 dc in ch-2 sp, ch 1, dc in 3rd ch of beg ch-3.

Rnd 3: Ch 3, shell in same sp, *[ch 2, shell in shells and V-sts with ch-2 between] 8 times, ch 5, rep between [] once, ch 2, [2 dc, ch 3, 3 dc, ch 3, 2 dc] in next corner shell, rep from * 4 times, ending last rep with 2 dc, ch 3, 3 dc, ch 2, join.

Rnd 4: Attach thread to center dc of corner, sc in same sp, ch 2, [7 dc in next shell, sc in next ch-2 sp] 9 times, ch 2, sc in next ch-5 sp, ch 3, sc in same ch-5 sp, ch 2, rep between [] once, ch 2, sc in 2nd dc of corner, rep from * 4 times, ending last rep with 7 dc in shell, ch 2, join in beg sc, fasten off.

Weave in loose ends.

— Designed by Loa Ann Thaxton

Victorian Floral

Shown on page 147

Experience Level: Intermediate

Size: Approx. 11" in diameter

Materials

- Bernat® Handicrafter® Tradition crochet cotton size 10 (200 yds per skein): 1 skein ecru #501
- Size 6 steel crochet hook

Gauge: 9 dc = 1"

To save time, take time to check gauge.

Pattern Note: Join rnds with a sl st unless otherwise stated.

Pattern Stitches

3-dc cluster (3-dc cl): [Yo, insert hook through sp, pull thread through sp, draw through 2 lps on hook] 4 times, yo, draw through all lps on hook.

4-dc cluster (4-dc cl): [Yo, insert hook through sp, pull thread through sp, draw through 2 lps on hook] 5 times, yo, draw through all lps on hook.

4-tr cluster (4-tr cl): *Yo twice, insert hook through sp, pull thread through sp, [draw thread through 2 lps on hook] twice, rep from * 4 times, yo, draw through all lps on hook.

Doily

Rnd 1: Ch 8, join to form a ring, ch 4, 3-tr cl in ring, [ch 5, 4-tr cl in ring] 7 times, ending with ch 5, join in 3rd ch of beg ch-4. (8 petals)

Rnd 2: Ch 3, 4-dc cl in next ch sp, ch 5, 5-dc cl in same sp, *ch 5, [5-dc cl, ch 5, 5-dc cl] in next sp, rep from * around, ending with ch 5, join in 3rd ch of beg ch-3.

Rnd 3: Ch 1, *[3 sc, ch 3, 3 sc in next ch sp] rep around, join in beg sc.

Rnd 4: Sl st in each of next 3 sc, [sl st in next ch sp, ch 15, sl st in same ch sp, ch 3] rep around, join in next ch sp.

Rnd 5: Ch 1, *[8 sc, ch 5, 8 sc] in next ch-15 sp, 3 sc in next ch sp, rep from * around, fasten off.

Rnd 6: Attach thread in any ch-5 sp, sl st in same sp, [ch 9, sl st in next ch sp] rep around, join in beg ch sp.

Rnd 7: Ch 3, 8 dc in same ch sp, [9 dc in next ch sp] rep around, join in 3rd ch of beg ch-3.

Rnd 8: [Ch 9, sk 5 dc, sl st in next dc] rep around, join in first ch of beg ch-9.

Rnd 9: Ch 1, *[6 sc, ch 5, 6 sc] in next ch sp, rep from * around, join in beg sc.

Rnd 10: Sl st in each of next 5 sc, sl st in ch sp, ch 3, 4-dc cl in same sp, [ch 9, 5-dc cl in next ch sp] rep around, ending with ch 9, join in 3rd ch of beg ch-3.

Rnd 11: Ch 4, 3-tr cl in next ch sp, [ch 5, 4-tr cl] twice in same ch sp, *[4-tr cl, ch 5] twice in next ch sp, 4-tr cl in same ch sp, rep from * around, join in 4th ch of beg ch-4.

Rnd 12: Sl st in each of next 3 chs, ch 4, [tr in 3rd ch of next ch sp, ch 4, tr in same ch] rep around, ending with tr at base of beg ch-4, ch 4, join in 4th ch of beg ch-4.

Rnd 13: Ch 1, [3 sc in next ch sp, ch 5, 3 sc in same ch sp] rep around, join in beg sc.

Rnd 14: Sl st in each of next 3 sc, [ch 9, sl st in next ch sp] rep around, join in beg sc.

Rnd 15: Ch 1, [6 sc in next ch sp, ch 5, sl st in first ch for picot, 6 sc in same ch sp] rep around, join in beg sc, fasten off.

— Designed by Nazanin S. Fard

Please review the following information before working the projects in this book. Important details about the abbreviations and symbols used and finishing instructions are included.

Hooks

Crochet hooks are sized for different weights of yarn and thread. For thread crochet, you will usually use a *steel* crochet hook. Steel crochet hook sizes range from size 00 to 14. The higher the number of hook, the smaller your stitches will be. For example, a size 1 steel crochet hook will give you much larger stitches than a size 9 steel crochet hook. Keep in mind that the sizes given with the pattern instructions were obtained by working with the size thread or yarn and hook given in the materials list. If you work with a smaller hook, depending on your gauge, your project size will be smaller; if you work with a larger hook, your finished project's size will be larger.

Gauge

Gauge is determined by the tightness or looseness of your stitches, and affects the finished size of your project. If you are concerned about the finished size of the project matching the size given, take time to crochet a small section of the pattern and then check your gauge. For example, if the gauge called for is 10 dc = 1 inch, and your gauge is 12 dc to the inch, you should switch to a larger hook. On the other hand, if your gauge is only 8 dc to the inch, you should switch to a smaller hook.

If the gauge given in the pattern is for an entire motif, work one motif and then check your gauge.

Understanding Symbols

As you work through a pattern, you'll quickly notice several symbols in the instructions. These symbols are used to clarify the pattern for you: Brackets [], curlicue brackets {}, asterisks *.

Brackets [] are used to set off a group of instructions worked a number of times. For example, "[ch 3, sc in ch-3 sp] 7 times" means to repeat the instructions inside the [] seven times. Brackets [] also set off a group of stitches to be worked in one stitch, space or loop. For example, the brackets [] in this set of instructions, "Sk 3 sc, [3 dc, ch 1, 3 dc] in next st" indicate that after skipping 3 sc, you will work 3 dc, ch 1 and 3 more dc all in the next stitch.

Occasionally, a set of instructions inside a set of brackets needs to be repeated too. In this case, the text within the brackets to be repeated will be set off with curlicue brackets {}. For example, "[Ch 9, yo twice, insert hook in 7th ch from hook and pull up a loop, sk next dc, yo, insert hook in next dc and pull up a loop, {yo and draw through 2 lps on hook} 5 times, ch 3] 8 times." In this case, in each of the eight repeats of the instructions included in brackets, you will work the section included in curlicue brackets five times.

Asterisks * are also used when a group of instructions is repeated. They may either be used alone or with brackets. For example, "*Sc in each of the next 5 sc, 2 sc in next sc, rep from * around, join with a sl st in beg sc" simply means you will repeat the instructions from the first * around the entire round.

"*Sk 3 sc, [3 dc, ch 1, 3 dc] in next st, rep from * around" is an example of asterisks working with brackets. In this set of instructions, you will repeat the instructions from the asterisk around, working the instructions inside the brackets together.

Stitch Abbreviations

beg	begin(ning)
bl(s)	block(s)
bpdc	back post dc
ch(s)	chain(s)
cl(s)	cluster(s)
CC	contrasting color
dc	double crochet
dec	decrease
dtr	double treble crochet
fpdc	front post dc
hdc	half-double crochet
inc	increase
lp(s)	loop(s)
MC	main color
p	picot
rem	remain(ing)
rep	repeat
rnd(s)	round(s)
RS	right side facing you
sc	single crochet
sk	skip
sl st	slip stitch
sp(s)	space(s)
st(s)	stitch(es)
tog	together
tr	treble crochet
trtr	triple treble crochet
WS	wrong side facing you
yo	yarn over

Basic Stitches

Front Loop (a) Back Loop (b)

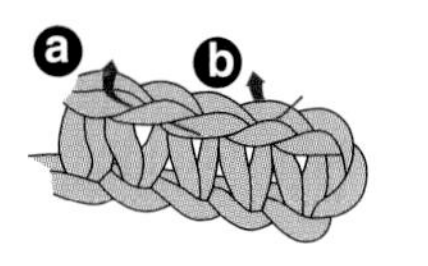

Chain (ch)
Yo, draw lp through hook.

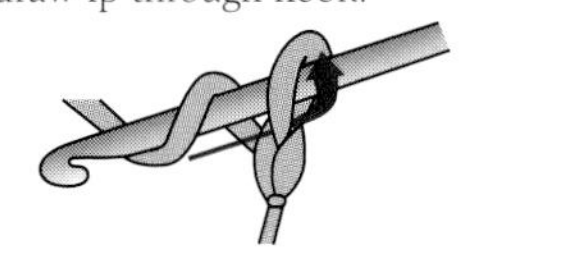

Slip Stitch
Insert hook in beg ch, yo, draw lp through.

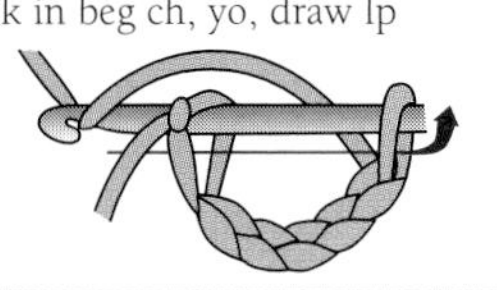

Single Crochet (sc)
Insert hook in st (a), yo, draw lp through (b), yo, draw through both lps on hook (c).

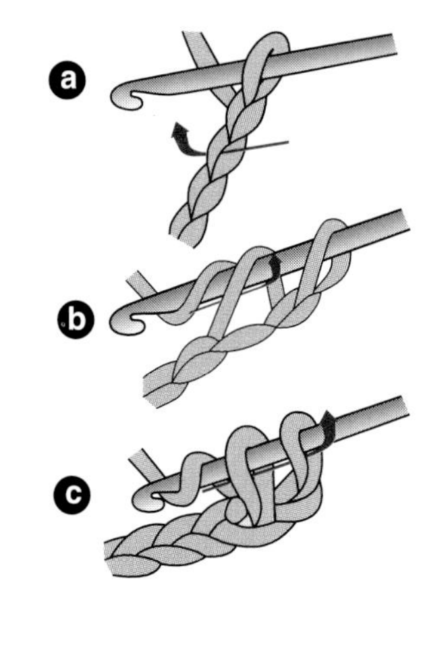

Half-Double Crochet (hdc)
Yo, insert hook in st (a), draw lp through (b), yo, draw through all 3 lps on hook (c).

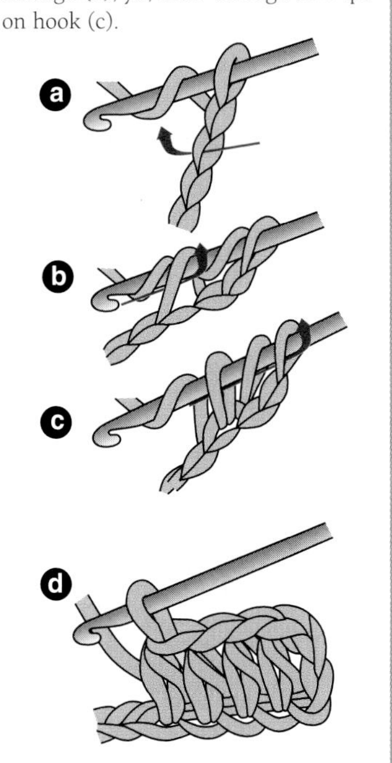

Double Crochet (dc)
Yo, insert hook in st (a), yo, draw through 1 lp (b), [yo, draw through 2 lps] twice (c, d).

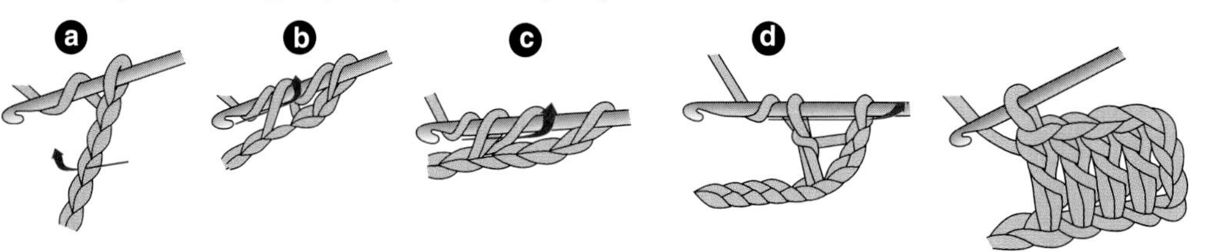

Treble Crochet (tr)
Yo hook twice, insert hook in st (a), yo, draw lp through (b), [yo, draw through 2 lps on hook] 3 times (c, d, e).

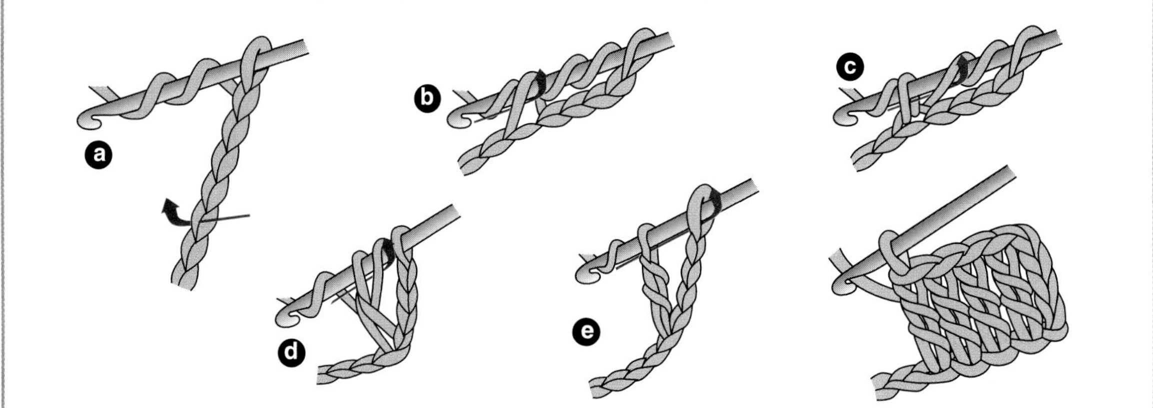

Double Treble Crochet (dtr)

Yo hook 3 times, insert hook in st (a), yo, draw lp through (b), [yo, draw through 2 lps on hook] 4 times (c, d, e, f).

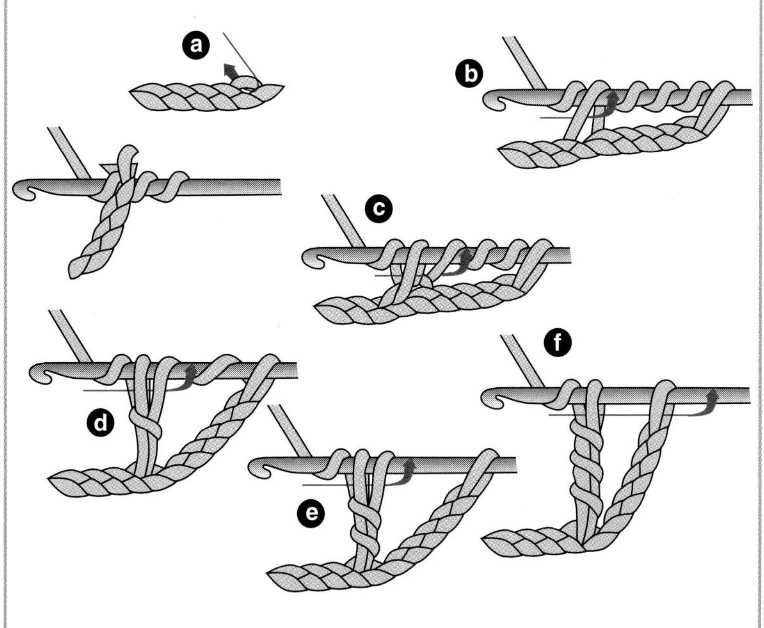

Decreasing

Single Crochet Decrease

Dec 1 sc over next 2 sc as follows: Draw up a lp in each of next 2 sts, yo, draw through all 3 lps on hook.

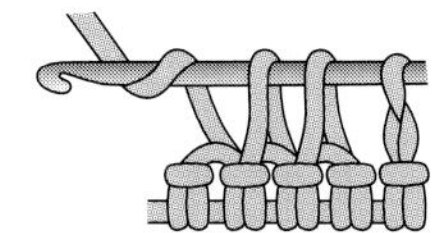

Half-Double Crochet Decrease

Dec 1 hdc over next 2 hdc as follows: [Yo, insert hook in next st, yo, draw lp through] twice, yo, draw through all 5 lps on hook.

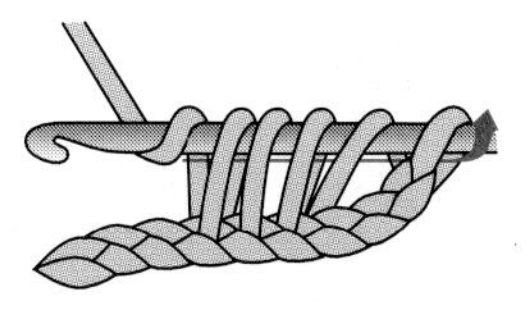

Special Stitches

Shell (sh)

[2 dc, ch 2, 2 dc] in next st or ch sp.

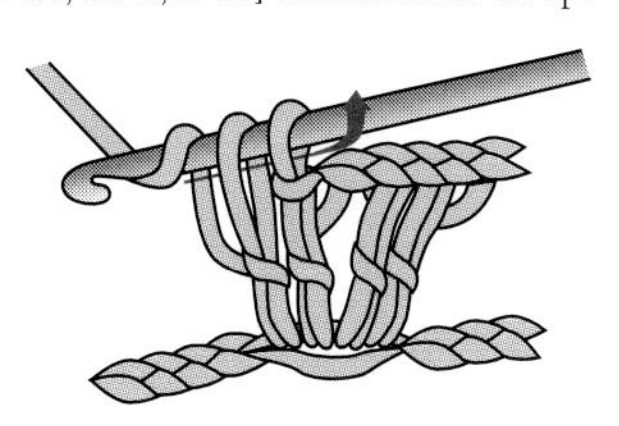

Reverse Single Crochet (reverse sc)

Working from left to right, insert hook in next st to the right (a), yo, draw through st, complete as for sc (b).

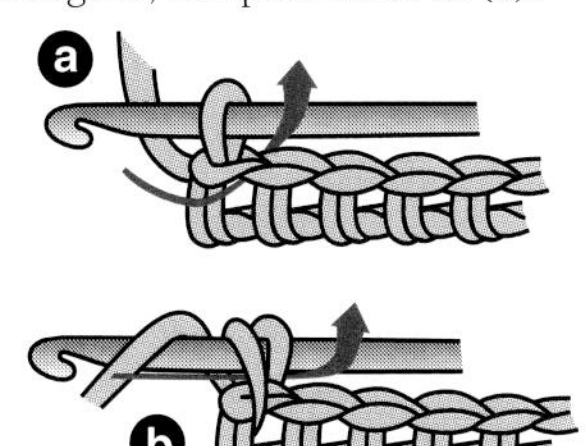

Picot (p)

Ch 3, sl st in 3rd ch from hook.

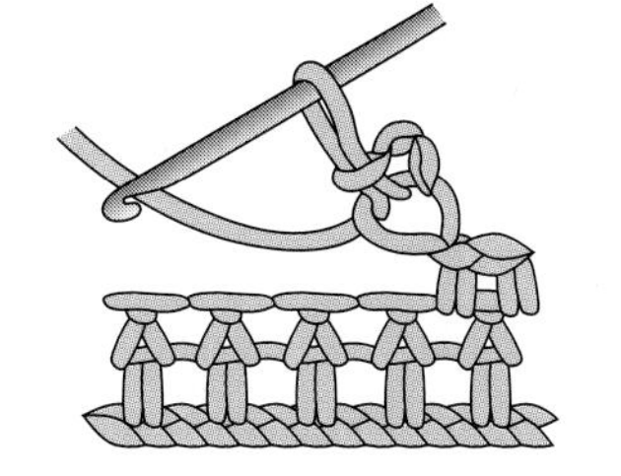

Front Post (a)/Back Post (b)

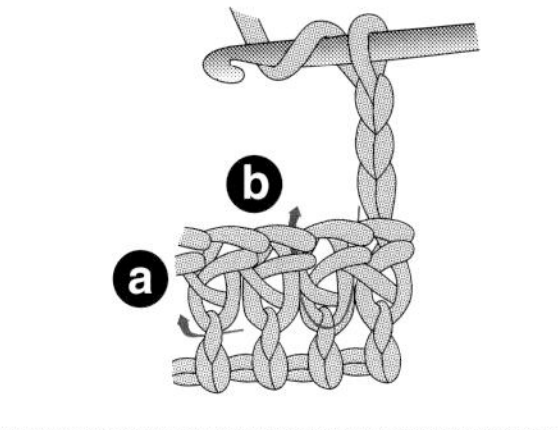

Chain color change (ch color change)

Yo with new color, draw through last lp on hook.

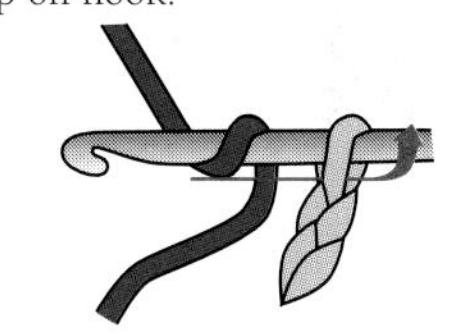

Double Crochet color change (dc color change)

Drop first color, yo with new color, draw through last 2 lps of st.

Yarn Conversion

Ounces to Grams	
1	28.4
2	56.7
3	85.0
4	113.4

Grams to Ounces	
25	⅞
40	1⅔
50	1¾
100	3½

Index